Job Searching with Social Media

FOR

DUMMIES®

by Joshua Waldman, MBA

WILEY

John Wiley & Sons, Inc.

Job Searching with Social Media For Dummies®

Published by
John Wiley & Sons, Inc.
111 River St.
Hoboken, NJ 07030-5774
www.wiley.com

Copyright © 2011 by John Wiley & Sons, Inc., Hoboken NJ

Published simultaneously in Canada

For general information on our other products and services, please contact our Customer Care Department within the U.S. at 877-762-2974, outside the U.S. at 317-572-3993, or fax 317-572-4002.

For technical support, please visit www.wiley.com/techsupport.

Wiley also publishes its books in a variety of electronic formats and by print-on-demand. Some content that appears in standard print versions of this book may not be available in other formats. For more information about Wiley products, visit us at www.wiley.com.

Library of Congress Control Number: 2011934640

ISBN 978-0-470-93072-4 (pbk); ISBN 978-1-118-13452-8 (ebk); ISBN 978-1-118-13453-5 (ebk); ISBN 978-1-118-13454-2 (ebk)

Manufactured in the United States of America

10 9 8 7 6 5 4 3 2 1

WILEY

About the Author

Joshua Waldman, MBA, is a consultant and entrepreneur who teaches technology and marketing skills to job seekers to help them get noticed and ultimately find jobs. He has been using social media to enhance his career and the careers of others since 2006 and has worked with unemployment office staff, MBA career center staff, and countless unemployed and frustrated job seekers. He founded the Career Enlightenment blog in 2009 with the mission of helping job seekers break away from outdated and ineffective job-searching strategies. Joshua's blog content has been featured on top career sites, including the International Business Times, Simply Hired blog, CAREEREALISM.com, and mediabistro.com. Exclusive extras and more resources for this book can be found at www.careerenlightenment.com/fordummies.

Joshua enjoys meditation, bodybuilding, vegetarian cooking, and bad kung fu flicks. He knows of the existence of Hannah Montana only because of his 13-year-old daughter. And he keeps his head on his shoulders only because of his wife's good sense.

Dedication

For my dear friend Lucretia, who faces each of life's challenges with a grin and a joke, who taught me that even if you're at the tail end of the line and even if the air gets thin, remember to keep walking. You just have to put one foot in front of the other.

Author's Acknowledgments

The story of how I came to write this book is a perfect example of the power of networking. My dad loves a professional networking group for small businesses called Business Networking International (BNI). As the president of its Rhode Island chapter, he's been trying to (unsuccessfully) persuade me to join the group. However, we both share a passion for social media and emerging technologies. When my dad found out that I blog on such topics, he put me in touch with Charles Westcott, a contact he'd made at his weekly BNI meeting.

Charles offered to introduce me to a friend of his at Wiley Publishing. After six months, I received a phone call from the *For Dummies* group, expressing their interest in publishing my book. So from my obstinate refusal to join my dad's networking group (and his patience with me), my book idea finally found its way into good hands at Wiley. So thanks, Dad. I don't doubt how hard fatherhood can be sometimes!

A few people I want to acknowledge include Pamela Slim, for inspiring me and believing in me, and Laura Roeder, for painting a picture of success in my head. Also a big thanks to James Alexander for delivering a ton of great research to my doorstep when I needed it most.

If it weren't for Wiley's awesome editing team, this book would sound like gibberish. In particular, my special heartfelt thanks to Jennifer Tebbe, Jennette ElNaggar, David Lutton, Jessica Smith, and Christy Pingleton. And thanks to my technical editor, Jane Finkle, who helped me make this material more accessible to a broader audience.

I also want to thank Michael "Dr. Woody" Woodward, Dr. Larry Chiagouris, Lauren Busley, Tony Deblauwe, Roy Cohen, Stuart Mease, Lavie Margolin, Dave Sanford, Stephanie Daniel, Courtney Hunt, and Katie Farrell for helping me get unstuck on the Facebook chapter.

Finally, I want to thank my family for putting up with my early mornings, early bedtimes, and working weekends. Shifting my entire waking existence back three hours was certainly a group effort. Your support and patience is truly appreciated. I'm sure you'll be happy to not have to stare at the back of my head all weekend.

Publisher's Acknowledgments

We're proud of this book; please send us your comments at http://dummies.custhelp.com. For other comments, please contact our Customer Care Department within the U.S. at 877-762-2974, outside the U.S. at 317-572-3993, or fax 317-572-4002.

Some of the people who helped bring this book to market include the following:

Acquisitions, Editorial, and Vertical Websites

Project Editor: Jennifer Tebbe

Executive Editor: Lindsay Sandman Lefevere

Copy Editor: Jennette ElNaggar

Assistant Editor: David Lutton

Editorial Program Coordinator: Joe Niesen

Technical Editor: Jane Finkle

Editorial Manager: Christine Meloy Beck

Editorial Assistant: Rachelle S. Amick

Cover Photos: © iStockphoto.com/Valua Vitaly

Cartoons: Rich Tennant (www.the5thwave.com)

Composition Services

Project Coordinator: Katherine Crocker

Layout and Graphics: Corrie Socolovitch

Proofreader: Laura Bowman

Indexer: Sherry Massey

Special Help

Christine Pingleton, Jessica Smith

Publishing and Editorial for Consumer Dummies

    Kathleen Nebenhaus, Vice President and Executive Publisher

    Kristin Ferguson-Wagstaffe, Product Development Director

    Ensley Eikenburg, Associate Publisher, Travel

    Kelly Regan, Editorial Director, Travel

Publishing for Technology Dummies

    Andy Cummings, Vice President and Publisher

Composition Services

    Debbie Stailey, Director of Composition Services

Contents at a Glance

Table of Contents

Part V: Executing Your Proactive Social Media Job Hunt Strategies 255

Introduction

*I*n the modern job market, no tool is more capable of shortening your job search and helping you become successful in your career than *social media* — online networks that foster interaction with other people. Social media tools have become key resources for hiring managers who, on smaller budgets, turn to their network to fill positions. Social media sites have also grown to augment business networking and have become vital marketplaces for the exchange of goods and services through trusted connections. *Job Searching with Social Media For Dummies* takes the topic most job searching books treat as a single chapter — using social media — and gives it the depth and focus it deserves in today's competitive job market.

When I was laid off for the second time in six months, I started to rely heavily on social media to get back on my feet. During that time, I developed a personal brand that worked for me, I began networking in person and online, and I started reaching out to people at companies I wanted to work at. Pretty soon the job opportunities started to open up, and I received several offers. But something inside me wasn't ready to start work again. That's when I started Career Enlightenment so I could help other people figure out social media and find jobs. Since then, I've watched countless clients slide right into the job of their dreams, using the tools and techniques I share with you in this book.

I know you have better things to do than read more books about job searching. In fact, you'd probably prefer to be out networking, cruising job boards, writing your résumé, or interviewing for that new dream job, right? I wrote this book with all that in mind. If you're hyper-focused on taking your career to the next level, if you prefer action over theory, and if you want to see fast results from your efforts, then this is your book.

About This Book

Job Searching with Social Media For Dummies is your go-to reference for all kinds of tips and tricks that reveal how to use social media to find a job. Whether you're new to social media or can surf Facebook in your sleep, you'll find information of value within this book.

Feel free to jump around to the subjects that interest you most. However, even if you think you know about a technology or tool, I encourage you to give each chapter a look. You may find new ideas or even old ideas used in new ways. These days, any new trick that separates you from the crowd is worth finding out about.

Conventions Used in This Book

Throughout the book, you'll notice that I use the terms *social media* and *social networking* interchangeably. The difference between the two terms is subtle and completely irrelevant to the purpose of this book.

I also rely on the following conventions to help make the text more consistent and easy for you to understand:

- ✔ All web addresses appear in monofont. Additionally, some web addresses I include start with bit.ly. This prefix is the most popular way Twitter users shorten their links to make room for more characters. Note that bit.ly links are case-sensitive, so be sure to copy them exactly as they appear.

- ✔ New terms appear in *italics* and are closely followed by an easy-to-understand definition. I also occasionally use italics for emphasis.

- ✔ The keywords in bulleted lists and the action parts of numbered steps appear in **bold.**

What You're Not to Read

The beauty of a *For Dummies* book is that you don't have to read every single word. In fact, you can skip over some parts of this book entirely. Feel free to pass over the sidebars (the gray-shaded blocks of text within some chapters). They provide context, extra detail, or happily ending stories, but you certainly don't have to read them to get the gist of a section.

Foolish Assumptions

If you're picking up this book, I'm guessing you're a frustrated job seeker. Perhaps you're just out of college and looking for your first job with little to no working experience under your belt. Maybe you're seeking to make the leap into a new field after spending several years in a different one. Or perhaps you never intended to find another job because you were so happy at your old one, but then life threw you for a loop and your job disappeared. If any of these statements accurately describe your situation, then this is the book for you.

I don't expect you to have a wealth of social media experience (although this book is certainly still relevant if you do). However, I do expect you to have access to a computer and the Internet so you can sign in to various social media sites.

Finally, I'm also assuming that you

✔ Want tips and tricks to accelerate your chances of finding your next job and you aren't finding answers anywhere else

✔ Are open minded about discovering new ways to approach the job hunt

✔ Are truly motivated to take action and that you take full responsibility for your career and your life

How This Book Is Organized

I've broken down this book into six distinct parts, each of which focuses on a particular theme so you can figure out exactly where to go for the type of information you're looking for.

Part I: Preparing for Your Job Search

In this part, you discover why social media has changed the way hiring managers hire and how successful job seekers get jobs. You also find out some of my favorite techniques for getting job-searching tasks done and staying motivated. And because landing a job tends to come down to who you know (or even who those people know), this part also provides you with a refresher on networking basics, both in person and online.

Part II: Marketing Yourself with a Personal Brand

If you don't brand yourself — in other words, if you don't present yourself online the way you want to be seen — someone or something else will.

Inconsistencies between your résumé and online profile can land you in the maybe pile faster than the weather changes in New England. This part helps you avoid that fate by not only introducing you to the concept of personal branding but also revealing how best to promote your brand and communicate your expertise to the online world. It even walks you through the steps for managing your online reputation so you can stay in charge of how you come across in Internet searches and on social media websites.

Part III: Crafting Web Résumés with LinkedIn, Video, and More

In today's world, you can't really get away with just a traditional paper-based résumé anymore. (You know, the one you type up on your word-processing software and mail out to hiring managers.) Nowadays, your résumé needs to exist in a format that's more social media friendly, which is why this part guides you through some of the highest-leverage ways to represent yourself online. In it, I explain how to repurpose your résumé for an online audience. I also show you how to make LinkedIn (a powerful online network for professionals), video résumés, and other types of web-based résumés work for you.

Part IV: Using Twitter, Facebook, and Other Sites to Find a Position

You may be using Facebook or Twitter already, but by discovering how to use these sites slightly differently, you can dramatically accelerate your career. In this part, I show you some tweaks and hacks designed to protect your privacy while helping you make connections that you never dreamed possible. I also introduce you to a bevy of other social networking sites that you may want to explore.

Part V: Executing Your Proactive Social Media Job Hunt Strategies

Technology isn't going to magically land you a job; you have to have a solid strategy in place. This part helps you synthesize all the technology I describe in earlier parts into a proven method for finding work. Namely, it shows you how to find the right people and companies, position yourself appropriately, acquire the full scoop about your target companies through informational interviewing, and interact with the people who have the power to hire you through various social media outlets.

Part VI: The Part of Tens

No *For Dummies* book is complete without the Part of Tens. Here, I feature some interesting top ten (or so) lists of information. Turn to this part if you want to find out more about how the job-search process has evolved, how to stay in the loop when it comes to the ever-changing world of social media, and what mistakes people tend to make on social media sites (and how to avoid them).

Icons Used in This Book

Keep your eyes peeled for the following icons, which I've scattered throughout the text to draw your attention to important paragraphs.

If you take nothing else away from this book, be sure to recall the information flagged with this icon.

This bull's-eye leads you to information I find to be particularly useful. After all, who doesn't like saving themselves a little time here and there or figuring out an easier way to accomplish something?

Pay special attention to paragraphs bearing this icon. The information they contain is there to keep you from making a potentially career- or reputation-harming mistake.

Where to Go from Here

If you're wondering where to start, take a look at the table of contents. Rest assured that wherever you choose to begin reading, you don't have to worry about feeling lost. Each chapter is self-contained and tells you what you need to know.

Obviously, if you really don't know where to start, you can always begin at the beginning with Chapter 1. Of course, if you already know why social media is important when it comes to the modern job search, and if you have a pretty good handle on your goal setting and organization skills, then why not start with Chapter 4 for an introduction to personal branding? For insight on putting the big three social media sites (LinkedIn, Twitter, and Facebook) to work in your job search, head to Chapter 9, 12, or 13.

Basically, head wherever the mood and your needs at this time lead you. Best of luck with your job search!

Part I

Preparing for Your Job Search

"Here's an idea. Why don't you start a social network for doofuses who think they know how to set a broken leg, but don't."

In this part . . .

Social media sites, such as Facebook and Twitter, are more than just venues for entertainment. Nowadays, they're places where people are finding jobs. In order to take advantage of social media from a job-searching perspective, you need to know how to use the social media tools available to you and organize your time.

Never fear. This part not only introduces you to the basic concepts of social media but also helps you set practical goals and organize the vast amounts of information coming at you at once. You'll feel much more in control of your job search in today's social media–focused world after reading about the concepts I share with you in this part.

Chapter 1

The Lowdown on Social Media for Job Hunters

....

In This Chapter

▶ Realizing why you need to have an online presence when searching for a job

▶ Showing recruiters and hiring managers what makes you uniquely qualified

▶ Using social media sites to host your résumé and manage your online reputation

....

*S*ocial media, sometimes called *social networking,* is nothing more than a technology that facilitates human interaction. Different than a website or a résumé, which are strictly one-way forms of communication, social media sites allow users to comment, share, or chat with each other, often in real time. Further, social media tools have lowered the barrier to publishing content online itself, and an army of bloggers, video producers, and article writers have found a voice. Social media has even given ordinary people a chance to build an audience or interact with their favorite celebrities.

Social media has also become an important tool for job seekers due in part to the new ways people are finding out about (and earning) jobs. As you may already know, most jobs come about through networking, not applying on job boards or aimlessly sending out résumés. Social media tools make networking much easier and much more powerful due to their interactive nature. Thus, when a job seeker really learns to use social networking well, his chances for finding opportunities multiply exponentially.

Nowadays, social media also plays a part in how hiring managers are conducting their research on candidates. More than 80 percent of recruiters use LinkedIn. Additionally, 50 percent of hiring managers can determine whether a particular candidate's personality is a good fit for their company just by seeing that person's social media presence.

In this chapter, I help you grasp the bigger picture of why having more than a basic online presence is essential. I also help you figure out how to do all the prep work necessary for job searching with social media, including discovering your personal brand and getting your résumé online. I even offer direction on where to go when you're ready to expand your online presence and how to keep your job search proactive with the help of various social media tools. Well, what are you waiting for? The job for you is out there — you just need to know how to find it and position yourself as the right person for it!

Discovering Why Having an Online Presence Is Important

Information for just about everyone can be found online by someone who knows how to conduct the right search. That's right. Personal information such as your name, address, and phone number are on the Internet. But if you really want to use social media as a tool to land your dream job, then you need to be willing to expand your presence online beyond just the basics. I explain why in the sections that follow.

Whether or not you can do the job you're applying for will certainly help you pass screening and get your foot in the door. However, final decisions about your employment will come down to your personality. Surveys have found over and over again that *fit* is the primary reason for hiring one person over another. And one of the best ways to prove how well you can fit in at one of your target companies is by using social media sites to reveal your personality. A printed-out résumé (or even one viewed on a computer screen through a word-processing program) can only witness to your skills; a profile on a social media site can demonstrate your passions, your personality, and your uniqueness.

Recruiters will Google you

Regardless of whether you search for your name online to see what comes up, you can bet that someone else will — namely the hiring managers at most (if not all!) of the companies you apply to. Recruiters from almost every field and industry take classes each year to find out about advanced Google techniques that can help them find and screen talent. In fact, many recruiters I've interviewed have told me that conducting Internet searches (mostly through Google) on the people they're placing is part of their due diligence and responsibility. In other words, they wouldn't be doing their jobs if they *didn't* investigate your online presence.

The unfairness of this situation is that most people don't know how to manage what information is found out about them online. So although you may be making a huge splash with great Google results from social media sites, your online presence may actually be a very serious liability. The solution? Proactively manage your online reputation by using the steps I show you in Chapter 7.

A job-searching-with-social-media success story

In January 2011, I interviewed Kathy for my blog *not* because of some lucky circumstance that befell her but because the story of how she got her latest job was a great, everyday example of how to use social media to run a job search. She strategically used social media to get her next job and did many of the things I show you how to do in this book. Here's how she did it (or if you'd rather watch the interview, head here: `bit.ly/Kathy-Job`):

- **Growing a network:** Kathy spent the majority of her job-search time growing her LinkedIn network, fixing up her profile, and meeting new people in person. When she met new people face to face, she added them to her online networks right away.

- **Staying on top of contacts' activities:** Kathy monitored updates to her network on social media sites daily. She knew what her new contacts were doing and was able to maintain and even grow her relationships by sharing information with them.

- **Using a social media–enabled job board:** Kathy used Simply Hired, which didn't just list job openings, it also listed who she knew on Facebook and LinkedIn at each of those companies (see `www.simply hired.com`).

- **Applying the right way and following up with a contact:** Kathy followed the company's rules and applied for the job online. After she applied, she e-mailed one of her LinkedIn connections who worked at the company. Because she had developed enough rapport and trust, Kathy was able to ask this person to pass her application directly to the hiring manager and bypass HR screening all together.

Within days, Kathy was on the phone with the hiring manager, and a week later, she started her new job at that company.

Hiring managers are cheap

During the great recession of 2008 and 2009 (and arguably longer), organizations made some serious cutbacks. The first people to go at many companies were the HR recruiters, which meant the responsibility of finding and screening new talent shifted to the *hiring managers* — as in the people who make the final decision about your employment and typically become your boss after you come onboard. In other words, hiring managers' jobs are primarily not about hiring new employees; their day-to-day role usually has little to do with hiring because they're paid for their performance at other functions.

What does that mean to you? Simply that hiring managers aren't going to spend tons of their department's time and money on fancy recruiting tools, databases, or placement firms. Most job boards are outside their budgets as well. Instead, they're going to rely on the cheapest and fastest ways of getting a stack of résumés, which often means leveraging their employees' referral network, LinkedIn, and maybe even Twitter. They want to get through the process of finding the right candidate as quickly as possible so they can focus on other priorities.

Having a positive, consistent presence on various social media sites makes it easier for hiring managers to find you. Plus, with all the relationships you're building through networking, an employee referral may take your résumé to the top of the pile.

Generic résumé blasts don't work

If your next boss is using social media to find talent, then you need to be on social media sites, too. If all you're doing is sending your résumé out to numerous companies via job boards and hoping for a phone call, I'm not certain you'll make it past the screening process at most companies or organizations. Why? Because the company may be wading through hundreds of other generic looking résumés. And when candidates send out general applications without really reading about the job, they can even get blacklisted.

An HR consultant friend of mine was hired by a large pharmaceutical company who wanted her to send three qualified candidates to fill a specialized role. She posted the job on a large, well-known job board. Each week she received an e-mail résumé from this lady who was so completely unqualified, it was like having a taxi driver apply to be a surgeon. After four weeks, my friend called the woman to find out why she kept applying to a job she was so shamefully unqualified for. The woman said, "I've never even heard of your company! I get a list of job opportunities and push a button that applies to all of them at once." The moral of the story? Don't start your job search with the job boards. Instead, spend time building your network on various social media sites, such as LinkedIn (see Chapter 9), Twitter (see Chapter 12), and Facebook (see Chapter 13).

Getting Ready to Start Your Search

Job seekers of earlier generations had one main tool at their disposal: the résumé. But thanks to the hundreds of social media sites out there, you have access to a lot more tools that can aid you in your job search — if you don't become distracted. If you've ever spent hours on Facebook by accident, checking out the "social" aspect of social media, then you know just how easy it is to forget all about why you got online in the first place. Fortunately, you can keep yourself from becoming distracted (and, therefore, take full advantage of social media sites and make progress toward finding a job) by doing a little prep work before you begin your job search.

First, establish clear goals for yourself. Start with your end goal (getting a job interview), and then work your way backwards, step by step. Each step must be clear and not complex to complete. By breaking down your goals into smaller chunks, you're less likely to feel overwhelmed. These smaller steps become the basis of how you spend your time, so every time you sit down to work, you know what to do.

It also helps to have some ideas for how you're going to manage your time. One way to go about that is by looking at your job search as a job in itself. Define the hours of the day you plan to work on finding a job and figure out how much time you're going to spend on certain tasks, such as profile writing, researching, or reaching out. I share a few time-management techniques in Chapter 2.

Naturally, you also need a way to keep all the information about your various contacts organized. After all, you're going to be meeting new people in person and adding them to your LinkedIn contact list, and then you're going to use Twitter and Facebook to discover what your network is up to. This information is a lot to stay on top of, but I help you figure out how to manage it in Chapter 3, which walks you through the basics of online networking.

Making Yourself Stand Out with a Personal Brand

Personal branding — the art of communicating what makes you unique — has been around for a long time. Everyone has a personal brand, even you, because everyone is unique. But not everyone is good at expressing this differentiation. Those people who are seem to prosper in any economic situation.

To figure out your personal brand, you need to take a serious look at your core existence. Really strive to understand your values, passions, and strengths. In other words, figure out what makes you you. (I present some exercises to help you with this in Chapter 4.)

After you're able to articulate what makes you unique, you can transform that knowledge into a value statement that expresses your worth and fit to prospective employers (I tell you more about value statements in Chapter 5). By expertly communicating your value statement across several different mediums, you can grow your credibility and your brand.

Blogs make an excellent medium for communicating your value statement because they also allow you to share your knowledge and opinions about topics that matter to your particular field of interest. An added bonus of blogging? Employers who see you passionately turning out articles, videos, or slides in the area of your expertise will see that you're truly passionate about your work and have a depth of knowledge that may help their organization. Also, not many other candidates are brave enough to put themselves out there and share their opinions. For pointers on blogging as a way to communicate your expertise to the social media world, flip to Chapter 6.

A huge part of branding is making sure your brand is represented accurately and consistently at all times. You, therefore, need to manage your online reputation by taking charge of the results that come back when someone does an Internet search for your name.

Here are the basic steps for managing your online reputation (for full details, head to Chapter 7):

1. **Assess your online appearance from the perspective of a hiring manager.**

   Try Googling yourself or searching for your name in a free, background check website like www.pipl.com.

2. **Build up enough content over time so Google's search results fill up with more relevant content.**

   Publish old slideshows or articles you've written to social sharing sites so that Google has more relevant content to display for your name.

3. **Monitor your reputation monthly.**

   If someone says something bad about you, you need to know about it right away. The only way to do that is by periodically searching for your name and seeing what pops up.

Putting Your Résumé Online

An online résumé can be searched and discovered by recruiters looking for talent, so having several of them increases your odds of being found. (Believe me, receiving a random call from a recruiter who found you online and who was so impressed that she wants an interview is a very nice feeling!) The beauty of online résumés is that you don't have to be a web designer to enjoy their benefits.

At the very least, you should have a LinkedIn résumé and a video résumé. If you want to have more than just these two online résumés, good for you! Head to Chapter 11 to find out about some additional online résumé options.

Writing an online résumé is very different than writing a résumé that you intend to print out and hand to someone. Don't think you can just copy and paste one into the other. (If you try that, your online presence can look stuffy, old fashioned, and hard to understand.) I give you the full scoop on the key stylistic differences in Chapter 8.

Why LinkedIn?

LinkedIn (www.linkedin.com) happens to be the highest-leverage tool for professional networkers today — period. With it, you have access to more information about companies and people than previous generations ever did — even if they paid for it! Study after study has shown that LinkedIn is the primary resource for hiring managers and recruiters to fill positions. If you aren't using it daily, you're making a huge mistake.

Of course, if you aren't using LinkedIn the right way, that's also a mistake. First, you need to make sure your profile is 100 percent complete (meaning it shows your photo, at least three recommendations, and all the details about your work experience and education). You also need to make sure the following parts of your profile are as appealing and informative as possible because these three parts are where recruiters look first (for help getting them in tiptop shape, see Chapter 9):

- ✔ Your profile picture
- ✔ Your professional headline (the line of text that appears below your name)
- ✔ Your profile summary (the larger text block that appears below your personal information)

To get the most benefit out of LinkedIn, don't just treat it as an online résumé. Instead, treat it as a professional networking tool. In fact, use LinkedIn as your networking hub. Sure, it may be easier to cruise job boards, but by regularly adding new people you meet to your network and getting so familiar with LinkedIn that you can use it in your sleep, you're going to have a better shot at finding a job at your target company.

Why video résumés?

Not every recruiter or hiring manager is going to spend time watching video résumés for fun. However, if someone already likes your application and wants to know more about who you are, offering him a video résumé is a great way to demonstrate your personality and communication skills.

The ideal video résumé addresses three key questions (I reveal the best ways to answer these questions in Chapter 10):

✔ Who are you?

✔ What motivates you?

✔ Can you do the job?

After you've produced a résumé that addresses each of these points, you're ready to upload it for hiring managers' viewing pleasure. In particular, I recommend uploading your video résumé to TubeMogul (which posts to YouTube). TubeMogul (`www.tubemogul.com`) allows you to share your video résumé on multiple sites with one simple uploading process, and YouTube is the second-largest search engine today.

Expanding Your Online Presence

As your online presence grows, so do your chances of getting discovered by a recruiter and receiving an unsolicited call. The more engaged you are online, the better off you'll be.

But where exactly do you start when you're looking to expand your online presence? Getting yourself on Twitter and Facebook, if you aren't already, is worth your while. Twitter (`www.twitter.com`), which I cover in Chapter 12, is hands down one of the most active recruiting tools (aside from LinkedIn, which I fill you in on earlier in this chapter). Not a day goes by that some HR recruiter or hiring manager doesn't hit up Twitter searching for talent. As for Facebook (`www.facebook.com`), which I cover in Chapter 13, you can discover the personality of the organization you're interested in by "liking" its Page, and you can even start engaging in conversation with it. That's a shortcut way to stand out from the crowd.

To cast your social media net even farther, start participating in some of the lesser-known networks. Your options range from general professional networking sites to niche networks, such as those for creative professionals and people seeking international employment. I share a wealth of such sites to explore in Chapter 14.

Going Proactive, the Social Media Way

Social media is pretty empowering to you as a job seeker. Think about it. Thanks to Facebook and corporate blogs, you can gather all kinds of research about companies to determine which companies (and positions) you really want to pursue. LinkedIn allows you to see how you may be connected to people who work at your target companies. If someone you know directly happens to know someone at one of those organizations, you can ask for an introduction to that contact. When you get it, *boom!* You now have a relationship with someone who, as long as you nurture and don't manipulate that relationship, can provide you with some real insight into XYZ Company.

Clearly, social media can be a job hunter's best friend — if you have a game plan for using it properly in your search for work. Fortunately, I'm here to provide you with just that. Here's how to conduct a proactive job search using the various social media tools at your disposal:

1. **Find companies (as well as people and opportunities) you want to target.**

    If you want the best results, you need to be very specific about what you're targeting in your search, whether that's a company or even a particular position at a company. You also need to know *who* in those companies you should be networking with. Fortunately, social media, as well as the tips I provide in Chapter 15, make it easy to hone in on your target company and identify potential decision makers.

2. **Get to know what the company and/or contact cares about and considers to be relevant.**

    Have you ever watched a good spy movie? The agent profiles his asset so he can understand what makes him tick. That's what you need to do in order to get noticed by very busy hiring managers in a very competitive job market. Start reading up on industry news, follow the company's various social media sites, and understand where you can add value. (For more specific advice, turn to Chapter 16.)

3. **Track down someone who's willing to give you time for an informational interview.**

    Just doing web research on the needs of your target audience isn't enough. You really do need to talk with other, low-stakes people at a target company. Use your network to bring your conversations offline. Talk to real people over coffee about what working there is like or set up time to converse on the phone if your contact is in a long-distance location. Ask them what about working for the company keeps them up at night. For in-depth guidance on tracking down the right contacts and conducting an informational interview, see Chapter 17.

    After you meet these info interview sources, add them to your social media networks (if they aren't there already). Doing so brings you one step closer to getting connected with a decision maker.

4. **Start interacting with people who have the power to hire you.**

The people who are going to be making a decision about hiring you are hanging out online. Now that you're armed with great information, you can reach out to them directly online and be confident in your ability to make a good impression. (For the full scoop on interacting with hiring managers online, head to Chapter 18.)

When you're reaching out to hiring managers, you still don't know whether you're a fit for the organization. So don't say, "I know I'd be a great fit for this job." Such a statement may easily turn off someone with the power to hire you. Remember that you're still in the process of gathering information, so just focus on making your interactions professional.

Conquering common objections to using social media in your career

If you have little to no interest in social media and are only reading this book because a friend or colleague thought you should, trust me when I say that numerous positive reasons exist for using social media in your career. For one thing, when you're trying to find a job, you need to be where the hiring managers are — and I guarantee many of them are using some form of social media.

Following are some common objections people pose to the idea of using social media in a career, as well as my thoughts on why those objections just don't pan out:

- **Social media is for kids on cellphones.** Au contraire! The fastest growing demographic on Facebook is 55 and older, and the average age of a Twitter user is 35. Also, all social media sites have desktop interfaces, so using your cellphone to access them isn't the only way.

- **I'm concerned about identity theft.** Honestly, you have more chances of getting your identity stolen from mail than from

hacked social networks. Plus, you don't have to give people your whole life story on social media sites. If you're smart about the information you reveal, you won't need to spend as much time worrying that an identity thief may steal your precious personal info. *Remember:* Keep the following to yourself at all times: your Social Security number, your mother's maiden name, and your birth date.

- **I don't have a lot of time, and I don't need another distraction.** Setting up your accounts on various social media sites may take some time, but from there on out, staying on top of social media shouldn't take that much extra time out of your schedule. If, however, time management is a serious concern for you, then turn to Chapter 2 for some tips and tricks.

Remember: My ultimate advice is to forget whatever judgments you have about social media and approach it with an open mind. Chances are you'll be pleasantly surprised by the results!

Chapter 2

Setting Yourself Up for a Successful Job Search

The various social media tools out there aren't magical — meaning they aren't going to lead you to your dream job if you don't put in a little bit of prep work. First things first: You need to have goals that inspire you, not frighten you. And when it comes to job searching, those inspirational goals tend to be smaller tasks so that you only have to think about one small piece of the puzzle at a time. I explain how to come up with such goals in this chapter. I also help you gather all the tools you need to run a modern job search and prepare a special space where you can focus solely on your job hunt.

If you're at all familiar with social media, you're probably well aware that you can easily lose track of time on sites like Facebook and Twitter. But that doesn't have to be the case. If you have a plan for managing your time, like the strategies I provide in this chapter, you can easily reign in the hours you spend in front of your computer instead of dragging them out. You can also save yourself some time by using one of the job-search organization tools I recommend. Finally, I offer some advice for keeping your motivation going strong on those days when job hunting is the last thing you want to do.

Developing Achievable Goals for Your Job Search

An achievable goal is concrete. In job-searching terms, having an achievable goal means aiming for positions that are equivalent to your work experience, not deciding you'll be president of a foundation within two years of graduating from college or declaring yourself the company's future CFO when your experience is all on the production side of the business.

Developing achievable goals helps give your job search momentum. More importantly, the small wins you make during your job search help turn feelings of helplessness into feelings of success. Aspiring after big goals can often lead to frustration. In many ways, it's much better to let aspirations be generally large and undefined and then be very concrete with the smaller, short-range goals.

The following sections help you figure out just how to set achievable goals for your job search.

Going with the flow

Mihaly Csikszentmihalyi (read: MEE-hy CHEEK-sent-mə-HY-ee), the author of *Flow: The Psychology of Optimal Experience* (Harper Perennial), carefully studied people's happiness in various life situations. Through his work, he discovered a state of mind called *flow* or *being in the zone,* which is characterized by a feeling of joy, purpose, and broad awareness with total immersion and focus. People report losing all sense of time when they're in flow. Perhaps you've had a flow experience before. Can you recall a time when you were so immersed in something that when you finished, you couldn't believe how long you'd been doing it? You can bring joy and flow into your job search by understanding the environmental factors needed to achieve flow and how to set goals in such a way that you're motivated and in the zone. According to Csikszentmihalyi, you need the following three conditions to create a sense of flow:

✔ **The activity you're doing must have concrete and worthy goals with clear next steps.** In other words, the reason you're doing what you're doing must have some value to you — it must be worth the effort. Clear next steps come from breaking down complex tasks into their smallest, least complex elements.

✔ **You must match your skills with the challenge you're facing.** The task facing you shouldn't be too easy, nor should it be too hard. Avoid boredom and anxiety.

✔ **You must have immediate and direct feedback from your activity in order to give you a sense of progress.** Tracking progress can give you a sense of accomplishment and direction. Also, knowing whether you did an activity well can help you do better the next time.

Looking at your current reality

Before you can set achievable goals, you must know where you currently stand. The best way to do this is by stepping back from your situation so you can critically analyze (A) what the situation is and (B) what you bring to the table. I once had a business coach ask me to list all my current assets. No, he didn't mean my stock market investments. He meant anything I have control over that can be leveraged to achieve an outcome. I included my skills, resources, experiences, web properties, articles I'd written, people I knew, and so forth. I didn't know how much I had until I spent time assessing my current reality.

Grab a sheet of paper and go through the following reality check before creating any goals related to your job search:

1. **List all the skills you have and can bring to the table in a work situation.**

   These skills may be as basic as typing and as advanced as certain technology, project management, or financial analysis skills. Don't discount public speaking, persuasion, or sales skills either. For each skill, consider how many years of practice you have.

   If you're having trouble figuring out what your skills are, head to www.onetonline.org/skills and check out the skills inventory.

   Don't stop listing skills until you have at least 20 written down. Yes, 20. Having to think of this many skills forces you to really take into account everything you can do well.

2. **Write down your most noteworthy accomplishments as they relate to your professional career.**

   Were you ever in the newspaper? Did you ever win an award? These accomplishments are important to celebrate and inventory. Also take into account any personal accomplishments that you're proud of.

3. **Note your 20 most important professional relationships.**

   Here you may include former bosses that you still keep in touch with or someone influential you once met. Examine your network and list anyone you know who may have more influence than the ordinary contact.

4. **List all your resources, whether they're people, groups, or objects.**

   Think about what's available to you that can provide you with support. These resources may be groups you're affiliated with, coaches you use, colleagues, friends and family who make you happy, or even software you own or subscribe to. This book is a resource. The local unemployment office may also be a resource.

5. Take your financial situation into account.

If you're unemployed, you want to understand how much time you have before you run out of money. Figure out how much you have in your savings and any secondary sources of income, and then subtract those amounts from your expenses.

Figuring out how long you can pay your current expenses with the money you have available is important. The last thing you need on your mind is the worry of how you're going to pay your bills. Also think about what expenses you can reduce or eliminate to give yourself an extra month or so. The goal here is to get to a number, in months or years, of when you're going to run out of finances. Doing so helps you establish a time frame for your most important goal: finding a job.

Students and recent grads may not have such dire financial concerns and familial responsibilities as the mid-level professional, apart from perhaps paying off some student loans. Remember, loans can be deferred, and if you can give yourself more time for the job search by doing so, then it's worth it. When you find the job you're looking for, you can pick your loans right up where you left off. The freedom from bills can open up new options for you, such as interning or temping, which often lead to full-time employment after several months.

After you write down all these lists, I want you to notice two things. First, notice how much support you have behind you. Not only do you have some amazing skills and accomplishments, but you have people who are willing to come to your aid. Second, you need to understand and know deep-down the kind of value you can bring to an organization. Coming from a place of confidence is important when you craft your personal brand (see Chapter 5). For now, use this information as the foundation for your goal setting. And ask yourself whether you have enough connections, skills, or resources to get you where you need to go. If not, then your first goal is to get yourself what you need.

Setting smaller tasks designed to help you reach your big goal

When you're conducting a job search, obviously your ultimate goal is to land a job. But the reality is that you aren't going to achieve that ultimate goal without setting smaller, intermediate tasks to help get you there step by step.

Just think about it for a moment. You can't have "get a job" on your to-do list without feeling a certain amount of anxiety. But if you chunk that larger goal down into smaller and smaller steps until you can't go any smaller, you'll reduce your anxiety level and feel a sense of accomplishment as you complete each smaller item.

How exactly do you go about breaking down the massive goal of getting a job into smaller tasks? Simply ask yourself, "What do I need to do that?" Ask yourself that same question each time you write down a new task. For example, you may come up with something like this:

> Get a job. *What do I need to do that?* Write a good résumé. *What do I need to do that?* Buy a résumé writing book. . . .

Buying a résumé writing book is a lot less scary than writing an entire résumé from scratch, and focusing on the smaller tasks first will help you not get overwhelmed with the big-picture goals.

The best way to track progress and get feedback about your goals is to use a scorecard. A *scorecard* is a spreadsheet that lists each step you take in order to achieve an outcome. As you can see from Table 2-1, a scorecard allows you to track your plan and record what actually happened.

Table 2-1		Job-Search Scorecard		
Milestone	*Task*	*Measurable Definition*	*Time Frame/ Measurement*	*Actual*
Get a new job		Receiving a written offer from a target company at the salary I want	6 months	
Have a good interview with a hiring manager		Interviewing with a hiring manager who's actively seeking to fill a position I want	1 per week	
	Apply to jobs online	Applying to jobs that I have a chance of qualifying for	5 per week	
	Attend networking groups with like-minded people	Meeting 10 new people per week and attending at least 3 events per week	Weekly	

(continued)

Table 2-1 *(continued)*

Milestone	Task	Measurable Definition	Time Frame/ Measurement	Actual
Update résumé		Having my résumé reviewed and approved by a professional résumé writer	Within a week	
	Hire professional résumé writer	Finding a résumé writer with recommendations who fits my budget	Tomorrow	
Build a personal brand		Looking consistent in all aspects of my job search	1 month	
	Come up with a value statement based on my strengths	Reciting it to people who seem interested in what I do	1 day	
	Polish up LinkedIn profile	Completing profile so that it's attractive and consistent with my résumé	1 week	8 days
	Write an article expressing my views on a professional topic	Receiving comments and feedback from my network	1 day	2 hours
Maintain my skills and industry knowledge		Volunteering in a role that requires my core skills	4 hours per week	
	Sign up for a continuing education class for a skill I need	Adding this skill to my résumé	1 month	1 month

Here's how to build your very own scorecard to keep track of your job-searching progress:

1. **Create a table like the example from Table 2-1, using word-processing or spreadsheet software or even just a blank piece of paper.**

2. **Write out your desired outcome, the measurable definition, and its time frame in the top row of the table.**

   A good example of a desired outcome is "get a job in three months." The measurable definition should explain what accomplishing this goal looks like in very tangible terms. For this example, that may be "receiving a written offer from a target company" because a written offer is tangible.

3. **Write down everything you think you have to do in order to achieve that outcome.**

   Don't check yourself at this point; just get your ideas out on paper. Keep asking yourself, "What do I need in order to do that?" as you go down the list.

4. **Group related tasks and identify goals that require more than one task to accomplish.**

   Goals that require more than one task are called *milestones* and are put in the far left column. Smaller tasks that can be finished without intermediary steps are put in the second to left column under Task.

5. **Group individual tasks under their related milestones and make sure each milestone has simple and concrete tasks under it.**

   Notice how in Table 2-1 the "Build a Personal Brand" milestone requires several intermediary steps? Each milestone will be like that. So the smaller and more specific you can make the task for each milestone, the better.

6. **Fill in the Actual column as you complete each step with how long it took you to complete.**

   By recording the actual time it took to complete a task, you're doing more than just checking items off of your to-do list. You're actually comparing the reality of a task with what you expected. From this comparison, you can gauge your level of commitment as well as the accuracy of your expectations.

Running a job search can be one of the most stressful things you ever do. So why not make it a habit to celebrate at least one accomplishment per week? When you pass a milestone, walk out from a good job interview, or finish a difficult task (like ranking in Google for your name), celebrate that success. These small celebrations can help you stay motivated for the duration of your search.

Setting Up a "Home Office" for Your New Job — Search, That Is

Job searching is almost a full-time job. And if you were running a small business from your home or apartment, you'd need a home office. So why not set up a home office to run your job search? Doing so helps you stay focused during tasks and reminds your family or roommates that you're not just playing around on the computer, but you're busy finding work and can't be disturbed right now.

Following are some basic rules to consider as you set up and begin using your home office for your job search:

- **Work in a separate space from the rest of your house.** If you don't have a spare room, then put up a curtain or separators in a corner of a room that's free from the usual hustle and bustle.

- **Establish boundaries with the people you live with.** If you have a door to the room you're working in, then when that door's shut, it means that you're not to be disturbed. If you don't have a door, make a sign to show that you're busy.

- **Get out of your pajamas and into your work clothes.** It sounds silly, but many people who work from home swear they get more done by dressing the part. If you're currently employed, this may mean that instead of changing into those comfy sweats right when you get home from the office, you opt for something that keeps you focused and in work mode.

- **Keep your work area well lit and clean.** Dark and messy places put up a psychological barrier. When you think about getting to work on your job search, you want a positive, clear-thinking feeling to arise, not a dark, disorganized one.

- **Use folders to file paperwork at least once a week.** Store these files below your desk or table. You want only things on your desk that you're currently working on.

- **Schedule your work time as if it were a job.** Tell yourself and your family supporters that during the same time every day, you're working on your job search. Scheduling time every day, whether it be a couple of hours or a full day's worth, ensures that you spend adequate time working on finding that dream job.

- **Avoid checking your e-mail first thing in the morning.** E-mail overload is a huge problem, and e-mails typically sidetrack you from doing the task you've set out to do. Check e-mail at only four or five scheduled times during the day and don't spend more than 25 minutes at a time reviewing your messages.

Of course, in addition to these ground rules, every home office requires some essential supplies. I describe what you need in the next sections.

Acquiring a working PC and Internet connection

If you buy only one item to help you with your job search, that item needs to be a computer or a *tablet PC* (a smaller, hand-held device with a touch screen). The good news is that every year, the cost of a computer goes down. In fact, you can have anything from a desktop computer to a *netbook* (a super small laptop, usually about 80 percent of the size of a standard laptop) for less than $300.

If you're willing to spend a little time on sites such as eBay and craigslist, you may be able to purchase a used computer for even less money than the cheaper new ones cost.

After you have your computer, you need to find yourself an Internet connection because the majority of communications you'll engage in during the hiring process will be via e-mail, and you may even have to fill out online applications for certain positions. Many affordable Internet options exist, ranging from free to $30 per month.

Want to get (relatively) free Internet? Most coffee shops these days offer free wireless Internet access. For the cost of a cup of coffee or a snack, you're welcome to sit in the shop for as long as you want.

If you want Internet at home, you have many options as well. Some cities now offer WiMAX services, also known as 4G, which is like cellphone service but used for data. It's essentially wireless Internet to your home. The leading provider of 4G Internet is Clear (www.clear.com), which has home Internet plans starting at around $30. Other options are cable and DSL from your local cable company. Cable companies offer promotions all the time, so make sure you ask for their current promotions when you call them. You may even say something like, "I'm looking for a new job and can't take on a large bill; what promotions can I take advantage of to become your customer?" (This works every time!)

Gathering the other essentials you need

After you have your computer and Internet situation figured out, you need to gather the other essential pieces of the job-searching-with-social-media puzzle:

✔ **A professional-sounding e-mail address:** Your e-mail address is the key to the world of social media because you can't sign up for sites such as LinkedIn or Facebook without one. And having an e-mail address with a professional ring to it tends to look better when filling out online applications. (If you don't already have a professional-sounding e-mail address, turn to Chapter 5 for tips on creating one.)

✔ **Word-processing and spreadsheet software:** Despite the emphasis on social networking sites in this book, you may, at some point, need to produce a résumé. For example, if you're submitting an online application, you'll be asked to attach a résumé, and you need a word-processing program to pull that résumé together. Spreadsheet software is good for budgeting, tracking milestones, and recording your target companies.

✔ **A phone number and answering machine:** Don't miss out on any opportunities by not having an answering service of some kind. You may not always be available to answer the phone.

✔ **A planner or task organizer:** Keep yourself organized and in control with some kind of web-based calendar and task management tool, which will help guide your job-hunting sessions each day.

Most job-search books say you need to *buy* MS Word, a paper planner, a phone, spreadsheet software, and an answering machine, but honestly, all you need is a free Google account. (And no, I don't work for Google, nor am I affiliated with the company in any way.) By simply creating a Google e-mail (or Gmail) account, you get the following free apps:

✔ E-mail with Gmail

✔ Word processor and spreadsheet software with Google Docs

✔ A phone number and answering machine with Google Voice

✔ A planner with Google Calendar

✔ A task organizer with Google Tasks

✔ A rolodex with Google Contacts

✔ Photo editing software with Picnik

✔ Translation software with Google Translate

✔ A library of free books with Google Books

Investing in business cards

Although I encourage you to network as best you can through a variety of different social media sites, all the social networking in the world isn't guaranteed to get you a job. You still need to put in some traditional networking time — as in interacting with people face to face at networking events. Some people firmly believe that all the best job opportunities truly come from the relationships you build with people as the result of networking.

If you plan on networking in person in addition to online, as I recommend you do, you're going to need business cards. Business cards are an extension of your *personal brand* (what makes you unique; more on this in Chapter 4) and are, therefore, important for helping people remember who you are.

The most common job-seeker business card comes from Vistaprint (www. vistaprint.com). Vistaprint offers new members 250 **free** business cards from a selection of 42 designs. However, as soon as you start customizing your card, it's not free anymore. I've been to networking events where three or four people have the exact same Vistaprint free card. Although the free option is a good starter, if you're serious about your personal brand, you may want to consider paying for premium or customized cards.

If you want some *nice* looking cards that get you comments at networking events, and you're willing to spend a little cash, then check out Moo Cards (www.us.moo.com). Moo Cards offers many modern designs and sizes on top-quality paper. The MiniCards are particularly popular these days.

Simplify your life with a single phone number

If you happen to have several phone numbers and they're getting confusing, consider simplifying your life by reducing those multiple phone numbers down to one. The free Google Voice service allows you to either import an existing phone number or generate a new one. Then, within the application, you can associate any other phone numbers to your Google phone number. This means multiple phones will ring when someone calls your Google Voice number.

Google Voice also provides these powerful features:

- Voice mail services
- Call screening
- Call recording

- Speech to text so you can actually read your voice mails as an e-mail or on your phone as SMS
- Free texting services
- Free calling anywhere in the United States
- Single number reach so you can get calls everywhere, even in Gmail

Even if you're happy with your cellphone service, I still suggest setting up a new Google Voice number to use for your job search. If an employer calls you, then you can screen the call and read his message instantly if you aren't in a place to pick it up. Having a Google Voice number also allows you to keep your job search separate from your personal life.

Managing Your Time in a Way That's Right for You

You may have broken your goals down into the smallest chunks possible and gathered everything you may possibly need for your job search (as discussed earlier in this chapter), but if you don't practice good time management, all those efforts may be for nothing. If you haven't yet experienced how easy it is to while away the hours on a social media site, trust me, it can happen without you even realizing it — and that's not a good thing when you're trying to find a job.

Because you've elected to look for a job by using all the social media tools at your disposable, you need to arm yourself with some strategies for staying on track. The following sections are here to help you out. I describe several strategies and encourage you to pick the one that makes the most sense for you.

The Pomodoro Technique

According to Francesco Cirillo, creator and author of *The Pomodoro Technique* (www.pomodorotechnique.com), the optimum chunk of time to work within is 25 minutes, the same time it takes to cook pomodoro sauce (a classic Italian tomato sauce). This observation led to Cirillo developing the Pomodoro Technique, an approach to time management that encourages you to work in 25-minute increments, taking short breaks after each 25-minute productivity session.

Here are the essential principles of the Pomodoro Technique:

- A *Pomodoro* (a 25-minute chunk of uninterrupted time) is indivisible.

- A task that takes more than five to seven Pomodoros is too big. Break it down.

- If a task takes less than one Pomodoro, add it together with other tasks.

- Time your Pomodoros with some kind of timer, being sure it rings at the end. You can buy software Pomodoro timers as well as kitchen timers that have been repurposed for this technique.

- Don't allow interruptions after you start the timer. If you do get interrupted, make a note of it.

- Once a Pomodoro is finished, you must stand up and take a three- to five-minute break. This break is important.

- The Pomodoro Technique shouldn't be used in your free time — enjoy your free time!

Looking at a big list of to-do's can be overwhelming. Because each Pomodoro is for focusing your energy, writing a daily list of to-do's can help reduce anxiety.

You can apply the Pomodoro Technique to your job search by following these steps for each of your job-searching tasks:

1. **Choose the topmost task from your daily task list to work on.**

2. **Set the timer to 25 minutes (one Pomodoro) and begin working.**

3. **Work on that task until the timer rings.**

4. **If the task is finished, cross it off; if not, put an X next to it.**

5. **Take a break, stand up, walk around, or do something else for five minutes.**

6. **Return to the task if necessary.**

   After four Pomodoros, take a longer break (about 30 to 60 minutes).

The egg timer method

If you find yourself online navigating from page to page, following this link and that link, or cruising around Facebook and before you know it two hours have gone by and you've accomplished nothing, then the next time you go online, practice the egg timer method. In other words, give yourself a time limit.

If you know that you have only one hour a day to spend on the Internet and you have a long list of tasks you need to accomplish for your job search, you'll be far more focused on using that time well. Of course, you'll need a count-down timer with a loud ring to make this one work. You'll have to be the best judge of how much time to take. So list out your tasks and estimate how much time you need to complete them, and then set yourself a time limit.

The shopping list method

If you're the type of person who typically enters a store with a list of items you want to buy, buys only those items, and leaves, the shopping list method may be for you. Just treat your time online the way you do when you're out shopping. Have a task you need to complete, stay online until that task is done, and then sign off. Be sure you don't put too much on your list. No one likes to spend two hours at the grocery store.

A note about interruptions

Interruptions to your work can become a real problem. They essentially rob you of your concentration and ultimately make your tasks take longer than they should. Specifically, it takes ten minutes to recover from an interruption. So in order to be truly productive, you need chunks of uninterrupted time.

Guard your work time selfishly and use some strategies for minimizing interruptions of either type.

✔ **Internal interruptions:** These types of interruptions are probably the most common and occur when you interrupt yourself.

Every time you second-guess your task list or priorities or start re-planning your job search, you take yourself away from your task. So if you suddenly feel the need to make an urgent phone call, don't. Unless it's an emergency, you can just write it down on your task list to be done later.

✔ **External interruptions:** True emergencies are rare, so if you get a phone call or e-mail, let it be. If someone comes into the room and wants to talk, kindly explain that you're busy at the moment but will get back to him when your work is complete.

Taking Advantage of Some Tools to Organize Your Search

Because most job searches follow a set pattern — find the opportunity, send in your résumé or application, follow up with a contact, go to an interview — using software to track your contacts and your steps on that path makes a lot of sense. Enter job-search organization tools. Not only do these babies help you organize the many moving parts, contacts, and job applications that are part of the job search, but they also allow you to store your data after you get your job. Later, when you're job searching once more, you can more easily pick up where you left off.

I profile a few different tools in the following sections. These tools have many similar features, so look at all of them and then choose one to use as your primary job-search organization tool (doing so will make your life far less complicated).

To make the deciding process easier, base your choice on the types of features the job-search organization tool offers and how well you like the user interface.

JobKatch

JobKatch (www.jobkatch.com) offers job seekers a powerful way to stay organized during a job search. It has built-in integrations with LinkedIn so you can import contacts and then track your interactions with them for particular jobs. As your list of opportunities grows, JobKatch helps you remember where you stand with each one. Here are some steps to using JobKatch:

1. **Find any job description or posting online.**

2. **Use the JobKatch bookmarklet to import that job description into the system and into your account to create a job record.**

   A *job record* is where job opportunities are stored.

3. **Add contacts into the job record and begin reaching out.**

   You can use the LinkedIn integration feature to speed things up.

4. **Take good notes about the company and opportunity so that you can apply with your best foot forward.**

   You can also rank jobs on a scale of one to five.

5. **Schedule follow-up calls or tasks and track your progress with each opportunity.**

6. **Watch the dashboard every day to see what tasks you've assigned for yourself that day.**

   Figure 2-1 shows you what the JobKatch dashboard looks like.

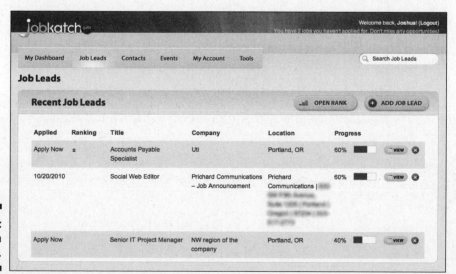

Figure 2-1:
JobKatch
dashboard.

Becomed

Becomed (www.becomed.com) bills itself as your job-search assistant. You can create specific job-search goals for yourself, such as how many applications you send a week or how many interviews you go to in a week. Then Becomed tells you where you stand against your goal as well as how you stand against other users (that's one way to stay motivated!).

As you enter job descriptions, link contacts, and upload documents, Becomed suggests possible next steps on your search. If you have a lot of contacts and job opportunities to keep track of, using Becomed is a great way to stay organized.

What I really like about Becomed is its report for unemployment offices. Many unemployment offices require some kind of proof that you're making an effort to find work. As long as you're tracking your activities in Becomed, you can print a report that most unemployment offices accept as proof of your efforts.

JibberJobber

My friend and mentor Jason Alba started JibberJobber (www.jibberjobber.com) in 2006 and can claim development of the first online job-search platform. By far, JibberJobber offers job seekers the most comprehensive set of tools for managing relationships, job searches, and careers. Here are just some of the features JibberJobber offers:

- ✔ Contact management tools so you can import contacts, see where they are in a map, and even show interrelationships between contacts

- ✔ A database of companies so you can quickly import target organizations or recruiters

- ✔ Job application management as well as job board RSS feeds so you can track the progress you make for each job

- ✔ Custom report building so you can take a summary view of your job search efforts or report to an unemployment office

- ✔ Interview preparation database so you can record questions you may be asked and how you plan to respond

- ✔ A library of articles and books, which you can download from or contribute to

- ✔ A log for your job-search expenses with a built-in budgeting tool to help you stay frugal during your hunt

CareerShift

If you recently graduated from college, you may recognize CareerShift (`bit.ly/Career-Shift`) because it supports many colleges' career centers as well as individual accounts. One of CareerShift's most impressive features is its job-board aggregation service. You can search every major job board from right inside your account, and the database is frequently updated with the newest opportunities.

What I think is the stunning value of CareerShift is that it actually tells you who you need to meet at each company, along with e-mail addresses and phone numbers for those people. This feature saves you hours of research identifying key hiring managers.

CareerShift also provides document management (so you can organize your résumés and cover letters) and campaign management (so you can keep track of which companies you've applied to). It also has a robust calendar feature that helps you track what you need to do each day of your job search.

Staying Motivated throughout Your Job Search

Motivation is the driving force that propels people toward a goal. And motivation during a job search, especially if you're unemployed, can become a real challenge. Mounting bills, unanswered résumés and applications, and other common job-search stresses make minced meat out of motivation sometimes.

Giving yourself time to heal after being laid off

If you just got laid off, don't expect to bounce back right away. A period of deliberate mourning for the loss of a job not only helps you heal but also helps you approach your job search with renewed interest and effort. So make sure you give yourself the time you need to heal. Often, people who are feeling frustrated during a job search are simply being too hard on themselves. You aren't a machine, so be realistic in your expectations.

I had a client who had just been laid off call me up urgently wanting to talk about her exciting new idea for a small business. When we met at the coffee shop, she started talking feverishly about this and that idea but not really committing to any one course of action. She got teary-eyed when we spoke about her old job and her anger for how unfair it was that she lost it. I could tell something wasn't right, so I said to her, "I can tell you're still upset about getting laid off. Have you really given yourself enough time to heal from that yet?" She immediately started to cry, shaking her head no. I prescribed a good month of not even thinking about her next job or business. After taking some time for herself, she pursued her small business idea and has now built herself a great independent income.

If you find yourself unmotivated, don't feel discouraged or start thinking you're lazy or lack ambition or will. All you have to do is find and understand the reason for your lack of motivation and then take steps to regain that motivation. Table 2-2 presents some possible reasons why you may lose motivation in your job search and what you can do to change it. Find yours and then apply the antidote.

Table 2-2	Combating Motivation Loss
Reason Your Motivation Has Disappeared	*How to Get Your Motivation Back*
Too much stress	Meditate. Studies show that just 20 minutes of daily meditation can significantly reduce cortisol levels in the body, which in turn reduces the feelings of stress. Exercise also reduces stress, so if you can't meditate, get to the gym instead. And if you really want to feel calm and confident, do both.
Skills deficit	Find out what skill you're missing and then take steps to acquire that skill, whether it be taking a class, attending a seminar, or brushing up on the latest trends in your industry.
Feeling overwhelmed	Break down the thing you're feeling overwhelmed about into smaller and smaller chunks. Then do one small piece at a time. Don't let feeling overwhelmed stop you from reaching your goals.
Feeling resentment	Take a step back and look at your situation dispassionately so you can solve the problem at hand. If you need to release some anger, go do that, but then come back to the table with a clear head. Also remember to not take things so personally. Keep focused on what you *can* control.
Procrastination cycle	Conquer procrastination by having clear next steps to a worthy goal. Record your progress and make sure your skills can meet the challenge. The real issue may actually be another item in this list. Find it and deal with it.
No clear next steps	Start with the outcome you want and then work your way backward by thinking of what it will take to make that happen. Break down each task into easily digestible chunks and take one step at a time.
No direct feedback from your actions	Use a scorecard to track your progress toward your larger goal. If you're just ticking things off a task list, you're not giving yourself enough feedback. Remember to celebrate each success, no matter how small.

Keeping a positive perspective during your job search is just one way to stay motivated. In the following sections, I help you find ways to clear your mind and not get overwhelmed with all the information being thrown at you or what may seem like a long road to meeting your goal.

Handling information overload

Give yourself a break! I mean an information break. Today, people are exposed to more information in a day than what someone who lived 100 years ago saw in a year. The human brain wasn't meant to take in so much, so fast, so consistently. Furthermore, most of the news you hear is negative and can wear you down.

Taking a day off from the phone and computer (and even the TV) is a great way to reduce your stress and recharge for more job searching later. Enjoy your free time without being tethered to a phone or computer or even thinking about your job search.

Looking at how far you've come

Looking at how much farther you have to go can easily overwhelm you. However, looking forward isn't the whole truth. Consider how far you've come and all that you've gone through to get to where you are now.

One of the lessons I learned while playing drums semiprofessionally in college was to practice, not out of desperation to get as good as one of the legendary drummers, but to be as good as I could be with the skill and time I put into it. After months of practicing four to six hours a day, I was on the verge of burnout when a saxophone player took me aside and said, "Look how far you've come!" I suddenly realized how much better a drummer I was. Instead of desperation to be great, I felt joyous at how much I'd accomplished. I still think back to that moment and am reminded to always balance aspiration with appreciation. So take a moment from striving for a job and look back to see and acknowledge how far you've come.

Take time to celebrate your progress. Every Friday, look back at your week and ask yourself, "What have I accomplished this week?" Then reward yourself for it. Not only is this a great habit to get into, but it will keep you going strong in your job search.

College grads, let your true self shine

College grads often find themselves in the doldrums not only because of the difficulties of finding a job but also because of not really knowing who they are and what they want to do. Call it an existential dilemma. Every year, more than 3 million people graduate from college, and the vast majority of them have limited or no experience in the workforce.

The key to staying motivated at such a chaotic time in life is to find your ground and really know who you are and what makes you unique. Think of the ideal of the Samurai who, in the midst of battle, keeps his mind calm and clear. If you're feeling pulled this way and that way or feel that you simply lack the experience needed to do what you want, then spend some time crafting your personal brand (I show you how in Chapter 5). Going through the introspective exercises required to develop your brand can really boost your confidence. Then turning that focus to researching industries and companies that interest you takes your mind off of your own stress and leverages all those academic skills you spent the last four years honing.

And if you worry about what you want to be when you grow up, realize that most adults never find an answer to that question. So don't get so bent out of shape about it. Just choose something that seems good enough for now.

Chapter 3

Reviewing the Basics of Online Networking

In This Chapter

▶ Discovering why online networking is as important as in-person networking

▶ Understanding the protocols of online networking

▶ Figuring out how to make your contacts' connections work for you

▶ Staying involved in your networks while employed

The essence of networking, either online or in person, is to listen and find ways you can be of service. No matter what tools you use or what your goal is, keep this fundamental principle in mind as you network. After all, you can't expect to receive help, introductions, or advice unless you're fully prepared to give those things to others first. Networking is all about building mutually beneficial professional relationships.

In this chapter, I help you understand why networking is the key to landing your next job. I show you how to network and manage all the contacts you'll make. And because not disappearing from your networks after you land that dream job is crucial, I reveal some easy ways to show the people who helped you get that job that you're still there for them, whatever they need.

Making Connections through In-Person and Online Networking

Only about 3.5 percent of job postings ever make it to job boards. So guess how most hiring happens? If you're thinking "through networking," you're exactly right. Most jobs, no matter what country you live in or whether you're a senior executive or an entry-level worker, are a direct result of networking. So if you want to have a successful career, you need to have a strong network.

But what exactly is networking? *Networking* consists of building your list of contacts, or essentially knowing a lot of people who you can easily call and invite to coffee or have a phone conversation with. Your network is people you know who know you and are willing to refer you to others. Traditional networking is when you go to an event and meet new people. Ideally, you want those initial meetings to grow into professional relationships where ideas and contacts are exchanged.

In the last several years, networking has taken an online dimension with the advent of social media. Social media has transformed an anonymous Internet into a social and deeply personal experience. Now more than ever, great networking can occur through meeting people online. I'm not saying online networking should replace in-person networking; however, I'm suggesting that, when used correctly, online networking can be every bit as powerful and effective to augment your in-person efforts.

Online networking has several powerful benefits, such as the following:

✔ You don't have to pay to get to the networking event.

✔ You can discover info about people before reaching out to them, thanks to their online profiles.

✔ You can connect with people much faster online than in person.

✔ You can have discussions with more people in a shorter amount of time online than you can at an in-person networking event.

You can't rely on online networking alone. If you use only online networking, your relationships may end up being quite shallow indeed. Meeting people in person is the best way to build relationships. Even if you're meeting new professional contacts online, find ways to meet them in person or at least talk to them on the phone. Although online networking is a great tool for growing your connections, it isn't a substitute for the real thing.

An easy way to turn a traditional, in-person networking event into an online networking opportunity is to send a note to your new contacts within the body of a LinkedIn invitation after you get home from the event. In essence, you're combining a "nice to meet you" with a "let's connect on LinkedIn" message. Most people who are active LinkedIn users accept invitations to connect, especially if they've already met you in person. As your new contacts make changes or updates to their profiles, your online connection allows you to engage with them outside of last week's networking event.

The Do's and Don'ts of Online Networking

Online networking — that is, meeting and interacting with other professionals via the Internet — is a relatively new thing. If you think about it, people have had millions of years to figure out how to interact with each other in person without being annoying. They shake hands as a symbol of friendship and consider interruption rude (in most cultures anyhow). But as people started interacting online, they had difficulty communicating with self-control and tact.

In the following sections, I share a set of protocols for networking with people online. Pay attention to them because if you can avoid being annoying in your online interactions, you'll be way ahead of the curve.

Avoiding online networking boo-boos

Whether you're networking with people on LinkedIn, commenting on a blog, or chatting more casually on Facebook, follow these guidelines to be sure you don't annoy people:

- **Don't ignore the unspoken rules of the network you're using.** For example, LinkedIn is a professional network, so don't share private information on it. Also, Facebook posts can be more casual, so don't be too formal in how you write.

- **Don't spam.** People are already bombarded with too much information these days. If you start interacting with someone too frequently, you may just annoy him or her. If someone doesn't get back to you right away, wait at least a week before following up.

- **Don't shout.** Using ALL CAPS in your online interactions is like shouting. No one likes to be shouted at.

- **Don't beg.** Networking isn't about you; it's about them. Never come across as desperate. Instead, show your passion and offer to help.

- **Don't be generic.** The worst thing you can say on someone's blog is, "Nice post." Instead, try being a bit more thoughtful by arguing with a point, calling out an example that applies to your life, or providing a quote.

- **Don't just add someone to your network without an explanation.** Although doing so is acceptable on Twitter, LinkedIn and Facebook connections deserve to get a reminder from you about how you met and why you want to connect. To avoid an awkward situation, consider sending a message first before asking for a connection.

Being an outstanding online networker

Beyond just avoiding being annoying online, you can do some powerful things to become an outstanding networker. In the end, you want your interactions with others online to grow your career and help you stand out from the crowd. Here are some pointers to keep in mind:

✔ **Be genuine.** Bring your authentic self to the table. Social media requires authentic communication, so show some personality when you write to people. And always make your intentions transparent.

✔ **Be respectful of people's time.** Long e-mails, LinkedIn requests, or other interactions often go unread. Get to your point quickly and keep your message short.

✔ **Show that you're listening.** Because getting information, news, and updates about the people you talk with online is so easy, you have almost no excuse for not knowing what's going on with a contact. If you demonstrate that you researched someone online before interacting, he'll respect you more.

✔ **Be positive.** Nobody likes to hang around with a complainer. Even if you disagree with what someone says, never take it personally. Try to keep all your interactions as positive as possible.

✔ **Be proactive.** Find forums, blogs, or new people to reach out to and interact with. If you're respectful, people will admire your outgoingness.

✔ **Make connections between people when you see similarities.** If you can make an introduction, go for it. If you find a link to an article that someone may like, share it. The greatest thing you can be for your network is a connector.

Taking Advantage of Your Connections' Connections

The power of networking, on- or offline, isn't simply who you know, but who the people you know know. In my own professional career, a lot of opportunities have come from those second- and even third-degree connections. In fact, a fifth-degree connection introduced me to the editors of this book! I'm sure if you look back at your own career, you'll find that your friends and/or colleagues are the ones who introduced you to other people who were of great help to you.

One way to start networking and assessing the value of the people you know is to look at the various categories of people in your life and make note of who you know in each category. Following are some basic categories most people have in their life; take a few moments to write down the people you know in each one.

✔ **Friends:** You hang out with these people casually. You may meet them at parties or speak to them mostly on the phone, or they may be parents of your children's friends.

✔ **Family or inner circle:** Within this group, you may have close or distant relatives, extended family, and then their business associates. Most people have relatives who've established strong careers for themselves, and their connections may be able to help you.

✔ **Current or past business associates:** Include former colleagues, assistants, or staff in this category. Also think about businesses you currently use; as a customer, you have a powerful business relationship you can leverage.

✔ **Professional associations and conferences:** You may already be a part of an organization that encourages networking. The contacts you make there are valuable even if you see them only occasionally. The same is true for any conferences you may have attended.

✔ **Fellow club or organization members:** Your alumni association in particular is a great place to network. After all, you naturally feel comfortable with people you share similar interests with. In this category, you may also include any athletic club members from clubs you or your children participate in. When I lived in China for a summer, I hung out at a local rock climbing gym and met some great new friends and potential business connections.

As you begin to build your network, you may want some way of organizing your contacts so that their information is easily accessible to you when and where you need it. The following sections provide advice for starting and organizing your contact list.

Using a CRM system to maintain a contact list

With the hundreds of online interactions you're likely to engage in, keeping a record of all the e-mails exchanged between you and a particular contact is incredibly helpful. Plus, these days, you also need a way of staying current with all your contacts' social media updates. Although LinkedIn is great for reaching out to new people and researching about companies, it doesn't offer the robust contact management features you need for a long career. Enter contact relationship management, or CRM. A *CRM system* is a software-based tool that stores interactions and organizes contacts. I recommend using one of the CRM systems described in the following sections.

Contacting everyone in your network at least once a quarter is a great way to stay connected, and a CRM system can help you remember to do that. It can also aid you in recalling which relationships require your attention. Set reminders in your calendar when it's time to scan your network for people who may need some attention.

Gist

Seattle-based software startup Gist (www.gist.com) provides one of the most robust systems for managing your contacts, tracking what they're doing online, and keeping detailed records of them. Gist is also the most hands-free and automatic system I've seen on the market. What's more, it's totally free.

What makes Gist unique is that it can automatically recognize people's names, add their social media profiles and their photos from Google images, and provide you with news feeds of the companies they work for. Better yet, Gist can start doing all of this for you pretty quickly because it doesn't take long at all to upload new contacts. Case in point: When I came back from a large professional conference and had 50 business cards of new contacts to process, I simply uploaded them to Gist, and in just a half-hour, I was able to follow all these people online. (To see for yourself just how easy this process is, check out this video: bit.ly/gist-video.)

If that's not enough to convince you that the potential for Gist (shown in Figure 3-1) as a job seeker's dream come true is enormous, then check out this CRM system's other interesting features:

- ✔ The ability to connect your current social networks in a single place by syncing Facebook, Twitter, or LinkedIn contacts into your Gist database

- ✔ An at-a-glance list of important contacts compiled by Gist based on an algorithm that guesses which people you need to keep on the radar on a scale of 1 to 100 (100 being the most important)

- ✔ An interactive calendar that links to your Google calendar, sends confirmation e-mails for meetings, and allows you to see your events and organize your day within Gist

- ✔ A *dossier,* or summary page, about your contacts that you can print and review before an interview or meeting

- ✔ News feeds about your contacts and the ability to interact with them without leaving Gist

- ✔ A way to keep track of important facts about your contacts, like whether they're mentors, clients, or hiring managers

- ✔ The ability to integrate with Gmail and see your most recent interactions with people, including a list of e-mails sent to them

- ✔ An info request form that allows you to ask your contacts for more information about them

Gist can feel a bit overwhelming at first because it displays an enormous amount of information on one page. Give yourself a couple of days to get comfortable with the interface. This tool can help you stay organized and be a better networker. Bookmark it to make sure you visit often.

Figure 3-1:
My user
interface on
Gist.

Plaxo

Many professionals use Plaxo (www.plaxo.com) to keep their contact records in order and monitor the online activities of the people they know. Plaxo was one of the first online contact management systems ever developed and is basically an online address book for professionals. Although you can connect with people on Plaxo and even see a stream of online activity from your network, it isn't technically a social network but rather a venue for managing contact information. Perhaps you've even received a notice from a colleague who uses Plaxo, asking you to verify or update your contact information on occasion, which wouldn't be surprising because the site has more than 20 million users.

The low-cost monthly subscription for full features on Plaxo includes

- ✔ Deduplication, in case you have the same contact recorded twice
- ✔ Syncing between Outlook and Google accounts
- ✔ Update-your-info reminders so your records are up-to-date
- ✔ Birthday reminders (if you have that information) and e-cards
- ✔ Backup services so, if you lose a computer, your contacts are safe

Batchbook

Batchbook (www.batchblue.com), from Rhode Island–based BatchBlue Software, is a traditional sales-based Customer Relationship Management system. Although built for small businesses to manage their sales funnel, some features may appeal to the ladder-climbing professional. This product was designed to optimize flexibility, so using it for professional networking is just as easy as setting it up for a small business. Batchbook has a small monthly fee for features that allow you to do the following:

- Track every e-mail you send to contacts (no matter what e-mail system you use) and then create follow-up tasks.

- Set up future tasks to remind yourself to stay in touch with someone.

- Keep track of where you meet people or what function they have in your network via *flexible tagging* (labels that you can assign).

- Pull a contact's social media information into a contact record.

Organizing your contact list

Not everyone in your contact list is created equal. And I mean that as non-hierarchically as possible. Some people serve as hubs and help you meet interesting people while others offer you great advice and are more like mentors. Here are different roles people can have in your network:

- **Promoters:** These people let you know about opportunities. They're the ones who call and say, "Did you hear that Widgets is hiring?"

- **Hubs:** These contacts connect you with other people you may want to meet, or they suggest new networking events for you to attend.

- **Mentors:** The people who guide your career, show you new things, or are brave enough to give you some direct, yet necessary, feedback are your mentors. If you have a wise voice in your life or even a coach, that person is a mentor.

- **Role models:** People who have achieved what you aspire to are your role models. They're the people you respect and value as being a part of your network. Role models may have a similar job to the one you're looking for, or they may just be excellent at what they do.

If you're using a tag-based CRM system to organize all your contacts, consider tagging each contact with one or two roles. What's great about tagging is that when you need someone to ask advice of, simply search for your mentors and see who you want to meet. If you're looking for an introduction into a company, search for your hubs.

Keeping a List of Online Networks You've Joined

The Internet is a wild and unstructured place. After surfing around for an hour, you may find yourself trying to remember where you read this or that. You may even forget what networks you've joined, which is a real problem when you're trying to conduct a job search in today's social media–heavy environment. The following tools help me stay organized, and I think they'll work well for you, too.

Your Google Profile

The Google Profile is a page that Google gives all its users to display their web presence, photos, and links. It links with your Picasa and Flickr accounts and lets you customize your messages. Anyone who has a Gmail login also has a Google Profile waiting to be customized.

To find your profile, just enter a Google search for "Google profiles." For guidance on customizing your Google Profile, turn to Chapter 14.

As you add more social networks to your pile, add their public links to your Google Profile so you have a list of all the networks you belong to in one place (as shown in Figure 3-2). Just click on Edit Profile and add a custom link. If you make a habit of adding each network you join to your Google Profile, you'll be able to easily keep track of all your networks.

Links

- About.Me Page
- joshuawaldman.net
- Cinta Media
- careerenlightenment.net
- Resume
- Linkedin Profile
- Follow me on Twitter
- YouTube - ngakalden
- Picasa Web Albums
- ngakalden
- Xing Profile
- Tungle.Me to get on my...
- Gist.com
- Viadeo
- Biznik.com

Figure 3-2: Links on a Google Profile.

Delicious

Delicious (www.delicious.com) is a web-based bookmarking tool that you can use to tag and keep track of all the social networks you join. Follow these steps to set up Delicious for yourself:

1. **Go to www.delicious.com and sign up for free.**
2. **Install the Delicious bookmarklet (button) for your web browser.**
3. **Use Delicious to tag any social network you join.**

   Be sure to use the same tag, such as "Social Network" or "Profile" for all the networks you join.
4. **Use your browser bookmarklet or go to your Delicious account to see what pages you've bookmarked.**

   When you search for your chosen tag, all the networks you've joined come up in a list.

Remaining Active in Your Network Even after You Land a Job

Here's a popular scenario (and one I know I'm guilty of): You start your job search and begin networking like crazy. You go to every event, exchange hundreds of business cards, and begin the long process of relationship building. Then you get hired, and no one hears from you again. You got what you were after and promptly abandoned all your contacts and online networks.

I understand that after you get a job, you don't have the same amount of time to devote to networking. However, consider the following three reasons to continue your networking efforts even after you move on to your next gig:

- ✔ **You never know when you'll need your network again.** With most jobs lasting about two years, needing your network for a job search may happen sooner than you think. By maintaining your network during employment, your next job search will be much smoother.

- ✔ **Because you now have a job, you're in a position to really help others who are struggling to find one.** Volunteering your time or leveraging your new position to help other people is an extremely upright and moral thing to do. Treat others as you want to be treated.

- ✔ **Most upward-moving jobs require a strong network.** Whether you're in sales, operations, or another part of a company, who you know matters to your career. You want to maintain visibility to your network not only to open new doors for projects or to get new clients but also to demonstrate that you're a leader and a contributing member of a community.

Planning your monthly networking events

To help you stay on top of your network in the face of a busy work schedule, set aside one day each month to plan and schedule some networking events to attend. For example, on the first Sunday of every month, I run through my event checklist so that I'm at least aware of and can make choices about what events I attend that month. As soon as I find an event I want to attend, I immediately add it to my calendar.

Create your checklist by listing out every place online where you can find local events. Create a document with active links to these sites so you just have to click down the list, look for cool stuff happening that month, and then put some of them on your calendar. This simple task saves you time from researching the event sites every month. You do it once at the beginning and just follow the checklist after that.

The frequency or intensity of your involvement and perhaps the groups you visit may be more industry-focused, but you shouldn't stop networking completely. The sections that follow provide tips and tricks for fitting networking into your life on a manageable basis.

Maintaining your momentum

It takes years to build a strong network. The longer you stay away from professional networking, the more career momentum you're bound to lose. And trust me, you can't afford to lose any momentum — unless you don't mind reinventing the wheel every time you start looking for a new job.

Here are some ways you can keep up your networking momentum without getting in the way of your new job:

✔ **Find the right mix.** Perhaps you choose three networking groups to belong to and be active with. Consider when and how often the groups meet and ask yourself whether you can commit to that. (Many professional networking groups meet quarterly after hours. Surely that's doable.) Maintain relationships from the groups via your social networks. At the very least, add them to your LinkedIn network.

✔ **Keep the right mind set.** If you think everyone you meet should and will benefit your career, then you won't make many friends. Instead, keep an open mind and see networking as an ongoing process with an unknown outcome. Perhaps you'll make a good friend or perhaps nothing will come of it. Whatever the outcome, enjoy the process.

✔ **Learn something new.** Many industry networking events also include some kind of lecture or guest speaker. Take advantage of the learning opportunity as well as the networking aspect. Then share what you learned with your online network through status updates or blog posts.

✔ **Set reasonable goals.** These goals may include attending at least one networking event a month and meeting three new people at it. Or you may set goals to help you stay in touch with your existing network. For example, commit to inviting at least one person in your network to happy hour or sending five LinkedIn messages just saying "Hi" each month.

✔ **Correspond with your e-mail list.** This task requires just a few minutes and keeps your relationships fresh. This approach is particularly useful when leaving an unemployment support group. Don't just disappear, but e-mail the leader of that group with any news about you. Group leaders love this type of news and usually share it with everyone else for you.

Giving back to your network by helping someone else out

After you achieve some degree of success in your career, helping others simply feels good, gives you a sense of hope and self-confidence, and shows that you're the type of person who gives back to his community and network. Here are some ways you can give back:

✔ Send an e-mail to a local job-search group and offer an hour of your time to look at people's résumés.

✔ Send job openings you hear about to people looking for work.

✔ Volunteer at a local unemployment office to teach a professional skill.

✔ Buy ten copies of a book (like this one!) that you found useful in your career and donate them to a group of motivated job seekers.

✔ Teach a class at the local community college.

✔ Volunteer for your local college's mentorship program.

✔ Interview high-school students who have applied to your alma mater.

✔ Pick someone you know who's struggling and reach out to her by offering to look at her résumé or sharing some of the tips you picked up from this book on using social media for your career.

Sending a regular newsletter

Sending your contacts an interesting, valuable, and consistent newsletter can keep you top of mind and active in your network. When done tastefully and with care, these professional (and sometimes personal) e-mail blasts can reconnect old contacts and build stronger relationships. Plus sending a newsletter really doesn't take much time or effort.

Don't send a mass e-mail to your entire contact list from Outlook or any other e-mail client. Doing so may be considered spam from a legal standpoint (and that's not a conversation you really want to have with a regulatory body). So always use an e-mail marketing client to manage large e-mail blasts. These companies ensure that your e-mail is delivered and complies with the most recent CAN-SPAM law.

The next sections explain how to find a system that can send your e-mail newsletter for you and how to pull together content for your newsletter.

Setting up your e-mail newsletter system

I particularly like the MailChimp e-mail newsletter system (`bit.ly/email-chimp`) because it's completely free to include up to 2,000 people from your contact list. Also the user interface is intuitive, and the newsletter templates are really nice. After you sign up for MailChimp, follow these steps to set up your e-mail newsletter system:

1. **Set up your e-mail list by clicking on Lists from the top ribbon and then clicking on Create List.**

   Follow the on-screen instructions to set up your first list. I recommend typing in "Networking Contacts" for your list name.

2. **Import your list of contacts into MailChimp.**

   You can import contacts into MailChimp by linking your Gmail account, uploading a spreadsheet, or simply copying and pasting.

3. **Start your first newsletter and choose how you want it to look.**

   MailChimp calls your newsletter, or any time you send out an e-mail, a *campaign.* It offers a wide variety of layouts and color schemes for your campaigns; see one for yourself in Figure 3-3.

Figure 3-3: A sample MailChimp newsletter setup.

4. **Send out your newsletter.**

   Keep on top of your newsletter by scheduling an hour each month (or quarter) to put together content to include in your newsletter.

Gathering content to send to your network

The biggest reason most newsletters fail after the third issue is that the author fails to plan. Planning your content strategy is critical, and it gets easier (and more fun) as you do it. Following are some tricks to help make sure your newsletter remains a consistent part of your networking and your career:

- **Bookmark any interesting articles you think your contact list will enjoy.** (If you're using Delicious to keep track of websites you like, you can tag it with "newsletter.") Later, when you're writing content for your newsletter, just go to your bookmarked websites (or your Delicious account and search for "newsletter") and attach them to your newsletter.

- **Link your personal blog (if you have one) with the newsletter by using MailChimp's RSS tag.** It automatically imports your most recent posts and populates your newsletter for you.

- **Keep a journal of your professional and personal news.** Evernote (www.evernote.com) is a good tool for journaling. When you're ready to write your newsletter, look at your journal and pick out three interesting things that have happened to you recently.

- **Tell an ongoing story.** One of my contacts, Jenny Blake, author of *Life After College: The Complete Guide to Getting What You Want* (Running Press), kept me updated through her newsletter as she wrote her book, found a publisher, and then started selling it. Each stage in her journey was interesting to read. You may tell an ongoing story of your job search and then continue with how your new job is going, or you may want to share in a professional learning experience or volunteer project for an organization. Some people are passionate about a particular cause that has affected their life. If you participate in a cause and are active in it, why not keep your network updated with it?

Part II
Marketing Yourself with a Personal Brand

The 5th Wave   By Rich Tennant

"I know it's a short profile, but I thought 'King of the Jungle' sort of said it all."

In this part . . .

Your personal brand isn't a tattoo that says, "Hire me! I'm a great employee." It's actually all the things that make you *you*. In other words, your personal brand is what makes you unique. This part puts you in touch with your personal brand; so after you figure out all the characteristics that make you who you are, you can start refining your brand and communicating those characteristics to potential employers.

A word of warning: If you don't brand yourself, someone else will, thanks to the ready availability of information about you on the Internet. That's why you have to be prepared to take an active role in managing your online reputation. This part also gives you the information you need to do just that.

Chapter 4

Personal Branding 101

· ·

In This Chapter

▶ Diving into personal branding and revealing why you need to take it seriously

▶ Realizing what goes into a personal brand

▶ Figuring out who you are in order to build your brand

▶ Delivering the right message to the right person

▶ Obtaining feedback on your brand from others

· ·

*1*f there's one thing you can do to improve your chances of getting a job, developing a personal brand is it. Yet despite personal branding's importance in today's job-search paradigm, many job seekers still don't understand what it's all about. This chapter is here to clue you in to what personal branding is and to relieve you of any misperceptions you may have about it.

After you have a solid understanding of what personal branding means and why it's so valuable, you can start working on building your own. Of course, that raises two questions: Should you look at the needs of your job market first? Or should you evaluate your own personal strengths? In other words, what comes first: you or your job?

The answer is you; a job seeker must always first understand herself. Your confidence as you walk into an interview room or networking event comes from self-understanding. Knowing what room to walk into comes from understanding your market. As Tom Peters (the man who essentially coined the term *personal branding*) once said, "You're not defined by your job title, and you're not confined by your job description."

So in this chapter, I also guide you through a series of fun self-discovery exercises, help you identify your target market, and reveal how to gather feedback that will help you refine your personal brand.

Discovering What Your Personal Brand Is and Why It's Essential

Personal branding is the culmination of your actions; it's an image that marks you as a brand. It is you, the entire package, outside and inside, in the sense that you're unique and distinguishable from others. Personal branding has a lot to do with the emotion someone feels when he or she thinks about you (something you can't control) but is rooted in self-reflection and integrity (something you can control by regulating your behavior on- and offline and by presenting yourself conscientiously).

Although obvious differences between you, as a brand, and a tube of Crest toothpaste exist, considering yourself as a brand can help bring objectivity to your job search and continuity to your career. In other words, building a personal brand gives you the ability to make career choices easily and consistently.

Every serious professional must consider his or her personal brand for the following reasons:

- ✔ **When you proactively define and communicate your brand, you're in control of it.** Most people have their brand handed to them by other people's perceptions and reactions alone. By defining your brand, you take back some control over this process.

- ✔ **Crafting your personal brand helps you figure out what makes you unique.** The process of finding and communicating your brand can therefore be pretty powerful.

- ✔ **A personal brand helps you appear more consistent online and avoid raising any red flags with recruiters.** Inconsistencies in how you appear online can put your career in jeopardy because hiring managers and HR professionals may view them as signs you aren't being completely honest about who you are.

- ✔ **When you have a personal brand, you can more easily make decisions during your career.** When you're presented with options that go against your brand — against who you are — then letting them go is easier, even if they're more lucrative.

- ✔ **A personal brand can even out the troughs between employment by being the one thing that doesn't change about you.** This is quite helpful when you consider that the average time at a job in the U.S. is about two years.

I delve further into each of these points in the following sections.

Branding yourself before someone else does

Branding is all about trying your best to manage other people's perceptions of you. Because you can't reach into someone else's head and tweak how that person sees you, all you can do is change your image, your messaging, your look, and so forth to better align with who you really are. If people who don't like you *really* got to know you, I'm sure their misperceptions would evaporate pretty quickly.

Instead of waiting for others to form random opinions about you that may or may not be accurate, help them out by sharing your well-crafted personal brand. Spending a few days figuring out your personal brand goes a long way in fostering understanding with other people and helps others see you for who you are.

Setting yourself apart from other job candidates

Differentiating yourself from all the other potential candidates for a job means being yourself, as in your authentic, true self — a task no one else can do for you. Personal branding allows you to let your true self shine by encouraging you to look inward and evaluate what makes you different from everyone else. Only after you complete this inner evaluation will you have enough information to say, "I'm better than anyone else going for this position because . . ."

Granted, looking inside and figuring out who you are can be very uncomfortable, which is probably why most job seekers avoid personal branding. But self-knowledge really is the key to building the confidence that helps you stand out and be unique.

I once lost a job opportunity because I didn't display enough self-knowledge. During a high-stakes interview at the end of my MBA program, the interviewer asked, "What are some subjects or classes that you really struggle with and why?" I answered with, "I get high grades in all my classes." So he pressed on, "What are three things you would want to change about yourself?" And I said, "I'd be a better speller, not have to use a calculator so much, and . . ." These answers were superficial and didn't show that I had spent a lot of time reflecting upon what I was really good at and what I needed to work on.

Maintaining a consistent online presence

Your online identity should be consistent no matter where someone looks for you. If you do your personal branding right, you become a single thought in the mind of a potential hiring manager. When you're done with the branding process, your LinkedIn profile will match your other online profiles. And if you get a chance to send a résumé, your brand will be visible there, too.

When recruiters start looking for talent, they typically start with LinkedIn. If they find you on LinkedIn and your profile appeals to them, they keep digging. They do background checks and Internet searches to find out more about you. If your online image has any inconsistency, you may find yourself in the *maybe* pile pretty quickly.

Why is it dangerous to have inconsistencies online? When someone's image is incongruent with what you expect, it can make you feel uneasy. Just think about cool, alpha male Tom Cruise jumping on Oprah's couch like a giddy schoolgirl.

Simplifying your decision-making process

Having a clearly defined personal brand can help make your career decisions easier. When career opportunities arise that you're unsure of, you can look back at your brand for guidance. For example, if you've determined that you prefer small companies and don't want to travel, then you know that turning down a job at a large, bureaucratic organization that sends its employees all over the place will contribute to your happiness, even if that job pays better.

Managing your career versus finding a job

To have an effective personal brand, you must think of yourself as the CEO of your own company. Any job you have is just a short-term contract. In the United States, where the average length of time at a job is two years, this viewpoint makes it possible for you to manage your career. Creating and maintaining a strong personal brand helps you minimize the gaps between jobs because you're doing the following:

- Continually networking, both on- and offline
- Maintaining your résumé and online profiles
- Setting short- and long-term goals by asking yourself where you want to be in three to five years and with what company, position, and level of responsibility
- Viewing your professional life beyond the confines of any single organization, which means you're reflecting on the personal and/or professional skills you need to further your career

Understanding How Social Media Affects Your Brand

The widespread adoption of social media has been the catalyst for personal branding's strong comeback. In the 12 years between Tom Peters's 1997 influential article in *Fast Company* and the heavy dose of personal branding literature in the early 2000s, personal branding was relegated to MBA types who had obscure notions of corporate branding and who had a public profile to worry about. Now the playing field has leveled because of social media, where everyone has a public profile.

Before social media, personal branding was really just a mental shift toward a feeling that you're a CEO in control of your professional life. The crux of the notion was that you controlled your image, position, and advancement. Personal branding was a shift from loyalty to a company to loyalty to your team, your project, your customers, and yourself. According to Tom Peters, when you had control over your brand, the ladder of advancement was what you made it. Naturally, elements of your public image were strictly relegated to your résumé, portfolio, how you dressed, and how you talked. Unless articles were written by or about you, you weren't going to have much public visibility.

These notions remained obscure until people began to realize how easy it is to get out there and be seen. Blogs, Twitter, and personal websites have changed the way most people feel about publicity. Nowadays, everyone has an online reputation to worry about, even if you don't think you do.

 As with any overused notion, the true meaning of personal branding is sometimes lost. People misidentify that personal branding is just a matter of making them look good online. Although online reputation management is certainly a large part of personal branding, nothing is more important than actually being who you say you are and being able to effectively communicate this.

Discovering the Elements of a Personal Brand

A brand, by nature, is a very abstract thing. Even companies struggle to put their brands into concrete terms. So this section isn't an exhaustive list of what a brand is. However, if you're new to the idea of a personal brand, having concrete examples of how your brand can manifest in your life is helpful.

In-person brand elements

How people perceive your brand when they meet you in person is based on the following elements:

- **The way you act:** Your actions are very much part of your image. Are you late, on time, or early? Is your body language confident? Do you smile a lot? Most importantly, are you really good at what you do?

- **The way you talk:** The tone, speed, and inflection with which you talk can tie into people's perceptions of you. Do you speak with a soft voice? Does your tone match someone of your social status or experience? Is your pace slow and confident or fast and high energy?

- **The way you dress:** Your attire can define you as a person. Are you casual or formal? What colors do you wear? Are you a thrift store junkie?

- **Who you think you are:** How you perceive yourself can come across to people subtly as they interact with you. What are you most proud of in your life? What do you value most? What are your special talents and skills?

Online brand elements

The purpose of online brand elements is to show people who don't really know you or have never met you in person who you really are. Your online brand elements manifest themselves in

- **The way you act online:** Your online behavior clues people in to what you may be like in person. The way you act may include the state of your LinkedIn profile, your blog, or the first three pages of a Google search result of your name. Do you have a story to tell? How frequently do you post messages?

- **The way (and how often) you talk online:** Your online voice reflects how people hear your offline voice. For example, are you posting status updates on your profiles? If so, do your updates add value or are they silly? Are you aware of your audience when you post?

- **The way you present yourself:** This may include the way your blog looks and how professional your pictures are. Is there a font you're fond of? If so, what does it communicate? Also, what do the colors in your blog or online résumé communicate?

Getting to Know Who You Really Are

Almost every decision anyone makes is based on emotions — yes, that includes hiring managers. If someone doesn't like you, she's probably not going to hire you. However, if someone does like you, she'll justify that feeling by looking at your good qualities. When job seekers don't show any personality, hiring managers often fill in the blanks with their imagination. So the more you can demonstrate who you are, the better off you'll be.

Personal branding allows you to let your personality — the only part of your application that can't be duplicated — shine in the eyes of decision makers. And it starts with self-examination. The more you know about who you are and the more gracefully you can share that knowledge with others, the easier it will be to advance and manage your career. This fact of life applies to everyone, from entry-level employees to executives. Just look at Cisco's John Chambers, the CEO with style. His warmth and presence has literally defined an entire company in the market. Many of Cisco's products are commodities, yet it outsells its competition every year.

If you can find the courage to venture into the world of self-analysis, you'll have an automatic leg up on your competition, and you may even shorten your job search by several months. The following sections help you through this process of self-examination.

Defining your life's values

Values — those fundamental principles that you believe in — are what drive your decision making, at least when it comes to the big stuff. For example, if you value sustainability, you probably aren't going to choose to work for an oil company, even if you're offered an impressive salary. Knowing your values makes it easier to establish goals, make career choices, and most importantly, make decisions about what you want your brand to be all about.

Spend a few days thinking about your values and what's most important to you in life. If you're a list person, you can head to `bit.ly/values-list` for a list of values that you can pick and choose from. If you prefer a more hands-on approach, try your hand at one of the following exercises designed to help you identify your values.

Creating this list of your own values helps you write your *value statement,* which is how you differentiate yourself in the job market. Head on over to Chapter 5 where I guide you through that process.

Who do you admire most?

A great way of discovering your life values is to think carefully about who you admire and what values you share. This person can be famous or as close to you as a parent. Sometimes you may find a value in another person that hasn't yet manifested in your life but is something you aspire to. That's okay too. To figure out who this person is, simply follow these steps:

1. **Make a list of five people you admire.**

   They can be icons, role models, or loved ones.

2. **List the reasons you admire them next to their name.**

   Was it something they achieved, something they sacrificed their lives for, or an ideal they stand for?

3. **Determine the value each of those people represents in you.**

   For example, say you put your grandmother on your list because of the compassion she shows others by spending a few hours a week visiting patients at a local children's hospital. Because of her example, you feel compelled to volunteer to help care for abandoned animals. So you may make a note that *compassion* is a core value for you.

What are you most proud of?

Thinking about the one thing in your past that you're the most proud of is a simple exercise that can work wonders. Many of my clients have found flashes of insight into their personalities and professional lives by doing this exercise.

Spend a few minutes writing down the whole story of your proudest moment. Then ask someone you trust to read it and give you feedback. Have that person tell you what you seem to value in that situation. Often, your deepest values emerge based on the events you choose to remember most. For example, one of my clients was most proud of a time she stood up to some bullies who made fun of her because of her skin color. Even though she was punished by her parents, she felt proud of having taken a stand. Through this story, she discovered that she very deeply cares about justice and taking personal risk in order to do what she thinks is right.

A real-life personal branding success story

I once had a client who was a brilliant engineer. His résumé was astounding, but he didn't really know, deep down, what he was good at. Apart from having an incomplete LinkedIn profile with no picture, he wasn't comfortable putting himself out there. As a consequence, he found it difficult even getting an interview.

I prescribed a heavy dose of personal branding. I challenged him to ask his friends and former colleagues for 360-degree feedback. (I explain what this is in the "Using the 360°Reach program" section later in this chapter.) I asked him to evaluate his values, passions, and successes.

Then we went shopping for some new clothes and took some glamour shots for his online profiles. After about a week of self-discovery, he was feeling much better about himself.

We then switched over to the second part of branding: understanding the needs of your audience. We dove into researching what his target companies were facing in the marketplace, and he discovered a personal connection he had at a new company. By demonstrating that he understood the needs of the organization and by changing his appearance in such a way as to be more congruent with his skill level, he got the interview.

Finish the sentence

Finishing leading sentences is a fun and creative way to elicit your values. What may seem like an obvious finish for you may be totally different for someone else, and realizing that difference helps you define your values. Finish the following sentences for a flash of insight into your deepest character:

> If I had 24 hours to live . . .
>
> If I had a million dollars, I would . . .
>
> Many people don't agree with me about . . .
>
> My best friends can be counted on to . . .
>
> People who know me think I am . . .
>
> If I could be any animal, I'd be a . . . because . . .

Write your own 75th birthday toast

Imagine you're at your 75th birthday party, and people who know you well are toasting you. Think about what you'd want that tribute to say based on your life up to this point and between now and age 75. Describe the setting, who's attending, and who's giving the toast, and then write the tribute, being as specific and detailed as possible. Consider talking about the following points:

- ✔ Your heirs — your genetic legacy — and what makes you proud of them
- ✔ Professional or charitable organizations you're a member of
- ✔ Various members of the audience; who else you'd have at the party
- ✔ Your most noteworthy accomplishment
- ✔ Something you always wanted to do but never did
- ✔ The impact you've had on the life of the person speaking, who that person is to you, and why he or she volunteered to toast you

Understanding your passions

Showing genuine passion can reassure a hiring manager that you are who you say you are and that you'll be as enthusiastic in six months as you are now, during a job search. This means that you need to know what your passions are and find a way to channel them in a constructive way. Having a firm knowledge of your passions helps you infuse your personal brand with authenticity and energy.

To discover your passions, ask yourself the following simple questions:

> ✔ What can I talk about for hours without getting bored?
>
> ✔ What really wakes me up in the morning?
>
> ✔ What do I do that makes me lose track of time?

Write down the answers to these questions in a notebook and then refer back to them when you write your value statement in Chapter 5.

Although you may discover that you really love to cook and can do it for hours without thinking of the time, that doesn't necessarily mean you should be a chef. It can simply mean that you love to be creative and work at a project that pleases others. Really think about what's behind the activity that you enjoy and use the core principle to help define your passions.

Giving yourself a sound bite

Perhaps you have a long list of words to describe yourself. That's great, but a hiring manager doesn't have the time (or the interest) to sit down and read through your list. You need to winnow down all those great, descriptive words into a short list of no more than three in order to create a memorable sound bite. Forcing yourself to choose three words also helps you prioritize your personal branding message. And this focus ties in to your value statement, résumé, and any other decisions about your image.

Take this opportunity to decide on the top three words that best describe *you*. Remember these words and hang them up so you can see them during your job search. They'll define you, drive you, and reassure you. If I were to call you on the phone right now and ask for the three words that define who you are, I'd expect no hesitation as you reply, "Integrity, helping others, and courage."

One of the best business cards I've ever seen was from a senior technologist who called herself a *database wizard with personality*. One simple phrase was really the perfect representation of her character, personality, and skill. The goal here is for you to have your own sound bite.

Taking the MAPP test

Online career assessments can help you bring objectivity to your inner search. The MAPP test, or Motivational Appraisal of Personal Potential, is a popular test for job seekers. It takes about 15 minutes to complete and asks you to agree or disagree with a triad of three questions. At the end, it tells you what your strengths and motivations toward different types of work are. You can take the MAPP test for free at `bit. ly/MAPP-test`.

Looking at Your Market

A brand is only as good as its perception, which means simple self-knowledge isn't enough. You need to understand the real needs of your target market if you want your personal brand message to really stick.

The secret to finding work that you love is to make sure that *what* you do and what you *like* to do overlap with what the *company needs* you to do. You achieve the second half of this by putting yourself in the shoes of a potential hiring manager, which I show you how to do in the following sections.

Identifying your niche with the blue ocean strategy

You want people calling you out of nowhere because they thought of you when a job opened up. So what can you say that really makes you stick out? Try using *blue ocean strategy* to figure that out. Blue ocean strategy is a way of differentiating yourself in a competitive market by changing the rules. After many years of business consulting and statistical analysis of more than 160 companies, W. Chan Kim and Renée Mauborgne wrote the seminal book on business strategy, *Blue Ocean Strategy: How to Create Uncontested Market Space and Make Competition Irrelevant* (Harvard Business Press). Some of their insights are valuable to job seekers competing in today's overcrowded market. Namely, they discovered that two types of markets exist:

- ✔ **Red ocean markets:** These markets are red because of the bloody battles of competition. Competitors vie for market share by offering cheaper or better products and services. For job seekers, this market exists when 50 MBA grads go for that big-name corporate position or when an entry-level position is announced on craigslist for the first time and 300 people send in their résumé.

- ✔ **Blue ocean markets:** These markets are blue because no one else is there to compete with you. The company has changed the value proposition so much so that it can't be compared with anyone else. For a job seeker, this type of market means that you're so different than everyone else going for the job that you're the obvious choice.

A blue ocean strategy is simply positioning yourself so uniquely that you don't have any competition. In other words, you separate yourself from the crowd by offering a different type of value to the hiring manager. You can create a blue ocean strategy by following these four steps:

1. **Eliminate factors in the market that everyone else takes for granted.**

2. **Reduce factors that can't be eliminated but can be lower than industry standards.**

3. **Raise factors that others aren't paying much attention to but that add value.**

4. **Create factors that the industry has overlooked.**

In real life, this blue ocean strategy played out with Southwest Airlines. The company focused on its strengths — low-cost, friendly service and access to smaller airports — and eliminated what other airlines compete on — meals, seating classes, and comfort. Then Southwest added a brand-new value to consumers by offering frequent departures. In a sense, Southwest is more competitive with automobile transportation than other airlines.

Grab a piece of paper or pop open your computer's spreadsheet program, create an *x*- and *y*-axis like you would for a graph, and then follow these steps, which show you how to use the blue ocean strategy to differentiate yourself in the job market:

1. **Think about a position you're going for — be specific.**

    Use this specific position to title your chart, as shown in Figure 4-1.

2. **On the *x*-axis, list about ten qualities, skills, traits, and other factors that may qualify a typical job candidate for that position.**

    Figure 4-1 uses obvious competitive factors, such as years of experience, education level, and skills.

3. **On the *y*-axis, draw in a scale from one to ten and map out the line where a typical candidate may be for each factor listed on the *x*-axis.**

4. **Fill in the data for two typical candidates.**

    Lines A and B in Figure 4-1 represents these two candidates. Drawing both lines helps you better visualize how you're different from the competition.

5. **Analyze which of these factors are unnecessary and which can be downplayed.**

    The person creating this chart is a career changer who doesn't have an advanced degree in the field, so he eliminates the importance of the years of experience and education level factors accordingly.

6. **Determine which factors can raise you to a point where no one else can touch you.**

    This person knows he can get a very high number of recommendations because people love working with him so much that they're willing to risk their reputations to support his career change. So he gives himself high marks for this factor and assumes that other job seekers have only the minimum number of recommendations.

7. **Create new value to get your line looking different from that of a typical candidate.**

   Look at other companies or functions within a company and see whether you can bring in other factors. Or look at the hiring manager's boss and see what he needs.

   In Figure 4-1, the candidate decides that this position really needs someone with high energy who can inspire and motivate others on the team. Consequently, he adds these factors to his chart and gives himself high marks because he knows how much enthusiasm he brings to the table compared to other job seekers.

After you have your chart, you can clearly see how you're different from your competition. Embed these differentiating factors into everything you do with your brand.

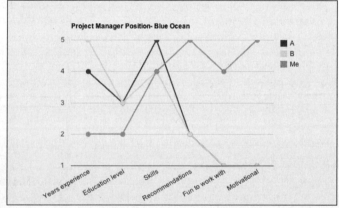

Figure 4-1:
A sample blue ocean analysis for a job seeker.

Finding "ins" with target companies and managers by collecting demographics

Demographic information about target companies and potential hiring managers can help you in crafting a powerful value statement later on. When writing marketing copy, such as your value statement or even profile information, being able to visualize your target audience is often helpful. On a spreadsheet or a piece of paper, list your ten target companies across the following dimensions:

✔ The company's mission or vision

✔ The company's top three goals

- ✔ The company's values

- ✔ Industry

- ✔ Location

- ✔ One to three main competitors

- ✔ The position you're looking for

- ✔ Size (revenue or number of employees)

- ✔ The top three struggles that the company or industry is facing now

If the companies you're targeting are publicly traded, all the basic information you can possibly need is included in their annual reports. If not, explore the companies' websites or LinkedIn profiles to find it.

Collecting these companies' basic information not only can help you write a strong value statement (see Chapter 5) but also may give you new insights on how to position yourself in the market. For example, a client of mine was going for a position designing eLearning for corporations. He discovered that the company's previous person wasn't very creative and the company had some pretty serious deadlines to meet. So instead of sending over a traditional résumé, he designed an eLearning about himself and about his experiences. It was an eLearning résumé. A critical component of this résumé was how little time it took him to do it. He addressed the company's two primary concerns — creativity and speed to implementation.

Now, you're going to drill a little bit deeper and try to understand the hiring manager at each of your target companies. Using LinkedIn's people search, try to find out who the hiring managers may be at your top ten companies (for details on how to use LinkedIn's people search feature to find hiring managers, check out Chapter 15). Look at their profiles, Google their names, and then fill out a demographic analysis on the following dimensions. (*Note:* Some items in this list require some speculation. That's okay for now. Just guess or make it up. The point of the exercise is to help you step into the hiring managers' shoes and see things from their perspective.)

- ✔ How old are they?

- ✔ Are they male or female?

- ✔ What's their career, rank, job position, or title?

- ✔ How much money do they make a year? (speculate)

- ✔ What's their education?

- ✔ What do they do in their spare time? (speculate)

- ✔ What websites or portals do they visit for information? (speculate)

- ✔ What are their professional activities outside of work, perhaps volunteering?

> ✔ What problems are they facing?
>
> ✔ How are they similar to you?

If you can answer these questions for your target hiring managers, then you have a shoo-in on making a huge lasting impression. Why? Because, like it or not, people are more comfortable with people who are like themselves. That's just basic psychology.

Case in point: Many years ago, I was going for a job that I was totally qualified for, but the guy who ended up getting it had more in common with the hiring manager. They both worked at the same company previously, encountered the same political problems, and were pushed out for exactly the same reason. I didn't stand a chance.

Use your demographic research not only to inform how you define your brand but also to keep track of at least one thing you can relate to about a person or company you're targeting. Then lead with that common thing when it's time to reach out.

Gathering Feedback for an Outside Perspective

Remaining objective about your personality and career can be a difficult task. This problem doesn't relate only to job seekers; even long employed professionals struggle with really knowing what they're good at and what they need to improve on. So a tool was developed called *360-degree feedback,* or *multisource feedback,* where the subject receives honest input from his peers and managers. Today, almost one-third of all U.S.-based companies rely on some kind of 360-degree feedback system to improve employee performance. As a job seeker, you want to take advantage of this type of feedback in order to better understand your strengths and guide your career search. After all, a brand is only as good as people perceive it to be. If you know how people perceive you, you have greater control over your branding choices later.

In the following sections, I show you how to ask your peers and colleagues for honest, constructive feedback and how to apply that feedback to your personal brand so you come out looking even better than you did before.

Getting honest feedback can be tricky

If you just go up to someone and say, "Hey, tell me what I'm bad at," you're not likely to get an honest answer. That's why you have to either put some time into crafting your questions or use a tool that asks the questions for you. I describe both approaches in the next sections.

Doing it yourself

If you plan to conduct your own 360-degree feedback, be sure you know exactly what you want to get out of your colleagues' feedback before you send out e-mails or develop survey questions. If you need this feedback to double-check your values, find out what your passions are or see whether the next job is really going to be a fit and then be sure to ask questions that get you the information you need.

For example, if you've done blue ocean analysis and a values-elicitation exercise (I explain how to do both earlier in this chapter) and the results show that you're enthusiastic and even optimistic, then you may want to make sure people really perceive you this way. So your questions may be something like this: "On a scale from one to ten, how enthusiastic would you say I am?" or "At any point, has my enthusiasm ever come across as inauthentic or annoying?"

You also need to pay special attention to the sensitivities of your friends and co-workers. They may not have the time to write feedback for you. Or they may be afraid of offending you. So before you blast an e-mail out to everyone you know, asking them what they think about you, follow some of these tips:

- ✔ **Frame your questions in the future tense.** Asking "What can I do to be better at . . . ?" moves the focus from feelings to future processes. People find it easier to respond honestly when they don't have to worry about offending you.

- ✔ **To respect people's time, offer them a chance to respond with numerical values.** "On a scale from one to ten, with ten being the highest, would you say I'm passionate about serving clients?"

- ✔ **Make it possible for people to provide anonymous feedback.** The more anonymous the feedback format, the more accurate the answers. You may consider using Google Docs (www.docs.google.com) to create a survey form or using SurveyMonkey (www.surveymonkey.com), which is a free online survey tool.

- ✔ **Keep your opinion on the feedback to yourself.** If you're receiving feedback from someone in person, the only two words you should say when they're done are *thank you*.

Conducting your own 360-degree feedback is great for keeping complete control over the types of questions you want to ask and is also much more personal than the form e-mails some tools send out.

Using the 360°Reach program

William Arruda, a personal branding coach and coauthor of *Career Distinction: Stand Out by Building Your Brand* (John Wiley & Sons, Inc.), developed a very handy little tool called 360°Reach, available at `www.reachcc.com/360reach`. It asks you approximately 100 questions about your values, who you are, and so forth. Then, you type in the names and e-mail addresses of at least 20 people you want feedback from. Reach then e-mails them and delivers the results to you.

Pick people who you know have time to respond to the survey and whose opinion you value. This group of people can be any combination of friends, family, and colleagues.

The response rate to Reach's e-mails aren't the best. Many times the e-mail lands in the spam inbox or the recipient simply doesn't know what it's all about or have the time to figure it out. So I strongly suggest that you give your list of 20 people a heads-up, telling them that you need their help and that they should expect an e-mail from Reach soon.

The benefit of using the 360° Reach program is that it gives the reviewer a sense of anonymity around giving you direct and candid feedback. You'll receive answers that may not come from more personal touches. And because the program is fully automated, all you have to do is log in, answer the questions, and wait for your responses.

Putting feedback into brand action

When you begin collecting the results of your 360-degree feedback, you may notice that who you *think* you are isn't exactly lining up with who other people think you are. For example, you may think you're confident or shy, but others may see you as arrogant or aloof.

These dissonances, as they're often called by psychologists, are painful. And not getting defensive is difficult. So keep a level head and show appreciation for this feedback. After all, you're going to use it to get better at what you do. The following sections help you figure out how to improve negative perceptions and build on positive perceptions.

Correcting negative perceptions

Negative perceptions can really get in the way of advancing your career, so you need to be on the lookout for them. Sometimes you can't do much to change innate parts of your personality, but as long as you're aware of them, you can manage them effectively. Consider the following strategies when faced with negative perceptions that may be a detriment to your personal brand:

✓ **Behave in the opposite way.** If you received feedback for being too cocky, then perhaps you don't have to show your confidence quite so much. Avoid self-aggrandizing language and tone down the confidence. If your feedback was that you're passive or indecisive, then maybe you should speak more loudly or be the first one to speak at a meeting or networking event.

✔ **Anticipate dissonance and admit it upfront.** If you know what the top three misperceptions about you are and how you generally rub people the wrong way, you can anticipate situations where these dissonances may occur. The best way to dissolve any potential bad feelings is to admit your weakness upfront: "I tend to get very excited about this topic, so if I come across as impulsive or hyper, just let me know and I'll check myself. I certainly don't mean to offend anyone." Or "I'm generally a quiet person, but that doesn't mean I'm passive. If I don't say much during this meeting, it's because I'm the type of person who likes to think through the whole problem. I'm actually very engaged and will chime in when I can."

Enhancing positive perceptions

Not all the feedback you receive will be negative. In fact, you may feel flattered at what some people say. If more than two people mention values, passions, or personality traits in their feedback, perhaps you have some brand perceptions you can simply augment rather than re-create. Or ride the wave, so to speak.

Ask yourself what perceptions people already have about you and what you can do to play those up. In my case, I was told by many people that I explain complex technology in an easy-to-understand way. So my brand is very much centered around making the obscure accessible through clear and practical advice.

Chapter 5

Crafting Keywords, Value Statements, and More

In This Chapter

▶ Doing a little keyword research so you get found online

▶ Creating a consistent value statement that tells others all about you

▶ Translating your value statement into a professional social media presence

---

Social networking is just like normal networking except it's done online. At a networking event, you may be asked to tell someone about yourself. If your 30-second elevator pitch about what makes you so great sparks the listener's interest, chances are you have yourself a nice conversation. As a job seeker, the goal of your coherent and consistent social media presence is to secure the interest of a hiring manager.

In this chapter, I help you figure out how to spark a hiring manager's interest so that you stand out from everyone else. I show you how to get noticed by search engines via killer keywords, put together a value statement that's social media friendly, and translate that message into a brand image that can be easily repeated throughout the Internet.

Conducting Keyword Research to Capture Attention

When you write online, you're not just writing for people; you're also writing for robots. Let me explain: Imagine the Internet is a large village of both people and robots. Whenever a person says something in this village, the words float through the air. Pretty soon, a robot grabs those floating words and takes them to a processing plant with millions of other words. These robots are the search engines of the Internet, and they're constantly scanning and categorizing online content — yes, even your LinkedIn profile.

The content producers who know how to write copy that attracts more search engines (robots) ultimately get more people reading their content. Good web copy is keyword rich. Think of a keyword as a noun that has more points with the search engines and a keyphrase as a series of keywords. In the following sections, I reveal how you can create content for a non-human audience by thoroughly understanding how search engines like Google spit out results, pinpointing the right keywords for your personal brand, and then keeping track of (and actually using) those keywords in your online profile.

The nouns, or keywords, you choose upfront become part of your personal brand. You not only use them in your value statement but also in your résumé, business cards, and so forth. The words you find in this section are going to help define and differentiate you.

Understanding how Google ranks its results

I remember career advisors handing me lists of power verbs to cherry-pick and add to my otherwise uninspired résumé. Using these power verbs was, of course, great advice for paper résumés. After all, the only consumer of a paper résumé is a human. But now we live in an online world where humans still love to read power verbs but robots prefer to read nouns, or keywords.

When was the last time you entered only verbs into a Google search? Your interactions with searching on the Internet are typically through finding people, places, or things. Imagine that when your future boss is ready to look for a new employee, he goes to Google or LinkedIn and types in the position he's looking to fill for the city where his company's located. He scans through the search results and clicks on the first few names that speak to his company's needs. If you want your name to come up in the search, you have to understand how Google ranks its results, because ultimately Google decides which people show up on that first page. This process is known as *Google Rank* or *PageRank*.

Google's legendary search algorithm has gone through several iterations over the years. With each cycle, Google's robot seems to get more human in its understanding of how people use language to convey meaning. In other words, the higher a page ranks on Google's first three pages, the more likely that site is relevant to the searcher. Let's face it, how many times have you searched in Google and found the results useless? Most of the time, Google gives you exactly what you're looking for.

Google is able to tell whether a website is spam and irrelevant or has great content. This determination is called *relevance,* and Google ranks websites based on relevance. Today, experts can boil down Google's search algorithm to the following on-site elements. ***Note:*** If you're knowledgeable about Search Engine Optimization (or SEO, which I cover in Chapter 7), then this explanation may appear oversimplified, but these points are the most critical for anyone writing profiles for social media networking sites.

- ✔ **Exact match of the search keyword/keyphrase:** Based on its appearance on the web page, Google ranks (or displays) an exact match first.

- ✔ **Semantic match of the search keyword/keyphrase:** Using a semantic match means that Google may rank a website based on the meaning of the nouns, even if it doesn't have an exact match. Think of a semantic match like synonyms for the keyword/keyphrase you used.

- ✔ **Appearance of the search keyword/keyphrase in key places:** These key places on the web page refer to headlines, titles, and bold font.

- ✔ **The readability of the text on the screen:** People who pack keywords on their page get penalized. Generally, Google prefers text that's easy to read.

- ✔ **The authority of the website that content is housed on:** This website authority is called *PageRank,* or *PR.* LinkedIn has a very high PR, which is why job seekers often see their LinkedIn profiles rank higher than some of the other websites they use.

The better keywords you choose and the more often those keywords appear in your profile, the better off you are.

Identifying your most powerful keywords

Because companies like to have high search-engine rankings, too, you may have a hard time competing with Fortune 500 enterprises for certain keywords. In order to improve your chances of getting found, start collecting and using *keyphrases* (a string of two or more keywords together). The following sections outline four specific strategies for uncovering the most powerful, high-leverage keywords/keyphrases to use on your online profiles. I encourage you to check out each of these strategies and then compile a list of at least ten powerful keyphrases. Keep this list by your side when you write your web copy.

Search engines don't process verbs very well; they much prefer nouns. Verbs are for people readers. During your keyword research, focus on coming up with a list of nouns that are the most relevant to the kind of job you want.

Use your brain

One strategy for coming up with killer keywords is to use your brain (and no, I'm not being cheeky by saying that). People often overlook their own common sense because the online tools are just, well, so convenient. But no online tool has the intuition you already possess about your desired role.

In order to come up with your keyword list, just imagine that you're an HR recruiter looking for someone to fill an open position. What words would you type into Google to find someone to fill that opening? For example, if you're an HR recruiter looking for a museum curator, you may search for the following words: *preservation professional, collection management, exhibition development,* or even *history enthusiast.*

Now, sit down with a blank piece of paper and brainstorm as many descriptive phrases as you can think of for your desired position.

Ask the government

Believe it or not, the U.S. government can be a good source for keyword inspiration. Every two years, the U.S. Bureau of Labor Statistics releases a publication called *The Occupational Outlook Handbook,* or the OOH. This huge volume can be downloaded or read online in small chunks at `www.bls.gov/OCO`.

The OOH contains information about job descriptions, responsibilities, and even career paths and compensation for most jobs. Each occupation description is divided into main sections, including the following:

- ✔ **Significant Points:** This section summarizes the key characteristics of the position.

- ✔ **Nature of the Work:** To find out what a person in that occupation actually does, look at the Nature of the Work section. You can find the best general keywords there.

- ✔ **Training, Other Qualifications, and Advancement:** Use this section to look for words to describe your education and training.

- ✔ **Employment:** This section tells you just how competitive the job is in the marketplace.

- ✔ **Job Outlook:** Gain a sense of a career path for the position you're looking for in the Job Outlook section. You may glean some words or phrases that managers of that position may use in their search.

- ✔ **Sources of Additional Information:** In this section, find out what professional associations are available for any given profession, what accreditation programs you can take, and so forth. Use the many links in this section as a launching off point for additional research.

Wondering how to put these categories to good use? Say, for example, that you're a museum curator. On the OOH website, type in "museum" in the Search OOH box on the left side of the page. Click the link for the top search result, which takes you to the occupation description as described in the preceding list. From that page description, you may find the following key-phrases significant:

✔ Museum technician

✔ Public outreach programs

✔ Long-term preservation

Explore job boards

I'm sure you already know a lot about job boards (Simply Hired, The Ladders, and Dice, to name a few), but did you know that job boards can have a hidden function? They're a great tool for finding out what language employers use to describe your desired position. For purposes of keyphrase research, find five or ten job postings that best match what you want to do. It doesn't matter where they're located or for what company. After you start reading these job postings, you may notice some repeating words and patterns. Write them down.

If you're a visual person like me, try using a word-cloud tool. A *word cloud* is a visual representation of the words used in a body of text, with the larger words representing higher frequency (see Figure 5-1 for an illustration of a word cloud for a sales position). Using a word cloud is an excellent way to find commonly used keywords for the job you want. Find a word-cloud generator you like (the two most popular ones are www.wordle.net/create and www.tagcrowd.com) and copy and paste the job posting you found to see what you get. Paste one entire job listing for each word cloud. Then save the image that's generated.

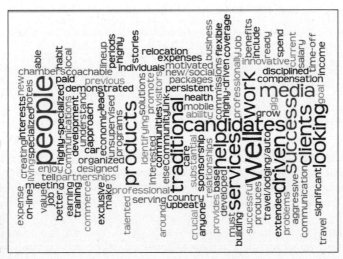

Figure 5-1:
A word cloud helps you visualize keywords.

Get familiar with Google's keyword tool

You may wonder why you can't just ask the search engines directly what words rank higher. Well, you're in luck. Google's External Keyword tool (shown in Figure 5-2) provides a way to do something similar to that. You can access this tool by doing a fresh Google search for "keyword tool" or by typing in the following address into your web browser: bit.ly/external-keyword-tool. By using this keyword tool, you can see which words are more popular than others and which words are similar to others. For example, if you enter "accountant," you may find that the word *bursar* is not just related but much more popular. So if you use *bursar* in your online profile, you have a good chance of being found in an employee search.

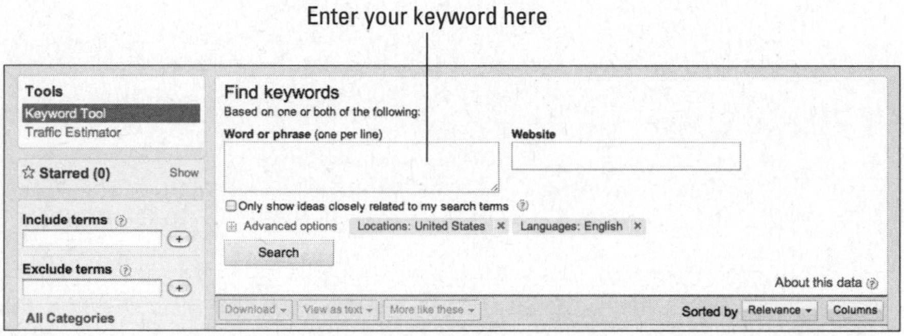

Enter your keyword here

Figure 5-2:
Google's
External
Keyword
tool.

To use the keyword tool, begin by entering one or more of the keywords and phrases you've collected from your research into the search box. Use the most basic words first and then progressively get more creative as you search for additional keywords. Also, make sure you check the "Phrase" box in the Match Types section in the left column (see Figure 5-3).

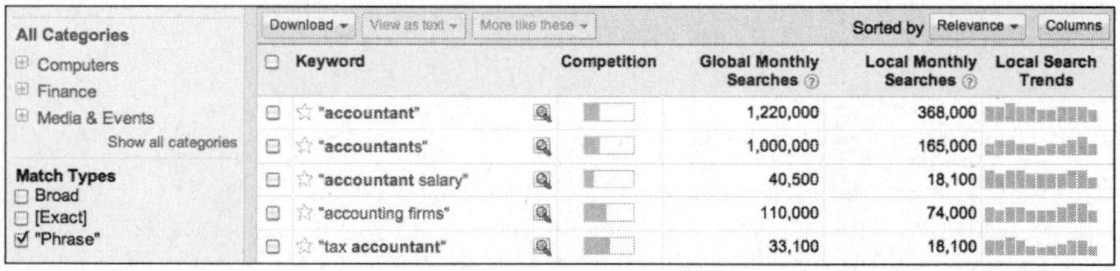

Figure 5-3:
Choose the
"Phrase"
Match Type
setting for
the best
results.

If you were to enter "public relations" into the keyword tool to see what Google suggests, you could then group by Similarity to Search Terms (click on the Group By button on the right side of the page at the top of the results section). As long as you're signed into Google, two results areas appear (see Figure 5-4). The first, called Keywords That Include Search Terms, includes the words *public relations* in the result. In this case, you discover that *careers in public relations* gets searched thousands of times per month.

The second results area is called Related Keywords. Here, Google uses its semantic brain and gives you related keywords. In other words, it brainstorms for you. For example, the words *media relations* and *public affairs* could be important alternatives to *public relations* — something to consider using in your résumé or online profile if you're interested in a PR position.

Figure 5-4:
Results
analysis for
a search on
public
relations.

Keeping track of and using your keywords for your job search

Good Internet copy writers keep a list of their top keywords next to them during the writing process. I suggest you do the same. Rank your keywords after you've done the research suggested earlier in this chapter and print a copy to keep by you. Then write your keywords into your copy when you prepare your value statement (I walk you through this process in the next section).

Note that merely listing one keyword after another won't help you. The copy should read nicely while weaving in your words. As you progress in your job search, you may come across other valuable keywords. Take note of them and try to use them in your next profile revision.

I find it helpful to make a note of where I use keywords and keyphrases online so that I use them all evenly. For example:

Keyphrase	Location 1	Location 2
Strategic communications	LinkedIn Professional Headline	LinkedIn Profile Summary
RPF writing	LinkedIn Experience section	DoYouBuzz Summary
Analyze sales statistics	Word doc version of résumé	LinkedIn Interests section

Putting Together the Value Statement

Your *value statement* is what you tell people about yourself. Some people also call this *the elevator pitch* because you should be able to deliver it in about 30 seconds, or the amount of time it usually takes to ride an elevator. In this section, I recommend you use the same value statement when you write about yourself online as you do when you meet someone in person. Providing the same information to contacts you meet through social networking and traditional networking allows you to maintain a consistent message, and that's really the heart of a strong personal brand.

You have several options for crafting your value statement. I walk you through them in the next sections (as well as how to write your statement), but the important thing to remember is that your value statement should help you establish instant credibility, curiosity, and likeability. Keep in mind that your value statement will change over time as well. For example, it'll change the more you use it at live networking events, and it'll change after you receive some feedback on your LinkedIn profile.

Choosing a value statement method that works best for you

Many methods are out there for writing value statements. In this section, I present three methods to choose from if you're getting stuck or looking for inspiration. These three methods are the fastest way I know of to help you find words around your personal brand. Pick any of the following methods for writing your value statement.

The Joel Elad method

Joel Elad, author of *LinkedIn For Dummies,* 2nd Edition (John Wiley & Sons, Inc.), offers a three-part model for crafting a profile summary on LinkedIn that's really applicable to creating a solid value statement and not limited to any one social media site. Elad's method maintains a who, what, and goals format. The first sentence answers the question of your current situation (*who* you are). The middle few sentences answer the question of *what* you've accomplished in your professional life. And finally, the last sentence describes your *goals,* or what you're going for right now.

Here's an example of a value statement using Joel Elad's method:

> I'm a project manager with experience in a wide variety of applications. I've run on-time and on-budget projects for both software deployments at XYZ Company and hardware installations for ABC Company. I'm excited about working for another insurance company that's looking for a dedicated and self-motivated PM.

The Jim Nudelman method

Jim Nudelman is an experienced sales trainer and a nationally known professional speaker based out of Portland, Oregon. He knows a thing or two about capitalizing on that brief window of opportunity when you make a first impression. Here's his four-step process for crafting a value statement:

1. **Begin with an action plan statement that describes what you do and not just your job title.**

2. **Add a one-sentence statement about what it is you do.**

3. **Give a statement of specific impact of your service, some kind of accomplishment.**

4. **End with a call-to-action.**

When I applied these steps, I came up with the following value statement:

> I am an Internet marketing wizard. I show job seekers how to trick the economy into giving them jobs by showing them how to use social media in the right way. People who use my five-step process or who attend my workshops tell me that they cut their job search in half and even get unsolicited offers. Please let any job seekers in your life know about me and have them sign up for my blog and newsletter.

The Corporate Layoff method

When the economy tanked in 2008 and I was laid off, my employer offered me wonderful outplacement services through a large international HR firm. I've used its method several times for crafting *positioning statements,* or value statements, not only for my own career but also for my clients. Here's the method as I remember it:

1. **Specify your desired job title.**

   Begin by simply mentioning what you want to do at your next job, but do it in the present tense, such as "I *am* a project manager . . ."

2. **Select an area of focus.**

   Every job title has its particular compelling focus areas. For example, an IT manager may have a focus on developing technology solutions for business problems, or a marketing manager may focus on developing high ROI campaigns in the CPG space. What is your area of expertise in the field?

3. **Give your statement some context.**

   No man is an island. In what professional environments were you the most successful? Did you really excel at a Fortune 500 company or was it the smaller startup that felt the most impact from your skills? Perhaps you found great joy in managing others rather than doing the task directly?

4. **Identify what makes you unique.**

   Approximately 16 people compete for the same job, so you have lots of competition. What makes you different from the other job seekers out there? This difference may be technical knowledge or simply an approach to problem solving that has served you well.

Here's an example of the Corporate Layoff method in action:

> I am a level 3 account manager with a focus on selling complicated business software solutions to large enterprises. I have been particularly successful in mapping large businesses' needs with Enterprise Resource Planning software solutions that I was responsible for selling. Not only were my customers extremely satisfied with their solution but also my vice president couldn't have been happier when I came in 150 percent over goal for 3 years in a row. My customers have told me that they felt I really listened to them and that's why they trusted me with their projects.

Surveying some tips for writing a strong value statement

As you start the process of writing your value statement, you may find yourself either stuck or unhappy with the results. Following are some tips to help you think about the writing process in new ways:

- ✔ **Use as many keywords/keyphrases as makes sense.** Write as many keywords in your value statement as you can without losing the flow of your sentences.

- ✔ **Incorporate analogies.** Analogies do wonders for making you memorable, so don't be afraid to use one.

   Do you remember the "Your Brain on Drugs" ads that aired on TV back in the late '80s? The purpose of these public service announcements was to turn kids away from drugs. The stickiest of these ads was the one where the actor cracked open an egg then fried it in a hot frying pan. As the egg got more and more distorted on the pan, the announcer said, "This is your brain on drugs."

Here are a couple of professional examples of a "Your Brain on Drugs" analogy:

> I am a financial plumber. I find your financial leaks and repair them. (Personally, I hate this one, and I think you can do better!)

> I am an organizational chiropractor. I put your company back in alignment so it can deal with any of the challenges in the marketplace.

✔ **Take advantage of the rule of three.** People remember things in threes: "Snap, Crackle, and Pop!" or "the good, the bad, and the ugly." Incorporating this rule of three into your value statement can make it more memorable.

✔ **Leave people curious and wanting more.** Finally, I maintain that the best value statements leave people feeling curious and wanting to hear more. After you craft your statement, do the curiosity test: Deliver it to someone. When you finish, stop talking and wait. If the other person says, "Tell me more," then you have a nice statement indeed!

After you've written a few versions of your value statement, present them to someone in your profession who you respect and ask for feedback. Remember that the value of your value statement is how it's perceived. If your audience likes it, it's a winner.

Transferring Your Value Statement to Social Networks

Your value statement translates to your social media presence in three ways:

✔ Headlines

✔ Profile summaries

✔ Profile pictures

If you've done your keyword research and written your value statement (I explain how to do both earlier in this chapter), all you have to do is copy and paste that statement into your online profiles. The sections that follow show you exactly how to transfer your value statement to the essential components of your social media presence. (I describe how to turn your value statement into a profile summary in the earlier "Choosing a value statement method that works best for you" section.)

Condensing your statement into a headline

The headline you use in LinkedIn, any online résumé, or the bio area in Twitter is connected with your name on almost every communication you send. It's therefore one of the first things anyone sees about you, so you need to be sure to get it right.

Think of your headline as a very boiled-down and condensed version of your value statement. It shouldn't be longer than 120 characters in LinkedIn or 160 characters in Twitter, including spaces. Make sure to use at least one of your keywords, two at best. And if you currently work for a company, mention the company and role by name. Otherwise, it looks like you're unemployed.

One way to separate ideas in your headline is to use vertical bars. Here are a couple of examples I found that I really like:

Web developer | Web designer | President of a local design interest group

Author | Trainer | E-learning visionary | Expert in improving corporate training programs

Branding is not only about what you like but also about what your audience likes. That audience may include potential employers, recruiters, peers — basically anyone who listens to you. Knowing whether your brand is successful depends on how your audience responds. So test a headline out for a week and see what kind of response you get. Then the next week, test out another one. Keep changing it until you get the results you want.

Whatever you do with your headline, don't beg for a job. Although the marketplace is filled with desperate job seekers, you don't want to be one of them (even though you may feel desperate). Differentiate yourself by showing your confidence. Make employers want *you*. Instead of saying, "I'm looking for . . . ," lead with how you can add value to their organization.

Also, be sure to include as much personality as possible. Would you rather be an experienced marketing professional or a marketing visionary who thrives on growing powerful brands through innovative teamwork?

Here's an example headline I used to use: "I specialize in helping MBAs who are frustrated with the traditional job search process to use social media for career management."

Dealing with your profile picture

The image you use on your social media profiles acts like an application icon on your computer. Just as you know that big blue *W* is for Microsoft Word, when people see the colors and shape of your image, they know it's you.

Don't look like an axe murderer!

An HR consultant friend of mine was approached by a job seeker with an interesting problem. He was a very experienced engineer, but no one would call him back for an interview. When she looked at his resume, she found several patents to his name, and he even had experience launching a successful startup. She didn't know what the problem was until she finally checked his LinkedIn profile. His picture was, well, a bit scary! He was staring at the camera straight-on with big eyes and no smile. She gave him $20 and said, "Take yourself to Target, wear a suit, and please smile into the camera." After the engineer posted his new profile picture, he received three job offers in the next seven days.

 Your social media photo serves as a visual reminder to your audience and shouldn't change that often. So take a good profile picture now and then forget about it for the next few years.

 A good headshot has interesting negative space around the head. Professional photographers ask you to tilt your head slightly or stand sideways and then look at the camera over a shoulder. Try several head tilting positions yourself to alter the negative space about your head. Oh, and remember to smile!

Creating a Professional E-mail Address and Username

When choosing e-mail addresses or usernames in social media profiles, retaining a consistent personal brand is important. Always opt to use your full name. Avoid kitschy e-mail addresses like `misshotpants123@hotmail.com`. Instead, find a way to use your full name as your e-mail address. If you need to start a new e-mail account for the purposes of your job search, know that it's worth it. The best option is to purchase your own domain name, which I talk about in Chapter 6.

In the context of social networks you join, the username you choose often becomes the web address for your public-facing profile. For example, if you choose FirstnameLastname as your profile's username, the public facing web address becomes `FirstnameLastname.sitename.com`. Keep this same username consistent across all your networks; for example, use it in your LinkedIn profile and VisualCV public *URLs*, or web addresses. (I describe these powerful social media tools in Chapters 9 and 11, respectively.) The more consistent you are, the more easily Google can deliver your online profiles in response to a search of your name. Also, consistency is key when a hiring manager is considering your application for a job.

Chapter 6

Communicating Your Expertise Online by Blogging

*T*he age of blogs as some kind of odd, private exhibition is over. Today, blogging is a respectable way of publishing ideas geared at a particular audience. If you have great content for that audience, you can easily build credibility online. By voicing your opinion, interviewing experts, or sharing new news, you're telling your readers that your topic is something you're passionate about and may even have some authority on. And the longer you blog, the more credibility you gain.

Your original blog content may, therefore, wind up becoming your biggest career asset. Many aspects of your personal brand are on the surface of things, like the picture you use and the value statement you develop. But a blog provides deep insight into your voice, your passions, your values, and your abilities. Blogging is the part of your personal brand that can't be duplicated by anyone else. And your blog is completely under your control. The amount and types of content you publish are reflections of your own volition and commitment to getting a job in that field.

In this chapter, I show you how to find something to write about and put it into an easy calendar you can follow. I also explain how to set up your blog and get people to comment on it. Finally, I reveal how to boost your online credibility even further by landing guest-posting opportunities on fellow bloggers' sites.

Developing Your Content Strategy

Less than a third of the millions of blogs out there remain active after the first few months, largely due to a failure to plan. Don't make the mistake of failing to plan what you're going to say.

When I tell job seekers that they need to blog, they usually object with, "I don't have that much to say." However, if you're passionate about your particular area of expertise, then you *do* have something to say. But without a plan, the fear that you don't can easily become a reality. I take it as my challenge to help you find something to blog about and keep your blog alive.

In the following sections, I help you figure out where your expertise lies, other ways to get your content out there if you're not much of a writer, and how to plan out your blog posts so that you're never left with nothing to say.

Recognizing your area(s) of expertise

Whether you think so or not, you're an expert at something. The shift from arm-chair specialist to outspoken expert is really just a mental shift. As long as you educate, inform, or even entertain your audience, your blog is readworthy. With social media's acceptance, everyone can have his or her day in the public spotlight, and you have a right to your say as well. Don't deny yourself this opportunity.

Finding what you want your blog to be about can be a difficult task; however, if you think about it in terms of your own passions, then it can be quite simple. Think about something you're good at. When people come to you for advice, what do they generally ask? Picking a topic you like and that you're knowledgeable about is important for the continuity of your blog as well. You want to pick a topic that keeps inspiring ideas for articles. If you're not particularly passionate about the topic, it'll eventually become impossible to generate new content.

A good friend of mine was a vice president at a local bank. He created several green banking products that provided discounted loans to businesses that used renewable energy or were involved with sustainability. These products were widely adopted by the bank and absorbed into their other products. So the unfortunate reward for his success was that his job became obsolete.

Through his experience building green banking products, he recognized that he developed some skills that other banks could benefit from. He turned his personal blog, which he posted to infrequently about random and often personal topics, into a blog that shared his professional knowledge. Soon, other banks got wind of him and hired him as a consultant.

The more specifically you can define your area of expertise, the better. General topics don't tend to develop strong audiences. Try to narrow down your topic to the point where it becomes different from what everyone else is covering. Often, you can simply put a new spin on an old idea or have a unique perspective when collecting artifacts. What you choose to blog about and how you represent it comes back to your personal brand because your name becomes associated with the topic.

If you're having trouble identifying what you should blog about, ask yourself these questions:

- What's a topic I can talk about for hours without ever getting bored?

- What's something I do that makes me lose track of time when I do it?

- What subject do I tend to have strong opinions about (apart from politics or religion)?

- What have I done for years, and maybe not realize, that I have amassed more experience than most people?

- Do I have a new interpretation of a concept or a new method of doing something that may benefit others? If so, what is that?

- When others come to me for advice, what do they ask? In other words, what can I write about that will resonate with others.

- Are there objects I like to collect and react to, such as funny ads, new products, or something else that relates to my career?

If you're getting stuck on ideas to build your expertise around, you may want to look at what other bloggers are writing about. Based on your survey of what blogs are already out there (and their quality), you'll be better able to identify your niche. The following list may help narrow your topics down:

- Business etiquette

- Business operations, theories, and practices

- Consumer package goods packaging ideas

- Creative design collections

- Financial news and analysis

- Green banking

- Holistic medicine and healthy living

- Leadership ideas and advice

- Personal productivity and time management

- Product reviews

- Project management techniques

- ✔ Public policy and social issues
- ✔ Technology reviews and predictions
- ✔ Writing tips and grammar

Identifying online mediums to publish on

Not everyone enjoys writing. Some people are just unable to adapt to a new style of writing to match online mediums. Blog writing is different than book writing or report writing, for example. The good news is that you don't have to write to publish online content. Here are other mediums you may also consider:

- ✔ **Podcasts or audio blogging:** This option is perfect for people who enjoy conversations or talking out their ideas. Just check out `www.blogtalk radio.com` to see all the different types of audio blogging topics out there.

- ✔ **Video blogging:** These unproduced, simple, two- to three-minute video conversations are a great way of building intimacy with an audience. Many great business leaders have taken to this medium.

- ✔ **Short blogs:** Short blog posts are between 50 and 100 words, or two to three sentences, and can be fun, to the point, and easy to read. Seth Godin virtually created this format. On his blog (`www.sethgodin.typepad.com`), he writes only one or two sentences every few days. They're usually high impact and poignant.

- ✔ **Facebook Fan Page posts:** These posts are another way to reach your audience by letting Facebook handle the technology. My good friend George Kao has turned his Facebook Fan Page into a highly engaging blog. He told me once that he doesn't really enjoy blogging, but that didn't stop him from building incredible expertise online.

- ✔ **E-newsletters:** These newsletters can be powerful to adding value to an audience, but they require you to build a contact list first. You can have a website that captures e-mail addresses and then actually delivers your content via e-mails. Some services now allow you to charge small amounts of money for someone to subscribe to your newsletter.

Using an editorial calendar to keep consistent

Every successful blog relies on an editorial calendar. An *editorial calendar* is a list of all the topics you plan to cover (via text, audio, or video) over a defined period of time.

According to ProBlogger's Darren Rowse, here are four reasons you need a content plan:

- ✔ **To combat writer's block:** You don't want to be stuck on publication day with writer's block thinking, "Here's another day I didn't post, and I still can't think of anything to write." Having a list of topics in front of you is a great backup plan.

- ✔ **To build good habits:** In the long term, you'll need to post consistently over the life of your blog. Planning ahead will force you to post regularly and respond to comments, which is good blogger behavior.

- ✔ **To be seen as a niche authority:** Remember that the name of the game is establishing your expertise on something. Publishing consistently about your topic is the best way to build an authoritative voice.

- ✔ **To get help with post ideas:** The process of sitting down and thinking about the next three to six months of posts gets your mind rolling. After a while, you'll notice that newer and better ideas emerge. Don't be surprised if you have to improve your content plan days after you think you've finished.

Creating your own editorial calendar is easy. Follow these steps to get started:

1. **Choose a niche topic that you feel very comfortable with.**

   All the techniques in the world can't help if you don't know your topic.

2. **Break your topic down into five categories or subtopics and list them at the top of a spreadsheet.**

   Think of a *category* in a blog as a chapter in a book. The categories I use for my blog (www.careerenlightenment.com) are LinkedIn Tips, Twitter Job Seeking, Online Résumés, Confidence Boosters, and Other Social Media Tips. I also have an Announcements category, but I don't need to plan for it because the content comes about as it happens. So when thinking about your topic, consider breaking it down into categories and then developing content to fit within each category.

3. **List the weeks down the left side of the spreadsheet.**

4. **Decide how many times a week you want to post.**

   Usually, you want to post between three and five times per week during your first three months. (Your blog needs to have a higher frequency of posting during the first three months than at any other time so you can grow your followers and they can trust that you'll stick around.) After the first three months, then you can consider tapering off to two to three times per week.

5. **Write down the titles of your posts under the appropriate categories and weeks, as shown in Figure 6-1.**

◇	A	B	C	D	E	F	G
1	**Career Enlightenment**						
2	Editorial Calendar 2009						
3							
4	Day	General Tips	General Social Media	Linkedin	Technical Posts	Personal Branding	Guest Post
5	Keywords		social networking	linkedin for job seekers	twitter for job seeker	personal branding	
6			using social media	linkedin tips	job search tool	image consulting	
7	Week of						
8	4-Apr					USP	
9	11-Apr						LinkedIn Employee
10	18-Apr	Be specific					
11	25-Apr		Becomed update				
12	2-May			Applications			
13	9-May				Twitter rules		
14	16-May					Make a Brochure	
15	23-May						Becomed owner

Figure 6-1:
A sample editorial calendar.

TIP

Pre-writing articles can give you a backup when you're out of ideas, so be sure to pre-write at least five articles before officially launching your content. Doing so gives you some cushion as you get used to this new part of your life. I like to batch my writing for a month so that I write 10 to 20 articles on the first Sunday. Find the schedule that works best for you.

If you're looking for additional structure around your content planning, I highly recommend you download Charlie Gilkie's blog post planners (shown in Figure 6-2) at www.productiveflourishing.com. (Click on Free Planners and then scroll down to find The Blog Post Planner and Calendar section.) Every month, Charlie publishes a new planner designed to help you think about what you're going to write about for each of your categories.

The Blog Post Planner
What Do You Want To Write About?

What conversations do you want to extend this month? Get your creative juices flowing by thinking about your blog's main topics.

February 2010
M T W Th Fr St Sn
1 2 3 4 5 6 7
8 9 10 11 12 13 14
15 16 17 18 19 20 21
22 23 24 25 26 27 28

Category/Type_____
Topic/Title   Scheduled

Category/Type_____
Topic/Title   Scheduled

O
O
O
O
O
O
O

O
O
O
O
O
O
O

Figure 6-2:
Charlie's Blog Post Planner sample.

Blogging as the Expert on Your Own Site

Having your own blog, where you control the look, feel, and tone of the site, is a great feeling. It's also one of the most powerful credibility builders for anyone's career. The sections that follow fill you in on all the basics you need to know to start blogging, from reserving the proper domain name to structuring your blog post so you get readers and comments.

Selecting the right title and domain name for your blog

The *domain name,* or *URL,* is the web address for a website. For a blogger, the domain name is the defining business card; therefore, it needs to be memorable.

Choosing a good domain name is closely related to choosing a title for your blog. Imagine that you're at a networking event and someone asks what the name of your blog is. You have to say it out loud! And if your domain name is different from your blog title, you may confuse people.

Follow these steps for finding a blog title and registering the domain name:

1. **Decide on a title that relates to your topic in some way.**

    If you can't think of one after trying for a while, just use your name (for example, John's Blog).

2. **Check your title with a domain registrar.**

    A *domain registrar* is a website where you can purchase domains. For an easy tutorial on buying and hosting a domain name, head to www.careerenlightenment.com/jobseekers-website-setup. Enter your domain name idea, and if it's available, you can purchase it.

    If the title you came up with is already taken, find another title and repeat Step 2.

If you get stuck, just use your name with the suffix .net, .com, or .me. As your blog evolves and you find your voice, a great name will come to you. You can always change your blog's name later and just redirect domains. For example, I started my blog using the domain name joshua waldman.net. Later, I came up with the name Career Enlightenment, so I purchased careerenlightenment.com and redirected my old domain to the new one.

Whether you come up with a creative blog title or just use your name, purchasing the rights to a new domain costs a minimal amount of cash. However, you're better off owning your own domain than purchasing one through a blogging platform because *you* want to be the one in control of your brand. If a blogging platform purchases your domain for you, then the blogging platform owns your domain, making it hard for you to leave its service later.

Setting up an attractive blog

Before you can start posting content to your blog, you need to make sure your blog looks attractive enough so that when people visit the site, they stick around long enough to read, watch, or hear what you have to say instead of scurrying off to another site simply because they can't stand your fascination with neon colors and flashing banners. Following are some basic blog-design concepts to be aware of:

- ✔ **Theme:** A *theme* is a template for the look and feel of a blog. It controls colors, typefaces, and layout. When you change the theme, your content isn't effected, but the way it's displayed is.

- ✔ **Page:** A *page* is static and may appear at the top of a blog for navigation. Pages can have subpages. (A page isn't to be confused with a post as described next.)

- ✔ **Post:** A *post* is where you publish your most recent article. When someone subscribes to your blog, what they're really subscribing to are your most recent posts.

- ✔ **Categories:** The *categories* of a blog are like chapters in a book. Typically, you don't want much more than five categories. This limit helps focus your writing and keeps you on topic. Use only one category for each post.

- ✔ **Tags:** *Tags* are like the index of a book. You can have as many tags on each blog post as you like. Readers can use tags to navigate to different posts.

A good blog keeps its focus on the content you're publishing. Some themes are beautiful but distract the reader from the content. When choosing a theme and setting up your blog, keep the following in mind:

- ✔ **Your theme is tied to your personal brand.** The colors and feel of the layout should reinforce the image you're trying to convey. If your personal brand is related to the field of education, then you may consider brighter colors than someone writing about finance.

- ✔ **Archives based on dates are useless for most readers.** If someone wants to read your past articles, they most likely want to do so based on category.

- ✔ **Tag lines or about-me boxes can help readers understand the purpose of your blog.** The easier you can make it for a new reader (like a potential employer!) to quickly understand what your blog is all about, the better. So make sure your about-me box talks about why you're blogging and what you blog about.

- ✔ **A photograph of yourself adds trust and credibility.** A photo can create a sense that you're talking directly to your readers. Choose one that best represents the voice you write with. If you write more formally, then use the same image as your LinkedIn photo. If you're more off-the-cuff with your content, then pick a more casual image.

Using e-mail to reach your blog readers

Only about a quarter of your readers will use *RSS feeds* (a way for your blog posts to show up in someone's news reader) to subscribe to your blog. Most people will want e-mail updates, so offering a way for readers to add themselves to your e-mail list is a good idea.

MailChimp (`bit.ly/email-chimp`) is a great e-mail marketing service for professionals.

It's free for up to 2,000 names on your list and is very easy to manage. After you sign up, you can create an opt-in form for your list to add to your blog and then send a newsletter to your list with new blog posts. MailChimp sends this newsletter automatically by populating an e-mail template with your most recent posts and sending them at a time you specify.

If you want to make your blog look as appealing as possible, I suggest you skip the other blog platforms and go right to WordPress. WordPress has more than 60 percent market share for blogs, has the largest community of developers, and is favored by Google in search results. Most importantly, you own your content when you use WordPress.

WordPress comes in two forms: `www.wordpress.com`, which is hosted by WordPress, and `www.wordpress.org`, which you host on your own hosting service. Hosting WordPress yourself requires more technical skills but is not unwieldy. It also allows you more freedom to customize the look and feel of your blog and offers a wider range of *plug-ins* (extra features you can load onto your blog, such as anti-spam filters for comments, a Follow Me on Facebook button, and more). For more details on WordPress, check out *WordPress For Dummies,* 3rd Edition, by Lisa Sabin-Wilson (John Wiley & Sons, Inc.).

Communicating effectively within your written post

Blog writing differs in many ways from other forms of writing, which is mainly due to the fact that most readers scan online content and don't spend a lot of time on any given web page. Also, readers are bombarded with catchy titles and flashing links that draw their attention away from your content. So a unique style of writing has evolved. The next sections break down some of the style elements for blog writing.

Topic

The *topic* is the single subject or idea that your post is all about. Generally speaking, you have only one topic for each blog post. When you first start to write, be sure you're crystal clear about the point of the post. Don't ramble or bring in too many counterpoints. Feel free to outline your post if you need more structure.

Title

The *title* is the name of your blog post. Always start by writing the title first. This technique helps me stay on topic. If I start rambling on and on in my post, I just look at the title and think, "Oh yeah, that's what I'm supposed to be writing about."

A strong title not only keeps you on task but also grabs the attention of your reader. In my experience as a blogger, I've found several formulas that seem to work as titles, including the following:

- **Numbered lists:** These lists always grab people's attention. Some examples include "Five reasons why . . ." or "Three mistakes policy makers make when . . ."

- **Quick tips:** Show your readers how to do something new or useful. By offering a learning environment, you can keep readers engaged for longer. Start titles with "How to . . ." or "Quick Tips to . . ."

- **Debunking myths:** This formula works really well! When you challenge popular opinion, you get readers excited and ready to watch a battle. You can grab readers' attention by starting with "Why most people are wrong about . . ."

- **Blatant controversy:** Controversies always make people curious. Saying something controversial, such as "Facebook will ruin your chances of getting a job" or "Why you should be afraid of getting Googled," can get people reading in a jiffy!

Hook

The *hook* is a journalism term that refers to the opening passage of an article. It's what keeps the reader reading. Because the hook in your blog post is an important part, it requires some extra time crafting.

According to ProBlogger's Darren Rowse, here are just a few techniques for writing strong hooks:

- **Ask intriguing questions.** When you ask a question, the reader tries to answer it in his head. Questions create curiosity; for example, "What does a project manager have in common with Papa Smurf?" or "Can you name the three reasons why most mutual funds fail?"

- **Tell a story.** This technique is probably the one I rely on the most. Telling a story brings readers into your world and provides context. I love sharing the story of where I got the idea for the post or an illustration of the main point. Try weaving in a personal story at the beginning of your post and then extract key lessons learned from it.

- **Use statistics.** Starting with startling facts that challenge someone's view of the world also creates curiosity. "Did you know that more than 40 percent of workers have never even met their boss in person?" To find interesting stats, subscribe to the Pew Research Center newsletter at www.pewresearch.org.

✔ **Upload a picture.** Sharing a picture on your blog helps support the point of your post. Provocative pictures keep an audience engaged and entertained. I like to scan Flickr for free image ideas, but for the best-quality images, check out www.istockphoto.com (this site charges a few dollars per image). The key is to find and use images that emotionally reinforce your topic and are visually interesting.

Headers

Headers are basically titles for the main points of your blog post. Because your readers are most likely going to scan your post, help them out by using headers to break up the article. Your blogging platform should let you format text as you write. The title of your blog post is usually an H1 header, the largest sized header, so use H2 or H3 headers for your subject markers.

If you've done any keyword research (see Chapter 5 for more on this), the headers are the best places to use a keyword or two. If you use a keyword in a header, you don't need to worry about using it again within the content.

Length

Most blog posts are between 300 and 800 words to account for readers' short attention spans, which means you need to be able to get to the point fairly quickly and then move on to the next point without lingering. If you plan on exceeding 800 words, consider breaking the post into two parts or writing a series. I write most of my posts in around 500 words.

Vary the length of your posts from time to time. Doing so helps you keep a fresh feeling on your blog and prevents your reader from getting bored. For example, if you usually write shorter, 300-word posts, then once a month, publish the mother of all posts to make a big splash at 800 words.

Tone

When it comes to the tone of your blog posts, forget what your fifth-grade English teacher taught you. Using first person in blog writing is completely acceptable, and you can even begin sentences with *and* or *but* for a more casual feel. In fact, your tone should be as intimate and candid as possible. However, writing conversationally doesn't mean you patronize your reader; it means you avoid jargon when possible and explain it when you can't, share your opinion, and use an everyday tone of voice — your own voice.

If you're having trouble finding your blogging voice, try visualizing your best friend — as in the person who usually has no idea what you're talking about when you start talking about your work — standing in front of you. Now write as if you were talking to him or her.

Call to action

A *call to action* is what you want your readers to do about whatever it is you're saying, and it's usually located at the end of your post. Do you want them to share a comment, rethink an idea, subscribe to a list, visit a website, or change a behavior?

The call to action in your blog post must be specific and transparent. Your readers aren't dumb or gullible. If they like what you have to say, they may want to do something about it. So make it easy for them to find out what to do.

Here are a couple of examples of calls to action: "If you resonate with any of the points in this article, I'd love to hear your opinion. Please leave me a comment below" or "Do these facts change how you lead project meetings? If so, try out my tips and see whether they work for you."

Getting people to comment and build your credibility

When you first start a blog, it can sometimes feel like you're talking to a wall. Don't worry if your page views are low or no one bothers commenting on your posts. Just remember that every website is vying for traffic and that many people are in the same boat you're in.

What really matters for you, as a job seeker, is that when people of importance see your blog, they get a good feeling about you. The point is this: People may not see your page-view analytics, but they do see whether other people are commenting on your blog. So don't get too worried about traffic. Instead, spend your energy producing good content and facilitating comments about that content.

How do you get people to comment on your blog? One easy way is to just ask them to. At the end of each post, say something like, "Please share your thoughts in the comments section below." Be sure to reply to each comment you get. When readers see that you read and respond to comments, they'll be more likely to join in.

Sometimes just asking for comments isn't enough. That's why I started something called The Comment Co-op (check it out at bit.ly/comment-coop) to allow job seekers to lean on each other to get comments on their blogs.

Every week, members of the co-op receive requests to read and leave comments on other members' sites. The more someone takes advantage of this service, the more comments they receive. After two or three people leave comments on your blog, other people can more confidently leave comments, too. It's like assuming that a restaurant is a good place to eat after seeing a line of people waiting to get in. A few engineered comments on your blog can really open up the floodgates to true and interesting engagement.

Another trick for jump-starting comments on your blog is to use a service called *Fiverr*. Fiverr is a community of people who will do anything for $5. Yes, anything. (Don't get any funny ideas, though). Most of the things people are willing to do are for traffic building, graphic design, or even video production. And, yes, people are willing to do some weird stuff, such as the guy who will dance to any song of your choice in a hot dog costume. But putting that odd stuff aside, you can purchase 20 comments on your blog for $5, giving you instant credibility. Here's how:

1. **Head to www.fiverr.com and either log in or create an account.**

2. **Type in "blog comments" in the search bar.**

3. **Hire the best provider based on reviews and whether they offer other services.**

   Don't worry if you don't like people's comments because you can delete them from your blog. Personally, I've had very positive experiences hiring people on Fiverr.

Don't rely too much on engineered comments that come from people you've hired (literally or figuratively). Welcome engineered comments only until you start seeing real comments and traffic coming naturally from genuinely interested people.

Scoring a Guest Blogger Gig

A guest blogger is someone whose articles are published on someone else's blog. Many bloggers struggle with creating enough content to fit their editorial calendars, so when a guest blogger reaches out with quality content, a lot of bloggers are happy to publish the guest's article.

Guest posting on a high-traffic blog can jump-start your public image, drive traffic to your own blog, and launch your personal brand. After you've established your own blog, your topic is clear, and you're comfortable with your unique voice, follow these steps to get your article posted on a top blog:

1. **Find top-ranking blogs that closely match your area of expertise or topic.**

   I note some places to find top blogs and guest post opportunities in the later "Finding high-authority blogs to guest post on" section.

2. **Narrow down your list to three or five blogs and thoroughly research them to make sure you can write on topic and to their audience.**

3. **Send an inquiry to your list of target bloggers.**

   I show you what a good inquiry e-mail looks like in the later "Crafting the perfect inquiry e-mail" section.

4. **Write an original blog post for each blogger that gets back to you.**

Don't write a guest blog post until you get an agreement from a blogger to publish it. Otherwise, you may waste a lot of time. Also, be aware that some bloggers want to reserve the right to review and edit your post before publishing it, so always talk to them in terms of sending a draft rather than a finished work.

In the following sections, I show you how to find a top blog to guest post on and how to compose an inquiry e-mail that shows off your expertise and pizzazz.

Finding high-authority blogs to guest post on

Unless you're running around to all the nerdy blogger events and networking with high-profile authors, you may need to research and cold-approach your own guest-posting opportunities. Following are some cool sites where you can find top-ranking blogs as well as guest-posting matchmaking:

- ✔ **Alltop:** Alltop (www.alltop.com) is a directory of top-ranking blogs on hundreds of different topics.
- ✔ **BloggerLinkUp:** This site (www.bloggerlinkup.com) matches bloggers looking for guest posters with article writers. You can subscribe to the e-mail list to see what blogs are requesting content.
- ✔ **BlogSynergy:** BlogSynergy (www.blogsynergy.com) is a directory of blogs looking for guest bloggers.
- ✔ **Jobs.ProBlogger:** This site (www.jobs.problogger.net) is actually a job board for bloggers. Companies and content producers post their jobs here, often looking for writers on particular topics.

Crafting the perfect inquiry e-mail

Your inquiry e-mail needs to be authentic and sound like you, so make sure you don't copy and paste a template when you reach out. Also top bloggers receive a lot of spam e-mails, so the less spam-like your message appears, the better your chances are that the person you're contacting will read it.

Follow these guidelines to boost the odds of having your inquiry e-mail read and seriously considered:

- ✔ **Get to the point in the subject line.** I like to use "Guest post inquiry for *Blog Name*" or simply "Guest blog post." If the blogger needs a new post, he'll gravitate toward your e-mail.

- ✔ **Prove that you did your research.** If you've read a person's blog for a while or if you heard about her (or her blog) through someone or some promotion she did, mention it. A generic "I love your blog" doesn't cut it. Make sure you can prove that you do indeed know who this person is and what she blogs about.

Many bloggers publish guidelines on how they want to be approached by guest bloggers. Search their blog to find these guidelines and then follow their instructions. If they have guidelines that you ignore, you just showed them that you really don't know much about their blog.

- ✔ **Build your credibility.** Mention any other writing experience you have, your own blog, or any other credentials to show why you're qualified to write on the topic.

- ✔ **Offer a title for your guest post.** Don't just say, "Do you accept blog posts?" Instead, offer a title that's both compelling and on topic for the other blog. Although you don't need to write the post until after the blogger agrees, you should offer a title for the post.

- ✔ **State what you want to get out of the guest post.** All you really want in return is a link back to your blog. You're not selling anything or using her blog as a platform for promoting yourself. Typically, guest bloggers link to their blog a few times during the article or at the very end in the author's tag line.

- ✔ **Close with a call to action.** End with telling the blogger what you want her to do. Usually, the call to action is "Please let me know whether you'd be open to seeing a draft of my original post."

The following sample inquiry e-mail puts all these pieces together. Although you may use it as a starter for your own message, be sure to use your own voice.

> Subject line: Guest blog post inquiry
>
> Hi Ms. Blogger,
>
> I saw your blog mentioned on the latest Techcrunch article and really enjoy your writing.
>
> I've been writing for my own blog on a similar subject at www.wanda right.com and want to know whether you'd consider an original guest post from me. One title I had in mind was "Three deadly mistakes people make when writing copy."

All I ask for is a link back to my blog in the author's section.

If you want to see a draft of this article to review, please let me know, and I'll send it on.

Thanks for your time. I look forward to hearing from you.

Wanda Right

Going national to really get noticed

The bigger your brand and the more people that see your name and what you do, the more chances you have of getting the attention of a recruiter or hiring manager. So if you're really comfortable with your topic, consider taking yourself to the next level by going national. Reporters from around the world constantly search for subject matter experts and personal stories to add color to their articles. Because your blog identifies you as an expert in a particular area, you're qualified to answer a reporter's questions about that subject.

You can put yourself out there to be found by eager reporters by taking advantage of one of several services designed to match reporters with sources, including the following:

✔ **HARO:** HARO (www.helpareporter.com) has grown to a massive 30,000 journalists and more than 100,000 active subscribers. It sends three e-mails a day to handle the volume. Chances are you'll find a request for your topic.

✔ **PitchRate:** PitchRate (www.pitchrate.com) is similar to HARO but you can focus your e-mails to your areas of expertise.

I was skeptical of such services at first, but after a client of mine encouraged me, I wrote back to a reporter's query with a quick pitch. I was then invited to an interview with a large national magazine. So you never know what can happen if you pitch to one of these journalists.

Chapter 7

I've Been Googled! Managing Your Online Reputation

....

In This Chapter

▶ Assessing your online reputation

▶ Figuring out what to do if your reputation is bad (or nonexistent)

▶ Keeping a spotless online reputation throughout your career

....

*W*hen someone conducts a Google search of your name, the information that surfaces about you makes up your online reputation. These artifacts can be articles written by or about you, photos of you, videos, or online profiles of people with your name. Even unwanted pictures of you from Facebook may pop up (think last year's Halloween party). Your online reputation is particularly critical when searching for a job in today's market. Why? Because hiring managers *are* going to Google you. Both large and small companies research candidates online before a job interview; indeed, Googling prospective hires is part of today's standard operating procedure.

Have you ever Googled yourself? If you have, you may know how misleading the results can be. Imagine a potential hiring manager Googling you and forming an opinion based on seeing your Grim Reaper costume. Scary, isn't it? Some people feel helpless in the face of this challenge and are willing to let Google's search algorithm determine their employment viability. But you don't have to be one of them. With the information I provide in this chapter, you can better control what people find out about you through Google or any other search engine. No longer will you be at the mercy of the robots. Instead, you'll be the master of your own destiny (and your online reputation!).

You can't tell Google what to display for search results, but you can feed it more content to consider. This process doesn't happen overnight. This chapter describes a long-term, career-long initiative.

Reviewing Your Current Online Reputation

Before you begin to build up your online reputation, you need to know just how much work to put into it. Consider this first part "reputation triage." You determine what your current reputation is, and then you align it to your priorities. For example, when you search for your name, you quickly discover how many folks share your moniker. The problem with this name-sharing business is that your prospective employer won't always know who *you* are. She'll just know that a criminal may be looking for a job with her. Building your online reputation is the answer.

I started seriously working on my online reputation about two years ago when I randomly searched my name and found that I was a New York lawyer, a gynecologist, and a convicted felon. The only accurate result that came up was on the third page about the spring dance concert at Brown University. (No, I didn't wear tights and dance around the stage. I was the technical director!) Clearly, these results weren't going to help my career. However, knowing how much I needed to work on my online reputation helped me pace myself when I began reclaiming my name.

You may be tempted to skip ahead to the later section about building up your online reputation, but I encourage you to read through this section first and follow the steps I outline to assess your reputation — no matter how painful it may be to see misleading information about yourself.

Taking your temperature: Is your reputation sick or healthy?

The most obvious way of assessing where your reputation stands is to simply step into the shoes of a potential hiring manager and Google yourself. When you do so, count how many times an accurate link to you appears in the results in the first three pages.

One of three things happens when you Google yourself:

✔ Information about other people with your name appears; info about the real you doesn't appear at all.

✔ Nothing related to anyone with your name appears.

✔ Bits and pieces about the real you show up.

If information about the real you shows up more than three times on Google's first page and you like those results, your reputation has a temperature of 98.6 degrees — pretty healthy. Chances are, however, that good information about you won't be so apparent in your search results, which means you have some work to do.

Try putting quotation marks around your name to get more accurate results. This tactic tells Google that you want results that contain both your first and last name and in that order. Savvy hiring managers know this trick as well, so you can bet they're searching for you in this way. Also vary your search based on a middle name or just the initial. Try seeing whether you can narrow your search results by adding qualifiers like the city or state you live in or a previous job title. The point is to think like a hiring manager who's trying to learn more about you. Based on your résumé, what information may the hiring manager try to use to narrow his search?

If you've ever changed your name, consider that each new piece of content you produce will have the new name. So if you want hiring managers to see some of the old results, you may mention your old, or maiden, name on your résumé. Doing so is a clue for them if they want to dig deeper. If you don't want them to find you with your old name, simply leave it out of your application.

The following list details two additional ways of quickly assessing your online reputation:

- ✔ **Try the Google Grader.** The free Google Grader tool available at Brand-Yourself (`bit.ly/google-grader`) is a great way to find out the status of your online reputation. When you enter your name, the program provides several pages of Google search results. You choose the results that apply to you and then click the Grade Me button. Not surprisingly, given the name, Google Grader then gives your reputation a letter grade. (The Syracuse University–educated creators of this tool must have very high standards because even though I dominate my Google results, I've never been able to get higher than a B+ with their system!)

- ✔ **Use the Online ID Calculator.** Developed by Reach Personal Branding, the Online ID Calculator (`www.onlineidcalculator.com`) offers more than just a letter grade; it tells you where you may be deficient and offers some practical suggestions for fixing it.

  After you log in (signing up is free, but you must provide your first name, an e-mail address, and some basic demographic information), the calculator asks you to manually Google your name and enter the results into the form. Depending on the information you enter, the program places you somewhere in a matrix of four possibilities: Dissed, Disastrous, Dabbling, or Distinct.

- ✔ **Check out MyWebCareer.** The newest and most advanced tool for figuring out your online reputation, MyWebCareer (`www.mywebcareer.com`) offers a fully automated reputation score based on your current social media profiles and Google rank.

  After you log in, you connect your various social networks and it tells you how relevant your name is in a search. The system offers practical suggestions for building your reputation and advanced analytics to monitor your progress.

Viewing your not-so-private information online

Even if you think you aren't online, you still may be. So you need to be aware of what people can find out about you through an online search. Even if you don't own a computer, people can use the readily available online tools in the following sections to find your personal information, including home address, phone number, and estimated annual income. Scary? Yes, it is.

Poking through your private data with Spokeo

Spokeo (www.spokeo.com) is one of the most popular search engines human resources (HR) departments use. If you're applying to a larger company, chances are the hiring manager will put your name into this tool for any last-minute background checks.

Spokeo pulls your name and other contact information from a huge database of public records to put together a demographic profile of you. And, yes, as unnerving as it sounds, results include your estimated income, political party, marriage status (and spouse's name), number of kids, and other personal data based on your zip code.

The results in Spokeo (or any other people search) are only as good as the sources of data the program pulls from. Spokeo draws assumptions about you based on its algorithm, so the assumptions may not be 100 percent accurate. Hiring managers know the results can be flaky, so they take them with a grain of salt. They're simply looking for any red flags that they can double-check on later.

To discover any red flags that are associated with your name, run it through a Spokeo search and see what comes up. You'll likely see others with your name. Find yours and see how accurate your profile is. In some cases, you may discover that your name doesn't appear at all. Although this scenario may please your inner privacy fan, it may not please the hiring manager trying to find out more about you. If you're in this situation, you may need to work twice as hard as the next guy to build your reputation simply because you don't have an online presence.

Even if you can't change Spokeo's results, at least you can know what other people are seeing about you, which gives you the opportunity to bring it up directly during your application process. You can keep it light, too, such as, "Well if you think I earn $250,000 a year, have 5 kids, and live in a mansion based on some online searches for my name, then this salary negotiation may be the best I've ever had!"

You can see only basic information from Spokeo for free. If you want a full report, you have to cough up a yearly fee. See the website for more details.

Zeroing in on your personal records with ZoomInfo

ZoomInfo (www.zoominfo.com) doesn't just aggregate information about you into a single personal record (unlike Spokeo, which I cover in the preceding section). Instead, it allows you to manually claim your profiles. In other words, some artifacts that show up in search results may be about you and others not, so you can claim the ones you want in order to create a more rounded profile of yourself. ZoomInfo pulls from current information, such as blog posts or news items, as well as static public records.

What's nice about ZoomInfo is that you can create an account and begin claiming profiles. Do this before someone else claims them for you. If any bit of information is inaccurate or irrelevant to your current job search, remove it. You have full control over what's included in your ZoomInfo profile. And ZoomInfo gives preference to profiles that are claimed by members.

Records that you manually claim and verify with ZoomInfo rank higher than unclaimed records, which means you have a good chance of showing an HR recruiter the real you online.

Being unique if your name is John Smith (or something else common)

Not everyone is as lucky as Ashton Kutcher when it comes to having a unique name (and good looks, as my wife likes to point out). People with unique names can much more easily rank in Google and build an online reputation. However, if you have a common name, like John Smith or Sarah Jones, don't fret. You can still differentiate yourself online. Just do the following:

- ✔ **Use your middle initial.** Your middle initial may separate you from all the other Johns and Sarahs. But keep in mind that, after you begin using your middle initial, you must use it everywhere to make this tactic work, including in your LinkedIn profile, website address, account profiles, business cards, and so on. In essence, you're rebranding yourself.

- ✔ **Use your degree or professional license or certificate.** Sometimes your middle initial won't work, so including your professional credentials, such as CPA, Leed Certificate, LPN, or NCC, is another way to differentiate yourself. For example, someone else with your exact name may use the same initial for her brand as well. Not to worry. You can always further narrow down the search by branding yourself with your degree or specialty. Those three-letter abbreviations after your name really do come in handy sometimes.

✔ **Create your own search button.** Going forward, you may as well assume that prospective employers will Google you. So rather than wait for some random hiring manager to type your name into Google and struggle to find anything relevant about you, why not give him a search button you've designed to return the most accurate results? You'll save him the time and hassle of trying to find you. After you create a customized search button, you can include it with your job application and e-mail signature.

You can use Vizibility (`bit.ly/get-vizibility`) to create a SearchMe button. This button helps you design your own Google search results page. You tell the tool what you want the search results to include, and then it creates a search query that produces those results. When someone clicks on the SearchMe link, it sends that custom search query to Google and delivers the results you designed. In other words, the SearchMe button is a specialized Google search query with predictable results that helps your searcher save time.

Taking advantage of social media search engines

Google isn't perfect when it comes to searching the social web because it doesn't deliver many results from real-time content such as Tweets, less-popular blogs, and frequently updated news sites. The danger is that these more obscure sites can still damage your reputation despite their lower Google rank.

That's where social media search engines come in. These search engines specifically search out the different social media sites and tell you (or a prospective employer) who's saying what about you.

Social media search engines look at more recent content, unlike Google, which still takes some time (up to a week) to index and deliver results. A bad reputation is a tricky situation. So if you have a few extra minutes to use these sites and be doubly sure that your reputation is up to snuff, I suggest you do so. If your reputation isn't what you'd like it to be, I show you how to spiff it up in the later section "Repairing a bad reputation."

Finding the social you on Social Mention

Social Mention (`www.socialmention.com`) searches the *real-time web,* which is online content posted recently, and the *social web,* which includes blogs, Tweets, news sites, review sites, and bookmarking sites.

Simply enter your name in quotation marks in the search field and choose All for the search. Within seconds, Social Mention delivers one of the most thorough analyses of your name you've ever seen. When I run this search for myself, I'm frequently shocked by how many times my name is mentioned, even just casually, on someone's blog.

As it's performing the search, the Social Mention program judges the search query by four metrics: Strength, Sentiment, Passion, and Reach. These dimensions are what Social Mention thinks are important for an online reputation. They're clearly explained on the site when you hover your mouse cursor over your scores. You also can see how frequently a mention of your name occurs. For me, my name was mentioned once every nine hours on average. You can even see which keywords are associated with your name and on which types of media a mention occurred. I like to click on the YouTube link to see what embarrassing videos my personal trainer has posted.

Finally, the Sources section clues you into which social network is talking about you the most. This information is great to have when you plan your campaign. If one network (or medium) dominates, then that's a great place to start building content.

Checking other social media sites for your name

Just for the sake of being thorough, here are a few other search engines you can use to see whether anyone's talking about you:

- ✔ **Pipl:** HR professionals commonly use this people search engine. What I like about Pipl (www.pipl.com) is that its search results page is thorough and includes public records, social media mentions, and multimedia mentions (such as pictures, for example).

- ✔ **Twitter Search:** This engine (search.twitter.com) is a simple way to search Twitter's real-time feeds to see whether your name has been mentioned. If you have a Twitter username, try also searching for that.

- ✔ **WhosTalkin:** This social media search engine (www.whostalkin.com) looks through blog sites, news sites, and other social media.

Repairing a bad reputation

If you don't like the results that come up when you search for yourself online, you have a bad online reputation. You also have a problem if no results about you show up, good or bad. Many people with a poor online reputation feel helpless and angry and just don't know what to do about it, but fixing this situation is far from impossible.

The answer to the problem is to simply bury the old, bad content beneath a barrage of new, good content. Or if you have no results, start building fresh content. Eventually the older search results will fall past the third page of Google and then into Internet obscurity. So get ready to face your bad rep head on and begin taking the steps I outline in the next section to rebuild your online reputation. (*Note:* The worse your reputation is, the more work you have to put into rebuilding it.)

Playing it smart with your online profiles

For older generations, sometimes the Internet can feel like the wild wild west. Younger generations grew up with the Internet, so their attitudes toward online privacy are much different. Because of this, the older generations are more at risk of looking dumb online, according to one study conducted by the Pew Internet Research Group.

Let me explain: The Internet generations know that what they post on Facebook tonight may come back to haunt them at gym class tomorrow. They're growing up realizing the direct impact of their online self on their offline self. Those of us who started using e-mail in our adult years often fall prey to the pitfalls of not understanding the consequences of our online actions.

Here are some areas to pay particular attention to when interacting online:

✔ **Be aware of your privacy settings.** Privacy settings change constantly and are different for each network. Understand the privacy settings of each network you use.

✔ **Be appropriate to each network.** Not all social media networks are the same.

Understand what's appropriate for each one. For example, pictures of your Halloween party are cool to share on Facebook but not LinkedIn.

✔ **Self-filter your comments and uploads.** Understand who may be seeing your profile and what the consequences are before you post anything online. For example, don't post pictures of the skiing trip you took while playing hooky from the office. If your boss or a colleague sees those pictures, you may get into trouble.

✔ **Don't get into a fight.** The Internet generations have lost friends and made enemies via e-mail and chat. So they understand the real-world consequences of such a mistake and try to avoid it. They don't fight online, and neither should you.

✔ **Show up and play.** Hiring managers *will* search for you online. Make sure something comes up when someone searches for you. The Internet generations you're competing with will have several results on Google. How many will you have?

Building Your Reputation and Increasing Your Visibility

I would be remiss if I didn't start my discussion about online visibility with the term *search engine optimization,* or SEO. SEO, the art and science of ranking websites on Google and other search engines, is accomplished by making subtle changes to a website's content, coding, and structure and by growing incoming links to the page. A good SEO campaign is rooted in thorough keyword research so you know which words are most important to include in your content. (I tell you all about keyword research in Chapter 5.)

In SEO-speak, two factors affect whether Google (or another search engine) delivers a particular site on the first page (the most desirable page):

✔ **On-site factors:** *On-site factors,* such as the content you include on online résumés and personal websites, are directly within your control. (Flip to Chapter 11 for details on these.)

✔ **Off-site factors:** An *off-site factor* is beyond your control, such as links pointing to your site, your content reprinted on other sites, or other people's mention of your name. However, you can post content to high-ranking Google sites in order to take advantage of their high rank and ensure your name gets seen by Google.

The sections that follow arm you with the tools and strategies you need to make yourself more visible online and in the way you want to be seen — whether you're building a reputation from scratch or rectifying negative or misleading content.

Ranking yourself in Google

The easiest way to rank yourself in Google is to generate your own content. Building your own website or writing your own blog provides content that gets you ranked — but only if you use your name in the appropriate places. For guidance on constructing an effective personal website, see Chapter 11.

If you don't want to build your own website or write your own blog but still want to rank in Google, here are some other tricks you can consider:

✔ **Customize your LinkedIn domain name.** LinkedIn (`www.linkedin.com`), a professional networking site, is considered a *high-authority website* by Google. (A high-authority website simply means that Google thinks its content is more valuable than other sites.) If you change your LinkedIn Public URL (domain name) to your full name, your name will start to rank in Google. Your domain name should look like this: `http://www.linkedin.com/in/yourname`. To achieve this, simply go to your profile, click on Edit next to the Public Profile section, and customize the domain (as shown in Figure 7-1). Often, as you build your online reputation, this minor change will be the first win you notice in Google's results.

Figure 7-1: How to change your LinkedIn profile's domain name.

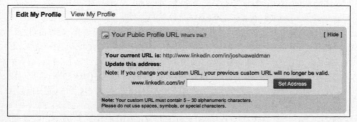

✔ **Customize your LinkedIn links.** With LinkedIn, you're allowed to link to three external websites. Most people use the default settings, like Personal Website or Company Website, but it pays to get a little more unique and specific. In Chapter 9, I explain how to customize the name of a link so that it says something like Joshua's Résumé or Joshua's Slideshows rather than the generic Company Website.

✔ **Make as much of your LinkedIn profile public as possible.** When you edit your public profile in LinkedIn, make sure you're including as much information as possible. Doing so ensures that Google will index more relevant information about you.

✔ **Buy your own domain name.** The fastest way to get your name ranking in Google is to have a domain name that matches the search query. For example, if a hiring manager is going to search for "John T. Jones" in Google to find out more about you, then purchase `www.johntjones.com` to be sure that page ranks. If you want to quickly dominate Google's first page, I suggest you read Chapter 11, where I walk you through the process of buying a domain of your own name. Then you can point that domain name to anything you want, such as an online résumé (like VisualCV or Innovate CV), your public LinkedIn profile, or an About.me page.

Everything you publish online is public record and will be there forever. So be sure that your links, articles, and anything else you publish falls within your personal brand, is professional, and is how you want to be represented online.

Skipping around the web: Making linking work for you

Linking (also called *hyperlinking*) is a way to reach another web page from the one you're currently viewing. You simply click the link and you're there. People who work with SEO for a living know that when Google sees a link on a referring web page, the destination web page is supposed to be related to the link itself. Even if you aren't an SEO master, you can use this technique, called *contextual linking,* to bolster your online presence. You should always link to other sites this way; it's considered best practice.

When you see the following two links, which one tells you exactly where you're going to end up when you click it? (The links are underlined for the illustration.)

Example 1: Click to see Joshua Waldman's Resume.

Example 2: Click HERE to see Joshua Waldman's Resume.

When Google comes across the first example, it expects to find my résumé at the other end. The search engine reads the domain name and the content on the page and expects to see the words *Joshua Waldman's Resume.* If it doesn't see those words, that link doesn't pass any magical Google juice (which is why the word *HERE* as a link doesn't work well). If it does, the destination page — in this case, my résumé — gets a higher Google rank.

The more you link all your online content together, the more Google juice you're passing around to yourself. So any time you link to anything else, use contextual linking. I don't want to see you using the horrible click here technique!

Repurposing your portfolio

Whether you're building, repairing, or burying your online reputation, at some point you'll need to generate new content. Creating a large quantity of new online content can feel a bit overwhelming. Who wants to write a new article or create a new video every week? Not me. Instead, I suggest that you first consider repurposing your old work content.

After all, don't you have old reports, presentations, or videos that show you in a good light? Have you ever put together a financial analysis or presented a group project? You may have to go back to your school days, but that's okay. Simply go back into your old boxes and records and look for the following types of content:

- Articles, essays, projects, or reports you've written or presented
- Business cases you've written
- Design projects you've worked on
- Marketing initiatives you're proud of
- Newspaper clippings
- PowerPoint slides you've presented
- Photos of you in action or in a professional setting
- Video clips or films that you've created or that show you in action

After you collect these artifacts, think about which ones best represent you and the quality of your work. Put yourself in the shoes of a curious hiring manager. He wants to learn more about you. Is any of this content self-explanatory and complementary?

After you gather and choose your content, you have to find a place to post it so that Google will index it and ideally display it when your name is researched. Many of the free content-sharing websites out there are not only indexed by Google, but they also let you upload various types of media. In the following sections, I fill you in on the best ways to post your different types of old content.

Publishing your written materials

For Google, content is still king. If you have written materials from past jobs or from your time at school, you're sitting on a gold mine of content that can help you rank. The best thing you can do with these materials is publish them on high-ranking, content-sharing sites. However, before you can publish your golden nuggets, you may have to tweak them so they're most effective.

If your content contains sensitive material from a company or anything that may harm an organization, you need to clean it out. Either remove any specific mention by changing the names of things (products or companies, for example) to fictitious names or find a way of altering the text so you can remove the sensitive parts completely without ruining the flow of the prose.

You also want to make sure your writing has the proper keywords and links. The most important keyword is your name. Make sure your full name appears at the top and bottom of the document with links to your other online properties.

Use this format for the top of the document:

Keyword-Rich Title

By Your Full Name (linked to an online résumé)

At the bottom of your document, include an *author's resource box.* In this area, be sure to include the following information:

- ✔ Your full name
- ✔ A brief description of what you do, including your value statement, if you have one (see Chapter 5 for more on value statements)
- ✔ Any relevant links, including your LinkedIn profile (remember to use contextual linking, not just "click here")
- ✔ A call to action, such as "call me" or "e-mail me"

Here's an author's resource box I sometimes use (the underlined bits of text are links):

Joshua Waldman, Founder and CEO of Cinta Media Group, helps businesses turn their struggling social media campaigns into winning lead generation strategies. He also blogs on his popular career blog Career Enlightenment, where you'll find a free video training that will change your job search forever. Sign up to his newsletter today.

After you've dolled up your written material, you're ready to post it to high-ranking sites online. Open accounts with each of these free services:

✔ **Docstoc:** This site (www.docstoc.com) promotes document sharing. The more you upload to Docstoc, the more documents you can download. In your case, each document you submit will be indexed by Google.

✔ **EzineArticles.com:** Marketers use this article-marketing database (www.ezinearticles.com) to get their links published. Bloggers also use it to look for articles to post on their blogs. When you post your writing on EzineArticles.com, expect thousands of people to click the links in your article.

✔ **Scribd:** This popular document-sharing network is also indexed by Google. You can invite friends to join your network, and then you can see when they post as well. You also get a public profile that you can customize. Check it out at www.scribd.com.

Keep your written submissions to about 500 words. Generally speaking, people don't read content longer than that online. If your material is longer than 500 words, break it up into parts.

Publishing your video materials

If you have any video footage of yourself in a professional capacity, consider posting it online. Why? Because YouTube, a video-sharing website, is the second-largest search engine in the world. And because it's owned by Google, videos often rank on Google's first page.

When I was building up my online reputation, I found a lot of archived footage of me doing public speaking. Most of it was raw footage, long and unedited. So I pieced together short segments from each video and created a short commercial for myself (check it out at www.careerenlightenment.com/social-media-job-search). If you have only raw footage, I suggest you produce a similar video.

When publishing online video, try to edit your raw footage down to three- to five-minute chunks. For tips on video editing, see Chapter 10.

After you've collected and edited your old video footage, make sure you post it to as many video-sharing sites as you can. TubeMogul, which allows you to post one video to 20 different sites all at once (including YouTube), makes publishing easy. Visit www.tubemogul.com for more details. I also explain how to use the platform in Chapter 10.

Google doesn't follow links inside the video itself. The power of posting online video is in the description, category, and tags that you assign to the video when you post it online. To help boost your online reputation, be sure to use your full name in the description and in the tags.

Publishing your slides and presentations

If you went to business school or gave presentations for past jobs, you probably have plenty of PowerPoint slides hanging around. You can repurpose these slides by posting them on SlideShare (www.slideshare.net), a slideshow-sharing social network that can get you ranked in Google. Not only does SlideShare have hundreds of thousands of fascinating presentations to go through and learn from, but it also lets you share your slideshow directly on your LinkedIn profile.

What makes SlideShare such a powerful Google ranking tool is that it actually reads and indexes the content of the slide and activates the links in the body of the slide. So if you use your name in the slide and include links to your LinkedIn profile and other online properties, that slideshow has a good chance of showing up when someone searches for your name.

Here are the steps to take when repurposing slides:

1. **Polish your slideshow.**

   Because you won't be around every time someone views your slideshow, it needs to stand on its own and be self-explanatory. Imagine someone going through your slideshow without you narrating it. Make sure that person can understand the content and get the point of each slide. If you have any doubt, make changes to the slideshow so that each slide has this level of clarity.

   I suggest looking at some of the more popular presentations on SlideShare and taking careful notes on how the authors make each slide communicate the point. Notice how the better slideshows get a single point across for each slide and aren't overly bulleted.

2. **Give your slideshow links.**

   Include live hyperlinks inside the slideshow itself. Be sure to link to your LinkedIn profile, online résumé, or other web properties. However, don't overdo it; one on each slide is enough.

3. **Include keywords, such as your name and field of interest.**

   You're trying to get your own name to rank in Google, so be sure it appears at least two times in your slideshow. You may also want to use some of the keywords you researched when forming your personal brand in Chapter 5.

   Use your name as footer text in your slides so it appears on every page without being obnoxious. For the most impact, create a footer for each slide that looks like this (with your full name linking to your LinkedIn profile): "Copyright 2011 <u>Your Name</u>. If you publish or borrow any of these ideas, kindly reference this link: www.YourBlogorResume.net."

4. **Submit your slideshow to SlideShare.**

   After you upload your slideshow, SlideShare converts it to an online format.

5. Add the SlideShare application to your LinkedIn profile.

You can link your SlideShare account to your LinkedIn profile by using a LinkedIn *Application* — a third-party plug-in on your LinkedIn profile. (I explain how to install applications on your LinkedIn profile in Chapter 9.) Doing so is a great way of showing a future employer what value you can provide to his organization by demonstrating your professional work.

Publishing your photos

Google's search results page has become more and more multimedia oriented over the years. A results page used to be a simple list of links to websites, but now you can choose from images, videos, maps, and social networks. So when you post photos of yourself, you're increasing your likelihood of ranking in Google.

In order for Google to correctly index and serve an image, the image needs to have a proper description. Creating a description for an image depends on the image-sharing tool you use. Here are two great photo-sharing sites you can post images of yourself to:

✔ **Flickr:** Flickr (www.flickr.com) is a photo-sharing site frequently indexed by Google. The site allows you to create a free account and then upload images. When you upload images of yourself, use your full name in the title of the image and in the description area.

✔ **Picasa Web Albums:** Picasa Web Albums (www.picasaweb.com) is owned by Google, so you can assume that images uploaded to the photo-sharing program get indexed pretty regularly. Although Picasa Web Albums isn't a social networking site like Flickr, it's still an easy way to get images ranked on Google's first page of search results for your name. Picasa Web Albums creates the title for your image based on the file name, so be sure to rename your image with your full name before uploading it. For example, before uploading an image, rename it like this: *full.name.presentation.jpg*. This step can help your Google ranking.

Picasa Web Albums was built for headshots. When you upload a headshot, the program allows you to name the face. You simply click the individual photo and name your face. Doing so adds a *meta tag* to the image. Google uses this tag to identify and index it.

If you're an advanced user of either of these programs, you can choose the *Creative Commons* (CC) license. CC tells Google that you give other people permission to use and reuse your image in any way as long as you're attributed as the source.

Publishing your creative projects

If you work in a creative industry like design or publishing, you probably have a stack of projects you've worked on or contributed to. Take a look through your stack and pick the best samples. Then upload them to Behance (www.behance.com), Carbonmade (www.carbonmade.com), or FigDig (www.figdig.com). These portfolio-building sites are for creative professionals (for more on each of these sites, see Chapter 14). Google regularly indexes projects from these sites, so you have a good chance of ranking on the first page of results.

When setting up a portfolio with Behance, Carbonmade, or FigDig, be sure to title it with your full name. Use your full name for the custom web address as well. By doing so, you create yet another domain with your name in it.

You don't need very many samples to make your point; aim for five to ten. You'll have choices of layout and privacy settings. As long as your project is made public or visible, Google will index it.

Before posting any creative project you've worked on, verify that you have the rights to reproduce each item. If you don't, ask the company for permission. It's better to ask permission and not get sued than to ask for forgiveness with a copyright violation fee!

Managing your content over time

Google is a pretty sophisticated robot. If you suddenly dump all kinds of new content with your name online, Google is likely to call foul. To avoid problems, make the process of building your online reputation methodical and consistent over many months. Don't expect to see results right away. You're running a marathon, not a sprint.

Base the frequency and length of your reputation-building campaign entirely on the results of your initial assessment (see the earlier section "Reviewing Your Current Online Reputation"). Ideally, you'll post content about once a week. But if you fall into the category of having a bad online reputation, you may even consider posting content twice a week for six months.

To help keep track of when and what you want to post, prepare an editorial calendar (just like you would if you were running a newspaper or a blog). In a spreadsheet, map out 26 weeks for the first half of the year. Then write down which piece of content you're going to post for each week. This type of preplanning helps you pace yourself, lower your stress level, and avoid getting on Google's bad side by dumping tons of content online all at once. (For help determining the pool of content you have to pull from, refer to the earlier "Repurposing your portfolio" section.) If you don't have enough repurposed content to fill up each week, consider generating new material.

Monitoring Your Reputation

Just as building your online reputation is an ongoing process, so is maintaining that reputation over the course of your career. When you monitor what people are saying about you, you can find inaccuracies before they spread, which gives you a chance to address problems quickly. Monitoring also helps you discover when people are saying good things about you so you can thank them.

Monitoring allows you to track your progress as you build your online reputation. When you see your content show up in search results, you begin to realize that you have more control over Google than you once thought possible. It's really cool to see yourself coming up more and more on Google week after week.

The following sections help you start the monitoring process by explaining how to set up alerts and make time for maintaining your online reputation on a regular basis.

Setting up alerts

Although it's a good idea to search for your name once a month, it's difficult to keep this habit up over time. You'll forget one month and then the habit will be lost. The best way to monitor what's going on in search results is to set up a Google Alert for your name.

A *Google Alert* is a reverse search. As soon as Google indexes a piece of content with your search term, you get an alert or notice from Google. These notices tell you when your search term (in this case, your name) is processed by a robot as soon as it happens.

To set up a Google Alert for your name, go to www.google.com/alerts and type in your full name in quotations. As you can see in Figure 7-2, all you need to do next is set "Type" to Everything and "How often" to once a day. Then have the alerts sent to your e-mail address. If your name wasn't indexed, you won't get an e-mail.

Figure 7-2:
The Google Alerts setup page.

If you want to monitor your presence in social media, you'll be pleased to know that you can set up alerts through Social Mention (`www.social mention.com`) just like you can with Google. After searching for your full name in quotations at the Social Mention site, choose the E-mail Alert link at the top-right side of the screen. With this feature, you get an e-mail every time someone blogs about you, tweets about you, or says anything about you in any social media site. *Note:* The results in your Social Mention alerts typically will be much different from those in your Google Alert (as I explain in the earlier section "Finding the social you on Social Mention").

Scheduling regular maintenance

Assessing and building your reputation may be activities you primarily focus on for your job search, but you also need to monitor and maintain your reputation throughout your entire career. Unless the Internet disappears (yeah, right), you need to manage your online reputation. Think of it as an ongoing chore, such as taking your car in for an oil change.

Somewhere in the calendar you use to schedule your time, create the following ticklers:

- ✔ Every month, review your Google Alerts and Social Mention alerts.

- ✔ Every six months, search your name using Google, ZoomInfo, and Pipl.

- ✔ Once a year, take stock of your online presence by using the tools and strategies I present in the earlier "Reviewing Your Current Online Reputation" section.

Part III

Crafting Web Résumés with LinkedIn, Video, and More

The 5th Wave   By Rich Tennant

RESUME
Robert Cosgrove
17 State St
Borgin Il 71661

SWM seeks successful
corporation for long
term relationship.

"My sense is that you're personalizing
your resume too much."

In this part . . .

Do you think the résumé is dead? I assure you it's not! The résumé has simply changed forms from a document that's printed on paper and handed to potential employers into a living, web-based document that you can share with anyone, including people you don't know directly (like those second-degree connections of yours on LinkedIn).

In this part, I help you take your current understanding of a résumé and translate it to various online media, such as LinkedIn profiles, video résumés, and other online résumé formats. Why? Because today's job seeker can no longer just rely on yesterday's résumé.

Chapter 8

Updating Your Résumé for an Online Audience

In This Chapter

▶ Fitting a traditional résumé into a modern job search

▶ Transferring your paper résumé to an online version

▶ Using and writing recommendations

*W*hen most people start a job search, they exclaim with some anticipation, "Now I have to update my résumé!" Although a traditional, hard-copy résumé *was* the pivotal part of a job search in the past, today a truly successful job seeker may never actually need one.

This chapter examines the way HR departments and hiring managers use résumés today. By understanding the function of a résumé, you can break out of the limitations it imposes upon you. This chapter also shows you how to transform yesterday's paper résumé into a modern, web-based version with greater impact on your personal brand. Finally, you discover how obtaining and writing recommendations works in the social media world (goodbye writing your own long-winded letters; hello short and sweet recommender-generated content!).

Understanding the Real Function of a Hard-Copy Résumé

A hard-copy résumé (as in the paper-based one that you create in a word-processing program on your computer and print out on a piece of paper) is a necessary evil. It's also an obituary. A traditional, hard-copy résumé tells employers what you did, not what you can do for them.

Nowadays, when potential employers ask to see your résumé, what they may actually be asking for is some kind of documentation that validates their opinion about you. Potential employers want an opportunity to get to know you better, and sending them a worn-out résumé may be a mistake because it doesn't do a very good job of demonstrating your personality.

Following are the functional purposes of a résumé in today's white-collar workplace:

- Fulfill some kind of process requirement with a company's HR software
- Allow a hiring manager to quickly assess your skills and abilities
- Provide an easy way to differentiate you among a stack of other candidates
- Allow a corporate recruiter to find a reason *not* to hire you
- Occupy a place-marker, a paper voodoo doll of you, on a person's desk

So what can you do to make the whole hard-copy résumé thing work in your favor? Make it look good on computer screens and be sure to include references to your online profiles so hiring managers can discover more about you. Your résumé should include just enough information to accurately represent who you are and offer options for readers to find out more if they choose to.

Discovering the Many Benefits of Online Résumés

By displaying your skills, qualifications, and abilities, a résumé used to indicate whether you could do a particular job or not. In the previous century, when most jobs were hands-on and less creative, answering the question "Can you do the job?" was good enough. But now that most jobs are knowledge jobs and business is so much more complicated than pushing buttons, employers need more rounded information on candidates. In short, you need more than your paper résumé to stand out from the crowd.

With social media, you have an opportunity to not only clarify whether you can do the job but also help a hiring manager determine your motivation level and whether you'd be a good fit for the company long before you reach the interview stage. In fact, if you've run your job search right by using the many social media tools available, you may hear a hiring manager say at the first interview, "I feel like I already know you."

Here are some of the benefits of supplementing a paper résumé with an online version:

- ✔ **You remain in control of the document.** If you make a change in one location, everyone reading that document can see the update. For example, if you get a promotion, you just have to update your online résumé to let other people know about it, rather than send out multiple copies of an updated hard-copy résumé.

- ✔ **You can show your current value, rather than just your past.** In other words, you can customize your online résumé to include more details about how you can help the company or hiring manager deal with a current issue or problem. You can also incorporate video, images, and color into your résumé to demonstrate your professionalism.

- ✔ **You can show some personality.** Because you're breaking away from the tired-out paper résumé format, you have much more flexibility to show your true colors. You can create a strong first impression as a likable guy or gal who's always motivated to do well at every undertaking.

Customizing Your Online Résumé

When transferring your résumé to the web, the last thing you want to do is simply copy and paste your hard-copy résumé into an online format. If you do, you miss out on an opportunity to demonstrate the type of person you are and how motivated you are. Also, people read a computer screen differently than a piece of paper. Consequently, the way you write and format your online résumé should change accordingly. The sections that follow show you how to convert a traditional hard-copy résumé (see Figure 8-1) to one that shines online (see Figure 8-2).

Hiring managers' questions reveal their thoughts

Has anyone used you as a professional reference before? If so, then you probably noticed that many of the questions you were asked had little to do with your friend's ability to do the job. Most of the questions were probably about his or her motivation and personality.

Hiring managers are clearly concerned with whether a potential candidate will fit in at the company and whether that person is a motivated individual. Thanks to all the social media sites out there, the Internet gives you the opportunity to demonstrate your personality and motivation level in addition to listing your abilities. So what's not to love about online résumés?

Jane Doe

1234 SW 56th Place, Portland, OR 97223 • 503.222.2222 • hiremenow@hotmail.com

Professional Profile

Seasoned digital marketing strategist and director with deep knowledge of brand stewardship. 17 years experience blending customer insight, creativity, and technology to forge visionary brand experiences. Adept at bringing new brands to market, demonstrating thought leadership and enabling cross-functional collaboration. Consummate presentation skills.

Professional History

Independent Contractor, Portland, OR Present
SOCIAL MEDIA CONSULTANT
Focused on social media marketing for B2C and B2B brands. Expertise covers all facets of social media: strategic planning, content development, influencer relations, program management, analytics/optimization and operations.

Watz it Creative, Portland, OR 2008 - 2010
DIRECTOR OF STRATEGY
Provided strategic marketing and digital brand management leadership. Worked with clients and internal discipline leads from account management, information architecture, design, engineering, media planning and business development. This includes using market research to fuel integrated marketing programs that utilize interactive, social media, traditional media, PR and events.
- Developed a social media and viral marketing practice
- Led in the development of methodologies and standards for the delivery of account planning and consumer research.

The Old Group, Portland, OR 2007 - 2009
DIRECTOR OF BRAND INNOVATION
Provided overall leadership, vision and direction for clients and company in relationship to digital brand communications. Partner with clients, executive management and department leaders in the development and execution of integrated digital programs. Champion thought leadership in audience research, experience design and analytics.
- Developed a social media marketing practice
- Stewarded company go-to-market strategy with prime focus on digital agency-of-record accounts

Independent Contractor, Portland, OR 2005 - 2007
DIGITAL MARKETING CONSULTANT
Applied consumer insight, cultural trends, technology and creativity to inform and deliver integrated, interactive and social media communication strategies and programs.
- Mapped consumer attitudes and media behaviors to the brand engagement cycle with a focus on the awareness, demand generation, sales and retention stages

Education

B.A. Political Science, Interdisciplinary Honors Program (Magna Cum Laude) – Temple University
The Wharton Management Certificate Program – University of Pennsylvania

HyperLife

http://linkedin.com/in/janedoe11

Figure 8-1:
A résumé
in the
traditional
format.

Professional Summary

Seasoned digital marketing strategist and director with deep knowledge of brand stewardship. 17 years experience blending customer insight, creativity, and technology to forge visionary brand experiences.

Jane Doe
Digital Marketing Strategist

Experience

Independent Contractor, Portland, OR Present
SOCIAL MEDIA CONSULTANT
Focused on social media marketing for B2C and B2B brands. Expertise covers all facets of social media: strategic planning, content development, influencer relations, program management, analytics/optimization and operations.

Watz it Creative, Portland, OR 2008 - 2010
DIRECTOR OF STRATEGY
- Developed a social media and viral marketing practice
- Led in the development of methodologies and standards for the delivery of account planning and consumer research.

HOME
1234 SW 56th Pl.
Portland, OR 97223

The Old Group, Portland, OR 2007 - 2009
DIRECTOR OF BRAND INNOVATION
- Developed a social media marketing practice
- Stewarded company go-to-market strategy with prime focus on digital agency-of-record accounts

PHONE
(503)-222-2222

EMAIL
hiremenow11@hotmail.com

Independent Contractor, Portland, OR 2005 - 2007
DIGITAL MARKETING CONSULTANT
Applied consumer insight, cultural trends, technology and creativity to inform and deliver integrated, interactive and social media communication strategies and programs.
- Mapped consumer attitudes and media behaviors to the brand engagement cycle with a focus on the awareness, demand generation, sales and retention stages

LINKEDIN PROFILE
LinkedIn.com/in/janedoe11

BLOG
DigitalGenious.com

TWITTER
@janedoe11

Education

B.A. Political Science, Interdisciplinary Honors Program – **Temple University**
The Wharton Management Certificate Program – **University of Pennsylvania**

Skills

Adept at bringing new brands to market, demonstrating thought leadership and enabling cross-functional collaboration. Consummate presentation skills.

Figure 8-2:
A résumé
in a format
that also
looks good
online.

Writing for an online audience

When you read articles online, do you tend to pass over large blocks of text? If so, then you're like most people who have a hard time sorting through dense paragraphs on a screen. When I first started blogging, I had to completely shift how I wrote. The truth is that most people scan online content most of the time.

Following are a few formatting guidelines to help make your online résumé easier to read:

✔ **Use bulleted points and lists as often as possible.** Bulleted lists are easy to scan, as you can see in Figure 8-3, which shows how you can easily convert a block of text into a bulleted list.

✔ **Shorten your blocks of text.** On the web, using single sentence paragraphs isn't uncommon (contrary to my daughter's seventh-grade teacher's advice). I tend not to write more than three sentences per paragraph for online writing.

✔ **Use headers.** Headers are just large, bold headlines used to break content up into sections. Headers can make your text more scannable and easier for the reader to follow your train of thought. For example, you may break up a big block of text, like your objectives, into two or three sections: "Who am I," "What can I do for your company," and "Three things that make me different."

✔ **Take advantage of hyperlinking.** The Internet was invented so scientists could link one article to another. If you mention something in your résumé, offer a drill down into more detail by linking to more information about it. For example, you may link to the corporate website of the companies you worked at or schools you went to. You can also link to your LinkedIn profile or even an online portfolio.

✔ **Put the most important content up top.** The *fold* is the bottom of what's visible on-screen in a web browser before you scroll down. You can read content above the fold without having to scroll down. Most people tend not to scroll down, so most content below the fold isn't read. So prioritize your writing according to this behavioral phenomenon.

✔ **Keep a little white space.** Reading big blocks of text on a computer screen is difficult. White spaces can break things up and give your résumé a fresh feel. Refer to Figure 8-2 to see how that résumé uses white space to frame the body of the content.

Changing the focus from verbs to nouns

A paper résumé may live only in your portfolio, but an online résumé can live anywhere — and, therefore, be discovered by just about anyone. If you can make your online résumé show up on a recruiter's Google search, then who knows what possibilities may open up for you.

To get your résumé found on Google, you need to practice *Search Engine Optimization,* or SEO, which is the art and science of making websites appear on a search engine's first page. (Flip to Chapter 7 for more information about SEO.) You can practice good SEO skills by sprinkling certain choice *keywords* — nouns that Google reads in a web page to determine the page's relevance to a search query — throughout your résumé.

Specialties
World travel, Challenging the status quo, Meditation, Entrepreneurship, Social Media Strategist, Career counseling, Social Media Strategy development, Professional Speaker, Author and Trainer, NLP and performance oriented relaxation techniques, Personal Productivity hacks

Figure 8-3:
A list of specialties before (top) and after (bottom) being broken into bullets.

Specialties
• World travel
• Challenging the status quo
• Meditation
• Entrepreneurship
• Social Media Strategist
• Career counseling
• Social Media Strategy development
• Professional Speaker
• Author and Trainer
• NLP and performance oriented relaxation techniques
• Personal Productivity hacks

Traditional job seekers don't write paper résumés with keywords in mind. Instead, they fill résumés with action-oriented verbs that describe what they did and what they're currently doing. But those verbs don't translate well to an online résumé because people tend to search for nouns. For example, a recruiter may search for "Houston Project Manager in Oil Industry" — notice, no verbs. Be sure to infuse your online résumé with powerful keywords that search engines can find and use to create a search results page.

Recognizing that your nouns aren't the only nouns

When job seekers discover keywords, they usually experience an aha moment that helps them grasp the importance of using nouns and incorporating search-friendly keywords in their online résumés. For example, I once had a client who called herself a volunteer coordinator. After some research, she discovered that the more popular way of describing what she did was *services coordinator*. I would have never guessed this, and if she didn't do her research, neither would she. By using a more popular keyword or job description in your online résumé, you're more likely to be found in an online search.

The sections that follow present alternative keywords for describing your current job that you may want to consider incorporating into your online résumé. Use these words to start brainstorming your own list of keywords (I show you how to conduct keyword research in Chapter 5).

Healthcare keywords

Health information manager

Interdepartmental communications

Medical and health services manager

Medical office manager

Practice administration

Regulatory affairs professional

Regulatory consulting

Higher education keywords

Admissions recommendations

Course administration

Education administrator

Education leadership

Human resources keywords

Compensation surveys

Cross-cultural communication

Industrial organizational psychology

Leadership development

Organizational development

Sourcing

Staffing

Training and development

Manufacturing operations keywords

Configuration management

Cost reductions

Distribution management

Just-in-time

Logistics

Materials coordinator

Operational efficiency

Operational excellence

Process improvement

Spares and repairs management

Supply chain management

Warehousing operations

Nonprofit keywords

Chief technical advisor

Communications director

Corporate giving program

Farm to market manager

Microfinance consultant

Policy research assistant

Program development activities

Social and community service manager

Technology professional keywords

Agile development

Application support services

Business continuity

Cross-functional team

Disaster recovery

Volunteer center

Global systems support

Hardware support

Help desk

Project lifecycle

Vendor relationships

Knowing what to include and what to leave behind

Selecting what to include and what not to include in your résumé is even more important for online résumés than for paper ones. Because your first impression is likely to be an online impression, and people make snap decisions, make sure your résumé displays the most relevant information possible. After all, you have only about 30 seconds (the average time a recruiter spends on a candidate online) to get and keep viewers' attention.

Just because a web page or profile page is infinitely expandable doesn't mean you should fill up pages and pages in order to store all your past experiences, interests, and certifications. If you've been in the workforce for a while, try to limit your work history to the last 15 to 20 years. Make sure every piece of information you reveal about yourself supports your value to the company.

Embracing the Modern Recommendation "Letter"

Along with most traditional résumés, people often included recommendation letters. Most employers require references to call at the very least. So smart careerists strive to collect agreements from former bosses to vouch for them.

In the old job-search paradigm, former managers and colleagues commonly asked people to write their own recommendation letters. I remember asking my boss to draft a letter for me, and her response was, "Why don't you write one for yourself, and I'll sign it?" That was fine then, but it won't work now. Here's why:

- ✔ The advent of online recruiting means that many of your recommendations appear online and in larger quantities than ever before. (If you want a higher search ranking on LinkedIn, you may even strive to have a minimum of 15 recommendations!) That adds up to a lot of recommendations you would've had to write yourself.

- ✔ The recommendations found on online résumés are much shorter than the old paper recommendations. The typical online recommendation is between five and ten sentences.

- ✔ Writing your own recommendation can look inauthentic to a recruiter who's trained to pick up on things like that. The key to social media is authenticity. If you try to write all your own recommendations, they may wind up looking the same (or at least suspiciously similar to the trained eye).

Having strong recommendations is essential, and having more of them builds your credibility online. You need to take advantage of this recommendation blitz by helping your connections write as many high-quality referrals as possible. The next sections help you figure out how to ask for web-appropriate recommendations and how to write them (because sooner or later, someone is going to ask you to return the favor).

Asking for an online referral

What do you do when you ask a former boss or co-worker for an online referral and he says, "Why don't you write it up for me, and I'll paste it into your online résumé"? Apart from letting him know that his attitude is a bit outdated, you can always softly explain that you've already written several versions of a recommendation letter and you're concerned about them sounding the same. Tell your former boss or co-worker that you'd appreciate if he could take just five minutes of his time and write a few sentences covering a few points you provide.

Offering your recommenders three points you'd like them to cover can help them collect their thoughts and organize their words. It also helps ensure that whoever reads the recommendation finds out what you want him or her to know. Case in point: I recently received a recommendation request where I was asked to talk about the unconventional approach to marketing strategies that the person possessed. I may never have mentioned that about this person if I wasn't asked to. When you give your recommender guidance, think about what elements of your personal brand you want to reinforce. And don't give everyone the same topic to focus on.

Avoiding the quid pro quo approach to recommendations

Because of the transparency in today's online job search, recruiters can easily see whether the number of recommendations you've received equals the number of recommendations you've given on LinkedIn and other online profiles. This equal number is a red flag for many professional headhunters. If someone recommends you, you aren't obligated to return the gesture. In fact, it may be wise to not reciprocate every once in a while.

Tip: Why not write someone you know an unsolicited recommendation? Doing so helps that person's career while simultaneously ensuring that your online résumé doesn't look like a quid pro quo for referrals.

When asking a former boss or co-worker for a recommendation, these tips may come in handy:

- **Expect a 50 percent response rate.** If you're aiming for three recommendations, send out six requests.

- **Follow up your request with a phone call.** Using e-mail or LinkedIn's request system alone can be ineffective.

- **Use the online résumé's recommendation system, if it has one.** I hate getting requests that require me to click around for five minutes just to find the spot where I'm supposed to write. Using the online résumé service's recommendation system makes writing recommendations easier.

- **Tell your recommenders how little time it takes to write a recommendation and how much it'll impact your career.** If you put your request into concrete terms, people feel a less perceived commitment. For example, you can say, "It will take only five to ten minutes of your time."

- **Make certain the person you choose can offer concrete examples to each of the points you want her to make.** A recommendation can look pretty weak without a real-life example. The person you ask should be in a position to draw from experiences with you.

This person did take time out of his day to help you. Show how much you appreciate his effort by sending him a personal e-mail to thank him.

Identifying who to ask for an online recommendation

Because online recommendations are much shorter than traditional ones and take much less time to write, employers expect you to have more of them. Having more recommendations is a credibility builder, and it tells LinkedIn's search algorithm that your profile is more important than other profiles, so it puts you on top of a search results page.

But this blitz for a larger number of recommendations doesn't mean you can ask all your best friends to write one. You still need quality people to write quality recommendations. Be sure you have a nice mix of the following business relationships as recommenders:

✔ Someone you reported to, such as a supervisor or boss

✔ Someone senior but who you didn't report to

✔ A colleague you worked with in the same group

✔ A colleague parallel in your organization but in a different group

✔ A customer or client who you helped

✔ Someone who worked for you or reported to you

Writing an online recommendation

At some point, someone will ask you to write a recommendation. Or you may just feel compelled to offer a recommendation, unsolicited, to someone you appreciate. Just be sure you recommend only people who you can honestly vouch for. Remember that your reputation is on the line, too.

Keep the following pointers in mind when writing online recommendations:

✔ **Be brief.** Your recommendation should be five to ten sentences or 150 words max.

✔ **Lead with a strong statement.** For example, "I've worked with Cathy on several projects, and each time, I come away inspired by her energy and creativity."

✔ **Remember that you're helping to sell the other person.** Don't be afraid to boast a little bit about the person you're recommending. Tell why she's so great and why an organization would be lucky to have her.

✔ **Back up your statements with concrete details.** Was there a specific incident that your person totally rocked at? If so, make sure to mention it.

✔ **Use the rule of three.** Keep to three main points and three supporting examples. Using three points and examples makes the referral easier to remember.

✔ **Be open to getting corrected.** The receiver of your endorsement may want to correct your memory of things. Be open if someone asks you to adjust some detail in a recommendation you wrote.

Chapter 9

Using LinkedIn to Put Your Best Profile Forward

*I*n today's connected job market, your first impression with a potential employer is likely to be an online impression. And LinkedIn — a social network for professionals — is one of the primary locations for an employer to find new talent online. Fortune 500 companies (including many of their executives), small businesses, startups, freelancers, and businesses from hundreds of sectors are on LinkedIn. At the end of 2010, LinkedIn had more than 85 million users, and more than half of them were located outside the United States. This number is even greater today because every second a new person joins LinkedIn. In fact, corporate headhunters now consider LinkedIn their primary resource for filling open jobs.

So what does all this information mean to you? The answer's simple. You need to seriously ask yourself this question: Is my LinkedIn profile strong enough, compelling enough, or just simply good enough to make the kind of impression on a hiring manager that can get me an interview?

After reading this chapter and applying my advice to your profile, the answer will be yes. That's because in this chapter, I introduce you to the rise of LinkedIn's use in the human resources world and explain just how this development affects your job search. I also reveal the most important elements of creating a LinkedIn profile for job-seeking success, what you need to do to get your profile looking great, and some powerful strategies for growing your network's leverage.

TIP Even if you're fairly experienced with LinkedIn, I encourage you to read through this chapter. You may find a trick or two that makes a positive differ-ence in your effort to find a job. (And for the latest on LinkedIn, head to www.careerenlightenment.com/fordummies.)

Understanding Why LinkedIn Is So Important

Put yourself in the shoes of a hiring manager in today's economy. Your com-pany is going through tough economic times. Your HR department has been drastically downsized, and you're being asked to find and recruit talent to fill your open positions — a task that you aren't even compensated for. Do you (A) pay a major job board $600 to $800 to post the job and get lots of spam and unqualified people applying, or (B) ask your trusted network, on- or offline, for free, to get qualified referred talent to fill your position?

Clearly, hiring managers prefer to leverage their social and professional networks to fill positions. Today, the highest-leverage social professional net-work is LinkedIn.

As with any social network, the power is not only with having a compelling profile but also with who you know, who those people know, and who those people know. Experienced networkers know that the best professional oppor-tunities come from second- or even third-degree connections. Several months ago, I checked my network statistics. I had more than 880 first-degree connec-tions, and from those connections I had access to more than 11 million people. This means that I'm more likely to have connections at companies I may want to work for and be able to ask for referrals into those companies. Building your LinkedIn network to this capacity is a very reasonable goal for any job seeker.

Are people *really* finding work through LinkedIn?

Because no global survey of LinkedIn users exists, I don't have statistics to share on how many people actually find jobs using LinkedIn. However, I actively collect stories — common, everyday occurrences — of people like you and me who find work through LinkedIn.

For example, David Smith was laid off in October 2010. He posted his predicament to his LinkedIn network — a network of about 900 connections.

In less than 12 hours, he had three network con-nections e-mail him. David was unemployed for a little more than a week and accepted a posi-tion with three others on the table to choose from. I hear stories like this daily. Do the right thing with your LinkedIn network, and this can happen to you. Granted, it may not happen as quickly, but it'll certainly happen much faster than if you didn't cultivate your online network.

Another compelling reason why LinkedIn is so important for your job search is that if you have a strong profile, you're likely to rank on Google's first results page when someone searches for your name. This fact makes a powerful LinkedIn profile the first step to building a strong online reputation.

Surveying the Elements of a Winning Profile

An employer looks at three key areas of your LinkedIn profile during the first few seconds of viewing (I show you where these elements can be found in Figure 9-1):

- ✔ Your profile photo
- ✔ Your professional headline
- ✔ Your profile summary

I call these elements "The Big Three." They're so important to your LinkedIn profile that I devote a section to each one.

Taking a good profile photo

Humans are visual creatures. In a matter of milliseconds, we draw conclusions, make assumptions, and form opinions about people based on how they look. The way we look, of course, shouldn't have anything to do with our eligibility for a position, but it often does. Hiring managers want to know who you are. They want to see whether you have leadership qualities and whether you're friendly and professional. They want to imagine what working with you may be like. All these attributes can be communicated to your advantage with a good profile photo.

Generally speaking, not having a profile photo on LinkedIn can cause you more damage than having a bad one. Many recruiters I talk to say that a blank profile photo lands many qualified candidates into the maybe pile. A faceless candidate communicates an incomplete profile, which is perceived as low motivation and a lackluster enthusiasm for finding work. After all, if you went to a dating site and read the profile of the mate of your dreams, but instead of a tall blond, you saw a blank, would you believe what that person says?

Professional headline

Profile photo

Figure 9-1:
A LinkedIn profile featuring the three winning elements.

Profile summary

A strong LinkedIn profile picture includes the following key elements:

- ✔ **A pleasant smile:** A good photo is warm and welcoming. Show those pearly-whites.

- ✔ **Professional attire:** Not every job requires that you wear a suit and tie, but you should dress appropriately. Think about the job you're going for and dress for your first day.

Turning age-related negatives into positives

Often, age discrimination occurs from the misplaced notion that younger people can be paid less to do the same job or that older people are resistant to change. If you're worried that showing a little gray hair in your profile image may cause an employer to pass you by, reframe age into something positive. Turn the negative association into a positive one.

For example, if you feel that age is associated with being "set in your ways," then find a way of showing flexibility and a willingness to adopt new things, such as social media. If you associate age with slowness to action, depict yourself in an action shot. Perhaps your profile photo shows you speaking, or walking, or shaking someone's hand. If you're concerned that age is associated with a high salary for a commodity job, then show yourself as a *sage* — someone whose wisdom and experience could save the company from a lot of unnecessary risk.

✔ **A pleasing background:** Each color and background texture alters the emotional quality of the image. Some people choose green or blue backgrounds, which convey trust and stability. One friend, a financial advisor, stood next to the Merrill Lynch bull to communicate an association with the financial industry.

✔ **An interesting angle:** Your profile picture isn't a mug shot, so don't look head on at the camera. Instead, try tilting your head slightly or look at the camera over a shoulder. You want to avoid symmetry around your head.

✔ **A sign of your personality:** A marketing friend of mine is playing her Rock Band guitar in her profile photo because she's in a creative marketing industry. Although you don't need a gimmick or prop in your photo, think about what you can do to show who you are and make your image memorable.

Don't crop your face out of your vacation photos. Take your profile picture seriously and find an hour or two to do it right. If you don't have a good camera, see whether your local department store has a family studio where you can get some good, professional shots.

If you're concerned that adding a picture of yourself to your LinkedIn profile may put you at a disadvantage due to ageism, racism, or sexism, consider this: If a hiring manager makes a negative determination about your employability based on a half-inch sized profile photo, then his company isn't the place for you. Clearly a culture of oppression is in that organization, and I'm sure you aren't anxious to jump into a shark tank. This type of organization can make it twice as hard for you to succeed, so let it go. The right place will come along.

Writing a professional headline

Your professional headline appears just below your name as well as on every communication you send in LinkedIn. It defines who you are and what you can do for an organization. That's why LinkedIn doesn't call this section *job title,* yet many people make the mistake of simply stating their role, such as sales executive or VP of Finance.

When you first sign up to LinkedIn, it puts your job title in the headline area. You need to edit this along with the rest of your profile based on the advice in this section.

In your LinkedIn professional headline, you have 120 characters to really communicate your identity — what you do, who you are, and what your level of motivation is. This spot is also your chance to show a hiring manager that you understand the needs of her business. What can you do to help her company?

Because LinkedIn's search algorithm indexes the headline first, be sure to include your most powerful keywords and keyphrases. (For more about how to find keywords and keyphrases and how to compose a winning headline, see Chapter 5.)

Here are some examples to consider for rewriting your headline:

> *Turn* Database Engineer *into* Capable CRM optimizer who thrives on finding efficiencies and saving organizations money

> *Turn* Marketing Professional *into* Effective Marketing Communications Specialist: Creating business value through focused messaging

> *Turn* Social Services Manager *into* Enthusiastic program manager who loves organizing outreach for the benefit of clients, volunteers, and the board of directors.

If you currently have a job, mention it by name in your headline. Employed people sometimes have an easier time finding other jobs. So take advantage of this trend by explicitly calling out your current employer and what you're doing there.

Summarizing what makes you different

The summary section of your profile appears just below the blue area at the top of your profile (refer to Figure 9-1). If hiring managers make it as far as your summary, they're essentially asking you to tell them more about you. So here's your chance to make an impression. Whatever you do, don't bore them. Only after reading your summary do hiring managers look at your experience and education.

Avoid overused LinkedIn buzzwords

LinkedIn announces the top ten buzzwords overused in profiles from the United States. So if you want to separate yourself from the crowd, avoid these words at all costs. For example, the list announced in December 2010 included the following words:

- Extensive experience
- Innovative
- Motivated
- Results-oriented
- Dynamic

- Proven track record
- Team player
- Fast-paced
- Problem solver
- Entrepreneurial

A good profile summary has these three characteristics:

- **It's short.** Keep your summary between five and ten lines on the screen, or three to five sentences. When read out loud, your summary shouldn't take more than 30 seconds to read. (And, yes, that means you need to read it out loud with a timer.)

- **It's concise.** Your summary isn't the place for bulleted lists of your accomplishments, but it should quickly tell viewers more about you.

- **It's unique.** Avoid jargon, buzzwords, or clichés.

- **It's a narrative.** You're welcome to use first person pronouns in your summary. Rather than referring to yourself in the third person, like you would in a résumé, tell your story with *I* and *my*.

Your profile summary is the first place you get to elaborate on your personal brand. And your brand should focus on the value you offer the reader. So feel free to use a clear and well-crafted value statement in this area of your profile. I go into great detail on writing value statements in Chapter 5. Go through one of the three methods for writing a value statement and then update your LinkedIn profile summary with the results.

Getting Your Profile in Tiptop Shape

Nowadays, first impressions between employers and potential employees are taking place on LinkedIn more often than not, which means you need to put the same effort into the way you look online as you do into your physical appearance when you're heading to an interview or meeting. But what I find when I speak publicly to various audiences about LinkedIn is that even though most professionals have a LinkedIn profile, the vast majority of them have done precious little with it. In many cases, 90 percent of the professionals I encounter haven't even bothered completing their profiles.

I don't want you to be among this group. I want you to have not only a complete profile — one that shows your photo, has at least three recommendations, and includes all the details about your work experience and education — but also an impressive profile that makes you stand out. In the next sections, I share with you the tools, such as applications and recommendations, that can help differentiate your profile from others.

If you don't yet have a LinkedIn profile and want basic details about how to set up an account, see Joel Elad's *LinkedIn For Dummies,* 2nd Edition (John Wiley & Sons, Inc.). Make sure your profile is complete before moving on to the next sections.

Installing applications

Because of the way LinkedIn is designed, the look and feel of your profile is, by default, very much like everyone else's. Fortunately, you can counteract this uniformity with LinkedIn's applications, which add a bit of color and personality to LinkedIn's baby blue veneer. *Applications* are third-party plugins to your profile that add additional functionality. Every month or so, new applications are released, and each one adds another layer of functionality to your profile. Following are some of the more popular applications:

- **The Amazon reading list:** This application allows you to tell the world what books you're currently reading, have already read, or intend to read.

- **The WordPress RSS reader:** This application streams your blog posts right onto your profile.

- **The SlideShare slideshow tool:** With this application, any slides you've uploaded to SlideShare can be displayed on your profile to show off your PowerPoint skills.

To access these and other applications, navigate to the More menu (in the gray banner at the top of the page) and choose the Get More Applications link (see Figure 9-2). From there, you can explore all sorts of LinkedIn applications. To install one, just click on the icon and then click on the Add Application button.

I recommend installing the Reading List by Amazon application (Figure 9-3 shows you what it looks like). When I went to university, I had a friend who always asked guest lecturers what books they were currently reading. And through this question, we were exposed to some of the best reading in our professional careers. The book you're reading now speaks volumes about who you are. Constantly reading and staying up-to-date about your industry is the best way to demonstrate your passion and motivation for that industry. Also the book covers add some color and personality to your profile. So pick two industry-relevant books that are easily recognized as new and cutting-edge and then add them to your Amazon reading list with a sentence below each stating why you think the book is important.

Figure 9-2:
How to access more applications on LinkedIn.

Figure 9-3:
The Reading List by Amazon application.

Requesting recommendations

Recommendations in LinkedIn allow you to send or receive professional references and display them on your profile. You need at least three recommendations to have a complete LinkedIn profile. The recommendations section is the one part of your profile that you don't have full control over because you have to rely on other people to write these recommendations for you. LinkedIn's search algorithm ranks profiles with more recommendations higher than others. If you want to be found, I highly encourage you to take your recommendations seriously.

As a general rule, you want to have recommendations equal to about 10 percent of your network size. So if my network has 280 people in it, I may strive for 28 recommendations. Of course, only half the people you ask for a recommendation will respond. So if you need three recommendations, send out six requests. If you want ten, send out 20. For details about how to improve your response rate and how to request recommendations professionally, see Chapter 8.

The trick with requesting recommendations on LinkedIn is to always personalize your request message. LinkedIn drops some standard language into the request form, but you need to tailor this note for each person you're asking.

Some people refuse to write original recommendations. They prefer that you write your own text, and then they just put their signature on it. In my opinion, this is an archaic and quite outdated point of view that's incompatible with social media. The theme with social media is authenticity. Writing your own recommendation and then putting someone else's name on it isn't very authentic. Such practices go against the philosophy of using social media and can backfire on you. And from a more practical standpoint, if you're the author of all your own recommendations, and you have ten of them, they may look too similar and people may notice. Try to explain this to the people who refuse to write a recommendation. If they still refuse to adapt to modern times and help you out, be prepared to let them go. What they may actually be communicating is that they don't have time to help you.

You're not obligated to return a recommendation. LinkedIn delivers a "Return the Favor" screen after you receive a recommendation, but you can ignore this. Give recommendations to only the people you feel compelled to give them to and who you're comfortable vouching for.

Answering questions

LinkedIn has a question and answer forum where anyone can ask a question and then anyone on LinkedIn can answer it. (Although you can choose to limit who can see and answer your question, this question and answer forum isn't necessarily limited to people in your individual network.) The asker of the question can then rank one answer as the top answer. Winners of the top answer get a green star right on their profile.

Earning a green star is a great way to build credibility, demonstrate expertise, and show that you're motivated in your industry. Finding new questions to answer can be a fun part of your online networking routine. And for five minutes a day, it can't hurt!

Any grammar mistakes or typos you make in the question and answer forum are seen by millions of people. So be sure to check your spelling and edit your answer (or question). Good, well-thought-out responses can do wonders for building your personal brand.

Asking smart questions makes you look smart

One way of expanding your network is to ask intelligent questions to the entire LinkedIn community. In the Answers section, choose the Ask a Question tab. When crafting your question, keep in mind that this is another part of your personal brand (what makes you unique — I tell you more about personal branding in Chapter 4). Some topics to consider asking about are how to get started in a new field, the top three challenges in a specific industry, or advice about a certain program. Here are a few examples of real — and in my opinion, good — questions posed by job seekers:

✔ What are you doing to make yourself more findable these days?

✔ What do hiring managers want to see on LinkedIn profiles for professionals in the marketing industry?

✔ What is the most important interview question you ask candidates interviewing for an accounting job and why?

Tip: Invite each person who answers your question to join your network. These people may be great sources for your informational interviews later on. (I fill you in on the job-seeker tool known as the informational interview in Chapter 17.)

To use the Answers section on LinkedIn, follow these steps:

1. **Navigate to the More menu in the top navigation bar and choose Answers.**

2. **Click on the Answer Questions tab at the top, which defaults to Open Questions.**

   For the questions in the Open Questions tab, the top answer hasn't been picked yet, so you still have a chance of getting the green star.

3. **Find a question you think you can answer intelligently and answer it.**

   You can browse by category on the right side of the Open Questions page to refine the questions to your area of expertise.

4. **Send a note to the asker and ask whether your answer was helpful.**

   In the same window where you type in your answer, you can include a private note to the asker. Most people don't bother with a personal note, so this personal touch may increase your chances of getting the green star.

Updating your status

LinkedIn's status update feature allows you to post a short message to share with your network (first- and second-degree contacts only — in other words, the people you're directly connected to and the people they're directly connected to). The functionality of status updates on LinkedIn is very similar to that of Facebook and Twitter. In fact, when you link your Twitter account to your LinkedIn profile, your LinkedIn updates can be sent to your Twitter feed as well. Think of the status update as a quick way of telling people in your network what you're up to. You can find status updates just below your professional headline at the very top of your profile (see Figure 9-4).

Figure 9-4:
Status updates are a good way to communicate within your network.

One of the most common objections I hear about using status updates in LinkedIn is that people feel doing so has no immediate benefit and is a real waste of time. However, using status updates can really accelerate your job search. Here's why:

✔ Due to the location of status updates on a profile, a hiring manager may read your update even before reading your summary.

✔ Updating your network with status updates keeps your name (think personal brand here; see Chapter 5 for more on this topic) at the top of people's minds. Your connections are more likely to think about you as an active member of their community when they see your status update.

✔ Appropriate status updates can demonstrate your personality and show a hiring manager that you're motivated and accomplished. Status updates add further personalization to your otherwise uniform profile.

As for the idea that posting status updates is a waste of time, that's completely not the case — if you do it right. Following are ways to maximize this activity for the biggest impact on your job search without wasting time:

✔ **Update your status at least once a week.** This frequency should appeal to you if you're more reluctant to use status updates. Try it for a couple of weeks and see what happens.

✔ **Don't update your status more than three times a day.** It just turns into noise at that point. (This advice is for you if you're a Twitter zealot who loves to share. LinkedIn is *not* Twitter. Don't pretend it is. For help turning Twitter into a job-seeking tool, flip to Chapter 12.)

Peering into the future of LinkedIn status updates

I predict that status updates will become more important in LinkedIn and in your professional online networking in general. At the time of this writing, LinkedIn is in beta testing of a new feature called *Signal* (www.linkedin.com/signal), which is a page that shows the real-time updates of people in your network, including top stories. Signal provides additional functionality to the LinkedIn home page, such as being able to filter updates by members of specific geographic locations, degrees of connection to you, schools, and even topics.

As LinkedIn's status update feature continues to improve, you'll find that these updates will become more than just short messages. Already you can share links and images via status updates. To make such sharing even easier, LinkedIn gives you a Share This Bookmarklet tool that allows you to share a website or news article to your network. All you have to do is click on the *Bookmarklet* from the website and it appears on your LinkedIn update. Go to linkd.in/linkedin-share and follow the instructions to install this time-saving tool.

✔ **Don't post casual content.** Keep your focus on your industry or professional interests. One way to achieve this is to share a link to an article you've read, along with your opinion of it.

✔ **Share links, observations, and activities that you feel may draw someone closer to you.** Before sharing, ask yourself, "If a hiring manager saw this, would he feel like he knows me better?"

Status updates aren't one-way messages. You can comment and share your thoughts on someone else's post and vice versa. Status updates are a good tool for starting discussions and staying relevant to people. Using status updates to communicate with others is also a nice way of deepening a relationship with someone in your network who you may not know very well and may turn out to be a valuable contact in the future.

Examining and Expanding Your Network

What good is having a beautiful and complete LinkedIn profile if no one gets to see it? Without an extensive network, your LinkedIn profile is just another online résumé. (I tell you all about online résumés in Chapter 11.) The problem is that trying to grow your network, and consequently your job-seeking leverage, can send you straight into some serious obstacles, such as the following:

✔ If you're looking to break into a new industry or specialty field, your current network may be very strong in the industry you're coming from but not so useful for the industry or new field you're trying to get into.

✔ Your network may be so small that finding new people to connect with is difficult.

Much like building an online reputation (see Chapter 7), building a useful LinkedIn network requires you to first assess your network's current state. After you know how strong or weak your network is, you can develop a strategy for getting where you want to go. I help you assess your network's current state and strategize how to improve it in the sections that follow.

Assessing your current reach

When you log in to LinkedIn, on the right side of that first page is a box telling you who else you may know, with the option to connect with them. This information is based on your current network and your past experience. Although seeing who you already know and who you can add is a nice feature, it doesn't help you grow your network in a new and strategic direction.

To see whether you're moving in the right direction to growing your network, look at your current reach. At the top main menu in LinkedIn, click on Contacts and then Network Statistics from the drop-down menu. (Figure 9-5 shows you what the Network Statistics page looks like.)

Scroll down and look at the Regional Access and Industry Access sections under the "More About Your Network" heading. In both of these sections, check for the following statistics:

- **The greatest percentage:** The greatest percentage should be in the area you want to get a job in. If the top region isn't where you want to work or if your industry connections aren't in the field you want to work in, then you have some serious network building to do.

- **The fastest growing areas:** These areas should match your job-seeking goals. Even if your top percentages don't match your goals, then at least the fastest-growing aspects of your network should match. If they do, this indicates that you're meeting and connecting with the right people.

Discovering the bare essentials of LinkedIn-style networking

If you determine that your current network of contacts can use a boost, the next step is to make sure you're fully using all your network-building options. To see what those options are, click on the Add Connections link at the top-right corner of your LinkedIn profile. When you do, you'll see the following network-building options:

✔ **See Who You Already Know:** You can import e-mail addresses from your e-mail clients, such as Gmail, Yahoo! Mail, Hotmail, or AOL, and invite your contacts to connect on LinkedIn. If you use a desktop e-mail client such as Outlook, you can upload a contacts file. Click on the Import Your Desktop Email Contacts link to upload the file into LinkedIn. The contacts who already have a LinkedIn account have a small blue *LI* icon next to their name. Be sure to add these contacts to your connections because they have networks that you can leverage.

✔ **Colleagues:** This tab looks at your profile data and shows you other LinkedIn members who work(ed) at the companies you indicated in your Experience section. Scroll through these lists and add anyone whose name you recognize.

✔ **Classmates:** This tab offers the same functionality as Colleagues but is based on the schools you indicated on your profile. You can even sort by graduation year to find your classmates.

✔ **People You May Know:** This tab is an extension of the box you see when you first log in to LinkedIn. Based on your network, experience, and interests, LinkedIn makes a guess on other members you may know. If you know them, send them an invite.

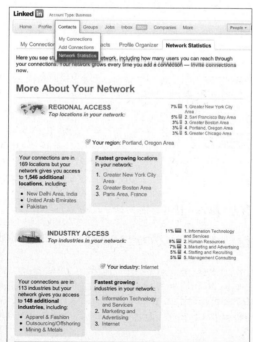

Figure 9-5:
A sample Network Statistics page on LinkedIn.

After you get home from an in-person networking event, professional meeting, or conference, sort through all those business cards you collected and add everyone to your LinkedIn network. Be sure to personalize the invitation message and remind people how you met and what you discussed.

Growing your network

The following statement may sound silly, but here goes: The more connections you have on your LinkedIn profile, the more likely hiring managers are going to trust you. They see your large network as a sign that others validate you and that you're worth getting to know.

When growing your LinkedIn network, you have to decide whether you're a Cat or a LION. *Cats* are more conservative networkers who add only people they know, and in some cases, they must have had at least a 15-minute conversation with them. *LinkedIn Open Networkers,* or LIONs, are more liberal networkers and can have networks as large as 15,000 connections or more. The following sections present some strategies you can use to grow your network in whichever category you find yourself in.

The magic number of LinkedIn connections is 143 — and not just because numbers that end in three are lucky! If you have fewer than 143 connections, chances are you're not going to have second- or third-degree connections in any of the companies you want to work for. If you have more than 143 connections, your next goal should be to get 500 or more connections. You add a lot of credibility to your profile by having a large number of connections. Recruiters see a lot of connections as a green flag.

The easy way: Become a LION

If you find yourself with fewer than 143 connections (or fewer than your target number), I suggest you take a more liberal approach to growing your network. Consider becoming a LION for a short time. At the very least, consider finding and inviting a handful of LIONs to join your network. Their large networks serve to increase your second- and third-degree connections substantially. So even if you don't want to add tons of strangers to your network, at least the few LIONs you do add can give you some substantial benefit.

The following are a few ways to promote yourself as a LION:

- Put "LION" next to your last name in your profile.
- Enter your e-mail address in your profile summary and say, "Invites welcome."
- Join several open networking groups, such as Lion500, TopLinked, or Open Networker. To find more, just do a group search for "open networking."

> To do a group search, simply click on Groups from the drop-down menu next to the search bar and type in your search keywords.
>
> ✔ Go to the Members tab at the top of any open networking group. In the search area, search for members in your area of interest.
>
> Invite these open networkers to join your network. Remember that if they didn't want to get your invite, they wouldn't be a member of a LION group.

Whenever your network reaches the size and depth you're comfortable with, simply stop being an open networker.

One disadvantage to being a LION for too long is that your network is filled with strangers. This means you're not in a strong position to ask for introductions to target companies. I highly suggest you use your LION status sparingly to just help you over the first few humps of getting to your target number of 143 or more connections. Also be sure to stop being a LION when you begin to actively reach out to hiring managers.

Although inviting open networkers to connect is fairly safe, you do risk the possibility of your account being flagged or blacklisted if LinkedIn thinks you're spamming. If you send out more than 50 invites a day, LinkedIn may flag you. If you send out invites and then many people respond with "I don't know," you may get blacklisted. If this happens, you need to write an apology e-mail to customer service. Next time, pace yourself.

The strategic way: Being a Cat

If you have a comfortably large network (any number larger than 143) and don't require the gung-ho networking of a LION, then you can afford to be a bit more catlike in picking who you connect with. (*Cat* doesn't stand for anything but is just a more careful way of growing your LinkedIn network.)

Strictly speaking, LinkedIn prefers that you connect with only people you know. However, unless you're networking like crazy and meeting hundreds of new people a week in person, this literal interpretation can get in the way. Another way to connect is to find new people online one-by-one rather than in bulk. And find those people in strategic places, such as from a group or alumni network.

Here are some steps you can take to strategically (and tactfully) grow your network:

1. **Click on People from the drop-down menu next to the search bar at the top-right corner of your LinkedIn profile, and then click on the Advanced link to access the Advanced People Search page.**

2. **Type in one of your keywords in the Keywords field or simply use your industry, such as advertising or accounting.**

3. **Put "LION" in the Last Name field.**

   LIONs are more likely to accept your invitation to connect.

4. **Click on the Search button.**

5. **Sort by Connections so that the people with the most connections in their network show up first because they're the most valuable to you.**

   Your search results list people in your strategic area who are open to connecting with you. Take your time and look at each profile. If you've joined any of the open networking groups, you may already be members of the same group and can invite them without using an e-mail address.

Generally, if people include their e-mail address in their profile, it means they're open to networking with you. Also look at the bottom of their profile at the Contact Settings section. Often, people say explicitly whether they're open to new connections. Always respect people's wishes.

Joining groups to increase your network's size

A LinkedIn *Group* is a collection of professionals connected around a common theme (see Figure 9-6). A group's main function is to facilitate discussions and networking within a trusted environment. The two kinds of LinkedIn Groups are *open groups,* where membership isn't mandatory to participate, and *closed groups,* where you need to join to read discussions and network. Some closed groups may accept your request to join automatically. Others require an administrator to approve your membership based on some criteria. For more on what a LinkedIn Group is and how to find one, check out Joel Elad's *LinkedIn For Dummies,* 2nd Edition (John Wiley & Sons, Inc.). For advice on how you can leverage groups to build your brand and grow your network for your job search, see the following sections.

Figure 9-6: A LinkedIn Group page.

Finding a worthwhile group to join

Because so many worthless groups exist, it pays to be careful about which ones you join. You can find useful groups by following these steps:

1. **Do a people search using a keyword or industry term.**

2. **Find people outside your network who are doing what you want to do at a desired company and view their profile.**

3. **Scroll down to the bottom of their profile and make note of any industry-specific groups they belong to.**

4. **Join the industry-specific groups you find.**

The easiest way to find a good group is to simply do a search in the Groups page. Navigate to the Groups menu in the gray ribbon at the top of the page and then click on Groups Directory. In the search box, type in a keyword or an industry-specific word, such as "ESL" or "Healthcare." Also try geographic terms, such as "Portland Marketing." Typically, the first page of results includes groups with active discussions and the most members. Groups with more than 1,000 members tend to be active.

Only about 20 percent of LinkedIn's thousands of groups are active, so be sure to look at the number of active discussions in a group before joining it. Only open groups allow you to see discussions without being a member. If you're interested in joining a closed group, you simply have to draw conclusions about its activity level based on the number of users in that group.

Most schools have active alumni groups that are eager to serve you. Try joining your school's alumni group and finding alums who are in your same industry. After you're approved, choose the Members tab and enter your industry in the search field. The results show fellow alumni in your industry; many alumni are willing to connect with you and even advise you. Invite some of these people to connect and be sure to customize the note in your invitation and lead by mentioning your common school. Also, always read their Contact Settings to be sure they're open to your connection.

Participating in groups the right way

As a job seeker, your primary focus is to stand out of the crowd and be seen. When it comes to LinkedIn Groups, participation is mandatory. Spend five to ten minutes a day cruising your top three groups and interacting with people in one or more of the following ways:

✔ **Comment on other people's posts.** On the group's page, look at the Latest Discussions as well as the Most Popular Discussions. When you find a discussion that interests you, add your two cents.

A good comment always adds to the conversation, whether in a LinkedIn Group or on a blog. Avoid pleasantries like "Good point" or "I like what you're saying." Instead, offer further examples or even dispute the points made with counter examples. You can take a person's point to a logical extreme, deconstruct it, or build it up. An easy commenting strategy is to tell a story from your own experience.

✔ **Share links with your group that you think are valuable.** If you aren't quite ready to post your own original discussion, then you may consider adding value to the group by sharing a news article or blog post that others may enjoy as well. Some people even copy and paste the first paragraph of the article with a link to read more at the bottom in order to build up curiosity. Add your opinion of the article and ask for participation.

✔ **Ask a question or ask for opinions.** Imagine you're at a networking event filled with industry experts. What would you ask them? Would you ask them how to get started in the field or for advice for someone in your situation? Perhaps you would ask them about an industry-specific issue or a news item that questions the status quo. LinkedIn calls this a discussion board for a reason!

✔ **Interrupt conversations.** Some discussions can get very heated. I've been in the middle of a few controversial ones, and it's fun. Jump into the fray. Back someone up who's making a controversial point. Challenge an assumption. Take sides.

Avoid sounding desperate when interacting with people online. A lot of people are out there looking for work. So answer the question of what makes you different and show the value you bring to the table. The LinkedIn Group's discussion page isn't your platform for sympathy or for asking for favors.

Using groups to connect with new people

After you're an active member of several groups, you have some credibility when you eventually ask to connect with other members. Members of the group begin to recognize your name and face and are, thus, more likely to accept your invite. Here's a great way to make a new friend in an active group:

1. **Keep track of the most active members.**

   You'll begin to recognize active members over a few weeks of monitoring discussions.

2. **Send a private reply to one of these contributors' posts or comments.**

   A *private reply* is a way to e-mail group members directly and privately, even if you're not yet connected.

3. **Tell this member how much you've enjoyed interacting with him or her within the group and that you want to connect.**

4. **Send an invite to connect (if the person agrees) and pat yourself on the back for finding a new friend who you've strategically and carefully vetted.**

Discovering Secret Ninja Moves for Your LinkedIn Profile

Some profile-optimization tactics don't fall into any real category but are still excellent, yet subtle, ways of making your profile shine. If you're ready to take your LinkedIn presence to the next level (and you've already followed the advice I present earlier in this chapter for sprucing up your profile and deepening your network), then the tactics I highlight in the next sections are for you.

Bulleting your specialties

The Specialties section of your profile (found just after your summary, as you can see in Figure 9-7) typically displays as a horizontal list, which means if you have a long list of specialties, this blob of text can be hard to read. You can make this section more scannable by putting your specialties in a bulleted list. Here's how:

1. **Open any word-processing application on your computer.**

2. **Copy and paste your LinkedIn Specialties to a new document.**

   If you don't have specialties yet, start from scratch.

3. **Edit the specialties into a bulleted list.**

4. **Copy this new bulleted list back into the Specialties section when you edit your profile.**

Too many specialties can be a turnoff. You don't want to list more than ten. And be sure to include some of your more important keywords (see Chapter 5 for details on finding your keywords).

Specialties
World travel, Challenging the status quo, Meditation, Entrepreneurship, Social Media Strategist, Career counseling, Social Media Strategy development, Professional Speaker, Author and Trainer, NLP and performance oriented relaxation techniques, Personal Productivity hacks

Figure 9-7:
Before (top)
and after
(bottom)
shots of a
standard
Specialties
section.

Specialties
• World travel
• Challenging the status quo
• Meditation
• Entrepreneurship
• Social Media Strategist
• Career counseling
• Social Media Strategy development
• Professional Speaker
• Author and Trainer
• NLP and performance oriented relaxation techniques
• Personal Productivity hacks

Embedding video into your profile

You can add a video résumé (see Chapter 10) or simply share an interesting video on your LinkedIn profile to give it some personality. Adding a video to your profile takes a little tweaking, but it isn't that difficult. Here are the general steps:

1. **Upload your video to YouTube (if you haven't already done so).**

   You need to be able to search for and find this video later.

2. **Log in to your LinkedIn account, choose More from the top menu, and then click on Get More Applications.**

3. **Select the Google Presentation app, install it, and make sure it displays on your profile page.**

4. **Sign in to your Google account in the Google Presentation app.**

   Your Google account is your Gmail or YouTube account if you have one. If not, you can create a Google account in two minutes.

5. **Click on Create a Presentation.**

   This button takes you to Google Docs where you can create a new presentation.

6. **Navigate to the Insert menu in the new blank presentation document, and click on Video.**

7. **Search YouTube until you find your video and then click on Select Video.**

8. Expand the size of this video to the same size as the slide.

9. Title the presentation and then click on Save Now.

10. Go to the Share drop-down menu and click on Publish/embed.

11. Navigate back to your LinkedIn profile and refresh the page.

12. Select your newly created presentation and click on Post to Profile.

Go ahead and double-check your profile to make sure the video shows up. Pretty cool, right?

Making your links more descriptive

LinkedIn's profile allows you to link to three different external websites. If you don't have any websites entered, you'll see a link called Add a Website just below your connections when editing your profile.

 When you try to add links, LinkedIn gives you some standard descriptive terms, such as Personal Website, Company Website, and Blog. These descriptions are pretty vague. If you want people to click on a link and find out more about you, then customize each link as described in the following steps:

1. Navigate to the Edit Profile page, click on Add a Website (or click on Edit to add more), and then choose Other from the drop-down menu.

2. Type the description of the link in the first new field that appears.

   If you're adding your blog, enter the name of your blog, such as "Batman's Nighttime Musings Blog." If adding your company's website, include the name of your company: "Bruce Wayne Enterprises." If adding your portfolio, use a description that tells viewers what the link leads to, such as "See Gotham City Prison's Lineup."

3. Enter the full domain name of the link in the second new field that appears, starting with `http://`.

4. Click on the Save Changes button at the bottom of the page.

SEOing for LinkedIn

Search Engine Optimization, or SEO, is the art and science of getting found when someone searches a term in a search engine like Google. LinkedIn uses a search algorithm that delivers results based on *keyword density,* that is, what percent of the time that keyword appears among all the other words on the page. If you want recruiters to find you on LinkedIn, just follow this simple checklist:

✔ **Know which keywords you want to be associated with.** (I offer tips on conducting keyword research in Chapter 5.)

✔ **Make sure those keywords appear in the following locations in your profile:**

- Professional headline

- Job title in current and three past experiences

- Summary

- Specialties

- Skills

✔ **Have at least six recommendations.** (The person with more recommendations wins in a tie for matching keywords.)

Some people take advantage of the simplicity of LinkedIn's search algorithm and do something called *keyword packing,* which is stuffing keywords into a paragraph as many times as they can. Because keyword packing looks horribly ugly, people often stuff keywords into the oldest experiences section in their profile, somewhat out of the way. Yes, their profiles rank, but I don't think they're playing fair. LinkedIn may start penalizing people who do this, so don't take the risk.

Exploring Other LinkedIn Features

LinkedIn has many features beyond the online profile. Many of these features are not particularly necessary to your job search, such as polls or the various collaboration applications. Other features are self-explanatory, such as the job board or contact organizer, and don't need mentioning. Several features you may not be aware of may have some usefulness in helping you find a job. I outline them for you in the following sections.

Organizing and participating in events

LinkedIn offers a full event management toolset, including invitations, payment options, and RSVP functionality. This is all well and good, but what makes this feature interesting for you as a job seeker is that your involvement in events shows up on your profile by default. Showing that you're organizing or participating in industry-relevant events on your profile is a great way to demonstrate your personality and motivation to a hiring manager.

To find events in your area, navigate to the More tab and click on Events. Next, click on Advanced Search where you can enter your zip code. When you find something potentially interesting, choose one of these three options:

  ✔ Attending

  ✔ Interested

  ✔ Recommend

Consider organizing your own event or just re-creating an event inside LinkedIn that's organized by someone else. The event shows up on your profile and makes you look like a valuable asset to a hiring organization.

Adding custom sections to your profile

LinkedIn now offers you greater flexibility with what types of content you can add to your profile. In addition to the standard Experience, Education, and Additional Information sections, you can also add the sections in the following list to reflect achievements and experiences (see Figure 9-8). To add sections, just click on the Add Sections link on you profile right below the blue box with your personal information.

  ✔ **Certifications:** Certifications are particularly important to highlight if you're an engineer.

  ✔ **Language:** Options include native or bilingual, professional working, and elementary proficiencies.

  ✔ **Patents:** Okay, Miss Smarty-Pants, so you have some patents under your belt. Go ahead and let everyone know how brilliant you are!

  ✔ **Publications:** Have you written any articles that have been published in a major newspaper or magazine? Adding these publications to your profile can really boost your credibility.

  ✔ **Skills:** This section indicates your skills and how many years of experience you have doing those skills.

You can reorder every part of your profile. After you add the new section, just drag it to the place where you want it to display.

Figure 9-8:
Adding new sections to your LinkedIn profile.

Add Sections	✕
Featured	**Enhance your Professional Profile**
Overview	Select a section or application from the left to preview and add it to your profile.
Sections	
Certifications	**Patents** — List your pending and issued patents to highlight your inventions. Show preview
Languages	
Patents	**Lawyer Ratings** — Are you a Legal Professional? Showcase your Martindale-Hubbell® Peer Review Ratings™ and Client Review Ratings™ to further validate your stated credentials and help you make the right connections. Show preview
Publications	
Skills	
Applications	
Blog Link	
	Have ideas for new sections? Send us feedback » · Close Window

Paying for LinkedIn or going free

A common question I get from audience members in trainings is, "Should I pay for LinkedIn?" LinkedIn has certainly made it easy for job seekers to do so by offering a discounted membership level. Additionally, I pay for LinkedIn and use the advanced features almost every day. However, my answer isn't so cut and dry. Many people find enormous benefit to the free version. So here's my advice: Use the free version up until you're limited by some restricted feature. You may need more Direct Messages, Invitations, or advanced search filters. If you're bumping up against this wall, then consider jumping into a paid account for the duration of your job search. You can always cancel and go back to the free version after you land a job, when you don't need to use LinkedIn so much.

Using the JobsInsider toolbar

The JobsInsider toolbar is a plug-in for your browser. When you're cruising job boards and find something you want to apply for, this tool (available for download at `linkd.in/linkedin-jobs-toolbar`) tells you whether anyone in your LinkedIn network works at that company. Using the toolbar, you can do company research and invite people to connect without leaving the job board you found the opportunity on.

Although knowing whether you have connections inside of a target company is a nice feature, I don't recommend randomly asking a hiring manager to connect with you on LinkedIn so casually. For a better strategy for connecting with hiring managers, head to Chapter 18.

Chapter 10

Producing a Compelling Video Résumé

Paper résumés, job applications, and even LinkedIn profiles do a great job of answering a recruiter's foremost question: "Can you do the job?" However, hiring managers may not be so sure about your presentation skills, leadership presence, or creative abilities. A video résumé allows you to showcase these attributes and can quickly launch you far ahead of any other candidates.

Video résumés augment your job application by letting you use visual, musical, and narrative elements to help you tell your story. They're ideal for demonstrating your professional presence, presentation skills, or creativity. A concise and memorable video can complement your application powerfully, and it may even be the determining factor in whether you get a callback for an interview.

In this chapter, I help you demonstrate to your next boss who you are and what working with you is like through your very own video résumé. I reveal how a great video résumé can make you a top candidate, detail what to cover in your video, and share how to keep it interesting — the last thing you want is to bore a hiring manager! Then I take you into some technical aspects of producing a professional video. Finally, I tell you how and where to upload your résumé.

You may notice that the primary emphasis of this chapter is *not* on the tools and toys of video production. Instead, I spend most of the chapter showing you what a job seeker needs to do and say on film for maximum impact on an employer. The camera and software you choose are secondary. After all, how you use the tools is what matters; anyone can buy a camera, but only a star candidate can produce good film.

Video Résumés 101

The unique limitations of online video make producing high-impact content in your video résumé even more imperative. Consider this: Hiring managers spend an average of just one to three minutes watching their top candidates on-screen. If you don't get to the point within the first ten seconds, they won't bother to finish viewing your film.

Hiring managers form their first impression of you from your video. Any sloppiness in production may be associated with you, and being characterized as sloppy isn't likely to lead to success!

Following are a handful of format limitations to keep your video résumé attractive to viewers:

- **Your video résumé should run between three and five minutes.** Generally speaking, the shorter the better.

- **The first ten seconds are very important.** Hook 'em at hello!

- **Your video will be watched online, where the screen isn't very big.** Small visual details may be difficult to discern.

- **The quality of the video reflects the quality of the candidate.** Don't make your video available unless you're confident it's a great reflection of you.

Dedicating time to write a strong script and set things up is critical. Your video must answer these three questions in both its form and its content:

- **Who are you?** What makes you different?

- **What motivates you?** What wakes you up in the morning?

- **Can you do the job?** Do you have the skills to do what the hiring manager needs done?

Just like with paper résumés, tailoring the content of your video résumé to the specific job opportunity is important. However, you may not identify every conceivable opportunity. That's why having one generic video résumé to post online is also a good idea. The cool part is that, after you finish a generic video résumé, you can use that footage as the basis for customized videos later.

Whether your video is general or job-specific, reading your résumé into the camera or making your video résumé a mirror image of your paper one won't take you far. Yet many tutorials on how to create video résumés suggest just that. Avoid boring your viewers at all costs!

Presenting the Chief Components of a Good Video Résumé

The first aspect of making a good first impression on video is presenting yourself well. In your video, make sure to dress professionally, as if you're on a job interview. (I recommend wearing neutral or tame colors to help bring out your face.) Also plan to wear some makeup to reduce the oils on your face. Yes, guys, too (if you need help, ask any lady in your life). For more information about how to present yourself for job interviews (and video résumés), take a look at *Job Interviews For Dummies,* 3rd Edition, by Joyce Lain Kennedy (John Wiley & Sons, Inc.).

Keep in mind that your video résumé supplements your job application — it doesn't replace it — and you only have a few minutes to tell your story. Therefore, you must be very choosy about what to include. A well-crafted script ensures that you include everything you need to say. Don't let the anxiety of being on film make you forget to say something. Be sure to evaluate your professional history and include the most critical and powerful examples. And take out the fluff — anything that doesn't add value to your candidacy.

In the sections that follow, I present the three most important points your video résumé should cover: your name and pertinent details, the position you want, and why you're right for the job.

Stating (or subtitling) your name and details

Stating your name is an important aspect of the video résumé, but the question is how to introduce yourself in a way that's memorable or unique. Many video résumés start with the standard "Hello, my name is . . ." approach. This approach isn't terrible, but it's not a great way to get someone's attention, either.

Depending on how bold you want to be, you have two great options for getting your name and other details across without being banal:

✔ **Simply display your name and details on the screen as you start telling your professional story.** You can add details, such as your education and work experience, as subtitles beneath your images on the screen as you progress. Bear in mind that a hiring manager watching your video résumé should also have access to your paper résumé, so you don't need to belabor these points.

✔ **Delay bringing in critical details.** Tell your story — the most compelling aspect of your video — first. Sometime between 10 and 30 seconds in, pause and say, "My name is _____ and I have 5 years of experience doing _____." In this way, you sandwich the critical details between the more interesting narrative elements of your script.

A more advanced technique for presenting your name and relevant details is to deliver them through *B-roll* — cutting away from the main footage to secondary footage in a way that adds meaning to the sequence. (See the section "Spicing it up with B-roll" later in this chapter for details.) A B-roll delivery of details may look something like this:

> An image of you pops up on the screen with you saying, "In 2008, I thought I was going to close the deal of a lifetime."

> The screen then goes blank and your name appears along with other relevant work experience or education you want to include (the text is white against a black background).

> You come back on-screen, saying, "What I didn't know at the time was that the market was on its way to a complete standstill."

> The video cuts to another B-roll with some market facts to support your statement.

> You reappear, stating, "But I didn't let that stop me! My passion for . . ."

You get the idea. Using this delivery method not only allows you to state your name and details but also sets the stage for you to show off your creativity and ability to create a professional-looking video.

For a wonderful example of B-roll as well as great transitions, check out `bit.ly/B-Roll-Example` to see expert video blogger Dave Kaminski's one-minute podcast on producing web video. Notice how his voice remains continuous throughout the film despite the frequent transition to other scenery or images. This video took him many takes, repeating the same script over and over again. The end product looks like a smooth delivery of audio through visually interesting transitions and background changes.

Making the position you want clear

Most organizations have multiple openings at any given time, and chances are you're a good fit for more than one of them. If your video résumé targets a specific position, company, or hiring manager, make that clear in one of two ways:

- ✔ **Use subtitles to display your desired position on the screen.** If, for example, you're interested in a marketing job, you can use a subtitle that says something like, "Looking for a marketing position with your company" or simply "Interested in the Marketing Communications Specialist opening."

- ✔ **State your desired role verbally in an interesting manner.** Opt for an engaging statement that tells the viewer more than just the position you want. Use active statements that show your interest, for example, "Your company is a great match with my passion for marketing communications" or "I'm interested in contributing to your company as a Marketing Communications Specialist." From here, you can go into more exact details about why you're such a great fit for the role.

Creating a boilerplate video that's general enough to fit most employers' needs in your industry is a good idea. This version is the one you share publicly. As you get better at video editing, you can switch out some of the general information with job-specific details that tailor your job search to a specific company or opportunity.

Communicating why you're a great fit

If you're interested in a posted opening for a specific position, chances are you already know the job requirements because they're usually included in the job listing. But doing additional research on the role and responsibilities of your target company and the job you desire is still a good idea. (In Chapter 15, I talk more about using social media to research your target companies.)

After you understand what hiring managers are looking for, think about your résumé script with the intention of directly answering that need. Here are some steps you can take to demonstrate your fit:

1. **Check out a handful of descriptions for jobs that are similar to the position you're interested in.**

   Looking at several job descriptions gives you a pretty good idea of what you need to say in your video.

2. **Make a list of the top five job requirements you think the position you want requires.**

3. **Map each requirement of your target position to a story or statement you can add to your video résumé.**

   Stories and statements help you show the hiring manager why you're a great fit. In particular, tell stories about accomplishments or that reflect innovation. Try to come up with five professional stories or statements that illustrate how you can do what he needs you to do. I recommend choosing the best three stories and devoting the most time to them; then you can briefly touch on the remaining two points.

Fit isn't just about your ability to do the job. Showing fit in your video résumé includes showing your personality and what motivates you.

Whether you're producing a traditional video or a slideshow commercial (see the later section "Turning to a slideshow if you're camera shy"), customize your promotional piece for each type of position you apply for. Even better, customize it for individual positions or companies. You can easily produce a generic video-résumé foundation and later insert a customized introduction for each job. With video-editing software, you can just pop in your custom intro and follow it with your common video.

Ensuring Your Video Résumé Stands Out

The art of storytelling may not come naturally to you. Sometimes you may feel like you're talking too much or getting off topic. Although you can ask others to read your script and give you feedback, your own feelings are signs that your script needs some touching up. In the next sections, I give you suggestions on how to refine your résumé script into a compelling film for your viewers.

Adding conflict to spice up your script

Adding narrative conflict to your video résumé allows you to capture the attention of your audience very quickly and keep them interested until the end. In narration, one thing happens after the next, in story form. With narrative conflict, you're telling a story about a transformative event. Until the conflict is resolved, most people remain curious to see what happens. People love the thrill of narrative conflict. Just imagine a one-hour TV drama where everyone gets along and gets everything they want — boring!

Four main types of conflict form the basis of most stories, and you can apply any of them to your video résumé:

✔ **A struggle between two or more people:** Think about how you may have beaten a competitor in the market or resolved a dispute between two co-workers. For example, did you go toe-to-toe with the competition in submitting a proposal to a client and emerge victorious?

✔ **A struggle against nature or uncontrollable forces:** Reflect on how you may have overcome the uncontrollable forces of the economic climate, a natural disaster, or political misfortune. For example, did you survive a round of layoffs by standing out?

✔ **A struggle against some aspect of society:** Consider how you may have changed a standard operating procedure to align with your customers' purchasing habits, overcome a restrictive regulatory environment, or brought diversity into your workplace. For example, did you organize an effort to correct some injustice?

✔ **A conflict of opposing forces within a person:** Think about a time you may have made a difficult moral choice, overcome a disability, or discovered a hidden talent that put you ahead. Have you ever turned a bad situation to your advantage?

Outlining and practicing your story

To make your video résumé easy to follow, tell the story linearly. Practice telling your story naturally so it flows well. Think of an interesting story you heard on the radio. That's how you want your script to flow.

Creating and revising an outline for your story helps you deliver your message effectively. Here's how to do it:

1. **Write down what you want to tell, how you want to tell it, and where you want to be when you tell it.**

2. **Practice the story with other people, including colleagues, to gauge their level of interest.**

3. **Evaluate your timing and whether you're talking too long.**

4. **Revise your outline as needed to keep your video succinct and to the point.**

Showing your personality

Your personality goes a long way in helping you stand out in today's job market. You know the old saying: Someone else will always be more experienced, more educated, or more qualified than you are, but there's never going to be another you.

Don't fall victim to the common notion that in order to be professional, you have to whitewash your personality. Hiring managers actually place great value on video résumés because video demonstrates a candidate's professional presentation skills and demeanor. When I bring this issue up with job seekers, their first reaction is to freak out. I'm not suggesting that you untuck your shirt and pepper your story with profanity; bringing your personality to the table simply means being yourself. And I'm not talking about telling personal stories. Your video résumé isn't the place for that unless the personal story adds significance to a professional one.

Here are some tricks to help you bring more personality into your video; note that I present the most helpful ones first:

- ✔ **Collect video testimonials from co-workers, managers, or customers — past or present.** Make sure you get their permission to use this footage in any way you want. Later, when you edit your video résumé and prepare to post it, you can simply splice in these testimonials to double the film's impact and demonstrate that other people have a positive opinion of you.

- ✔ **Express your passions.** Talk about what work you love to do and why you love it. If possible, demonstrate this passion on-screen. Remember that video allows you to show off your presentation skills. Speaking faster and becoming more animated during this portion can show the viewer how much you care about the subject.

- ✔ **Use your sense of humor.** You can always edit out a bad joke later, but the overall feeling that you're having fun with the process can still come across indirectly. Remember those old Jackie Chan movies where, at the end, you see outtakes of Jackie being a total goofball? The fun that he has during filming comes across in the final edited film even without those deleted scenes.

- ✔ **Interact with others.** You may feel more comfortable with another person on the camera. Try setting up a mock TV interview with a friend or co-worker. Alternatively, have someone off-camera ask you questions and just film your replies. You can edit out the questions later, leaving behind your naturally delivered answers.

- ✔ **Be yourself.** While taking a storytelling class, I noticed that the students who rehearsed the least performed the best at the end. Unlike scripted theater, the main point of storytelling is to appear natural and spontaneous, yet still prepared, skilled, and professional. Writing out a script is fine, but you don't need to stick to it rigidly. (Yes, I realize this is contrary to most of the advice you find online. Trust me on this!)

- ✔ **Be confident.** The most confident people are relaxed. Keep your arms and legs uncrossed. Smile, but don't force it. Make eye contact but don't stare. Vary your rate of speech. Use your hands to emphasize a point but keep in mind that too much hand movement can be distracting.

Always get a second opinion from a professional in your field about your final product before you publish it. Ask your reviewer whether the video captures your personality while still portraying you as professional. You want your reviewer to say, "Yeah! That's exactly what working with you is like."

Turning to a slideshow if you're camera shy

Some people simply don't do well on camera. I've known people who come across quite well in person but simply don't look good on video. If you fall into this category, all hope isn't lost. You can still demonstrate your presentation skills and professionalism with a *slideshow commercial*, which entails presenting your story audibly and supporting it with images and words. I love making these presentations, and I think you will, too.

You can use common slideshow software, such as Microsoft's PowerPoint or Apple's Keynote, to put together a commercial for yourself. Regardless of which program you use, the steps are pretty much the same:

1. **Write out a script that's a maximum of three to five minutes in length (about 750 words).**

   Each sentence of your script should narrate a different slide. In the "Notes" section of each slide, paste in one sentence from your script.

2. **Include an image or impact word for each slide.**

   Images speak a thousand words, and when used in a slideshow, they emotionally reinforce your spoken point. Note that taking this approach is quite different from going the usual bulleted-list route. Don't be afraid of having nothing more than an image on the screen. Check out Flickr (www.flickr.com) for copyright-free content you can use. Also be sure to include at least one picture of yourself.

   Note that some slides work better with impact words, either in addition to an image or on their own. Impact words are the main topic, or the essential meaning, of what you're saying at a given time. If you're telling a story about a success, consider showing an image of someone jumping for joy with the words on the slide proclaiming, "150% of quota!" and then fade to black with nothing more than the words, "But it didn't end there . . ."

3. **Edit the transitions between slides.**

   Make sure the words appear on the screen the way you want them to with each click. The last thing you want to worry about when you're reading and recording your script is what happens when you click. Click one time per line to simplify.

For example, you can structure your transitions like this: "Hi, I'm Joshua, and I love managing large, complicated projects" (click, new slide shows up). "Let me tell you about a time when . . ." (click, words appear on the new slide), and so on.

4. **Take a practice run when your slides are done.**

The goal is to reach the end of your script while progressing through the slideshow easily. Make sure the slides transition smoothly the way you want them to.

5. **Run through your presentation, script, and slides while recording the screen.**

Screen recording software simply records everything happening on your computer screen as a movie. It can record a video of you if you have a webcam, as well as your voice. Companies use it to demonstrate their software. If you don't already have screen recording software, download Jing (`www.techsmith.com/download/jing`), a free program that records up to five minutes at a time.

Make several different versions and remember to save each recording at the end. Then you can splice together the best parts of each take.

6. **Upload your commercial to the video sharing sites of your choice.**

Recording software allows you to save the recording on your computer for uploading. From there, you can share your video with the world!

You can check out an example of a slideshow commercial I created for my personal branding e-book at `bit.ly/personalbrandingebook`.

Concluding the Video

The end of your video is very important. Hiring managers tend to remember the last few moments of your video as they review candidates for a position, so you want to make sure your video goes out with a bang. If you manage to make an impression and enable the hiring manager to get in touch with you, chances are good that you'll get a call back. I help you figure out how to do both in the following sections.

Always end your video by reaffirming your excitement and passion for the position. That final blast of energy will carry you far. Practice saying things like, "I'm confident that my background and skills are a great match for your organization."

Adding a call to action

Every good marketing piece needs a clear call to action. Because your video résumé is essentially a three-minute infomercial about you, you need to make clear what you want the hiring manager to do after watching your video. I'm guessing you want him to call you, so make sure you give him a good reason to do that. For example, you may say, "So if you're looking for an energetic and passionate accountant with an eye for detail on your team, *please give me a call right away.*" (The words in italics are the call to action.)

Consider ending your video with a question. Curiosity is one of the most powerful human emotions. Asking the viewer a quiz question and then saying, "To get the answer, set up a call with me," can be a playful yet powerful way to get the call back. Do you know any weird factoids about your field that people may be interested in?

Relaying the best way to contact you

Your call to action (see the preceding section) leaves the hiring manager ready to reach out to you, so make doing so easy by sharing your contact information. Because a hiring manager is most likely going to view your video during normal business hours, give your daytime phone number or your e-mail address and note that you'll respond to any inquiries as soon as possible.

If you ask a hiring manager to e-mail you to set up an appointment, make sure you have a professional e-mail address. That Hotmail address you set up in middle school, `misshotpants123@hotmail.com`, just doesn't cut it. Make sure you use your name or some combination of your name and numbers (see Chapter 5 for more on this). Also, if you give out your phone number, be sure your voice mail is professional.

Producing Your Video and Tying Up Loose Ends

By the time recruiters watch your video résumé, they already have some sense of who you are as a candidate. So your video's job is to answer other questions about you, including your level of professionalism. The production quality of your video implicitly answers this question, which means your film needs to not only have good content but also look good.

Hiring a pro to produce your video résumé

If the technical aspects of producing a video résumé seem overwhelming to you, seek out some professional help. You can likely find several freelance videographers in your area. Most charge anywhere from $50 to $150 an hour, but the good news is that an hour of their time is all you need. Or you can check out these online resources for video production (mention my name if you use them, and you may get special treatment!):

✔ **BlazitResume:** BlazitResume (`www.blazitresume.com`) edits, crops, and

produces your raw footage for you to make a nice-looking video résumé without much hassle.

✔ **Resume Blimp:** The folks who run this site (`www.resumeblimp.com`) offer workshops where they coach and film groups of job seekers with professional cameras.

✔ **videoBIO:** This site (`www.videobio.com`) is a great service that helps you write a script, shoot your video, and then edit that film into a sharp, modern video résumé.

To produce a quality film, you need to take a look at the basic elements of production, such as camera options, lighting, and timing. Remember that the spit and polish you add to your video shows hiring managers that you take pride in your work and are a serious professional. After you have these basic components down, consider incorporating an appropriate soundtrack and/or a B-roll to spice things up a bit. Implementing these elements well can make the difference between a boring, amateurish video and a well-produced, fun-to-watch résumé. I walk you through all these video-production elements in the sections that follow.

Producing your video is easier if you have a trusted friend help you out. Make sure you give him clear instructions on how to frame the shot. And be sure to use a tripod. You're not filming reality TV. If your friend holds the camera, the video will look shaky.

Having to watch a video that has a "wizzzzzzz" sound in the background is beyond annoying. To prevent this sound from creeping into your video résumé, either mic yourself or get as close to the camera as you can. If the buzzing sound still slips in, your editing software may be able to help you reduce it. Remember, too, that you can mask poor audio quality with a mellow soundtrack. (I fill you in on how to create a soundtrack later in this chapter.)

Looking at camera, lighting, and editing software options

For most people, the best part of producing video is getting to play with all the toys. So here we go. Assuming that you've thought long and hard about your script, your setting, and your attire, choosing the appropriate gear is the next important step. With the following tips, not only can you get great gear, but you can get it at a very affordable price!

Cameras

A portable video camera untethers you from your computer's built-in webcam and takes better film, too. I recently got my wife a new smartphone for her annual upgrade. I was shocked to realize that it took better pictures than the camera I bought three years ago. Video and photo technology is getting better and more affordable. With a minor investment of around $150, you can buy a high-definition (HD) video camera that plugs right into your computer. Search for "flip cam" on Amazon.com (www.amazon.com) for some great camera options.

When you're filming, mount your camera on a solid surface to avoid shooting wobbly footage. You can get a tripod very inexpensively on Amazon.com.

Lighting

Lighting yourself during your shoot is an important aspect of looking professional. Professionally lit film is hard to miss. Shadows are almost absent on the speaker's face. The speaker is backlit so she doesn't look two-dimensional, and the light is bright but doesn't wash out the contrast of the image. However, professional lights can cost you thousands of dollars. If you're on a limited budget, keep the following lighting tips in mind:

- ✔ Use light from the front and the back to give your image some depth. Avoid light from directly above (this type of light creates shadows).
- ✔ Shoot between 9 a.m. and 11 a.m. or between 3 p.m. and 5 p.m. for best results when filming outdoors.
- ✔ Arrange indoor lighting with care, with a frontlight (like a spotlight) and a milder backlight from behind you from the floor.
- ✔ Experiment with combinations of cold (white) lights and warm (yellowish) lights until you get the look you're going for.

If you want to invest in some extra lighting to make sure you're seen clearly on camera, check out the $40 Might-D-Light on Amazon.com. It points more than 80 low-watt LED lights at you, and the rechargeable unit comes with AC and DC charging adapters.

Editing software

Video-editing software allows you to put text on the screen, split video from audio tracks, and handle transitions between scenes. Most PCs come with video-editing software these days, and all Macs come with iMovie. If you don't have video software, you can edit your video online with a service called Animoto (www.animoto.com). The basic version is free, and you can upgrade to full features for a marginal fee.

Video editing is really fun and can consume huge amounts of time. If you're new to it, expect at least a three-hour learning curve.

Adding your soundtrack

The soundtrack to your video résumé defines your candidacy more subtly and more powerfully than any other video production technique. When you think about the soundtrack for your film, keep these suggestions in mind:

- **Vocal music takes away from a script.** In most movies, the music with words usually plays when no one is talking. Consider using music without lyrics.

- **Some music has cultural implications.** For example, gangster rap may have negative connotations because the culture around it espouses law-breaking activities. Conversely, classical music may imply an excessively conservative culture. Think about the cultural implications of your soundtrack. My advice: Avoid the extremes.

- **Keep it happy.** Choose a soundtrack that has a simple melody and an upbeat tempo. I tend to alternate between a single acoustic instrument and a compelling electronic musical composition.

- **Pick music that has the right licensing.** Most of the music you listen to on the radio is copyrighted. Because your video résumé is for public use, using copyrighted music without permission is illegal. Even though you can't use your favorite hit single, you can still use appropriately licensed music for free as long as you reference the artist at the end of your film. Do an Internet search for "Creative Commons Music" to find the best sites for legal soundtrack downloads.

- **Embrace ducking.** *Ducking* describes a technique whereby the volume of one soundtrack gets really low as another track comes in. Most video-editing software lets you duck the soundtrack so when your voice comes in on the other track, the music automatically gets very soft. Just make sure the music isn't competing with your voice.

When using video-editing software, experiment with different transitions. Your options include *crossfading* (when the next scene blurs onto the current scene), simple *cutaways* (a sudden cut to the next scene), and *fade-to-blacks* (where the current scene fades to a black background before the next scene comes in). You'll probably use the first two quite often. If you want to denote a full change of scene or passage of time or if you want to create chapters in your video's sequence, you can try using a fade-to-black. For instance, when you change topics or move from introductory material to more detailed material, fade-to-blacks give the film some space. With only three to five minutes, however, I don't recommend using this type of fade more than three times. Whatever you do, don't get too fancy with your transitions. Things like spiraling fades and flashing lights take away from your content.

Spicing it up with B-roll

Many video résumés are a single shot taken with someone sitting in front of a camera going on and on about who he is. These videos look amateurish. To avoid this fate and visually spice up your video résumé, try adding some B-roll. *B-roll* entails cutting away from the main footage to secondary footage. A video résumé that uses B-roll may take you, say, to someone introducing herself outside her house, moving to her piano bench in the next scene, and then moving again to a desk chair to complete the talk. These scenes are filmed at three different times, in three different places, with the subject wearing three different costumes, but the scenes are edited together in a linear way to give the film fluid continuity. I give another example of using B-roll in the earlier section "Stating (or subtitling) your name and details."

Using B-roll is also a great way to cover up a bad take or a mistake. Suppose you're delivering your script just fine until you mess up on the second-to-last sentence and scratch your face. Record that sentence again, but then edit the video so just words appear on the screen when you say the face-scratching sentence. The transition from seeing you talk to a black screen without any interruption in your script is a B-roll. Then, when you splice the two shots together, no one will know a blooper occurred. In fact, your video will look great in the end!

Here's how you can incorporate B-roll into your film:

✔ Record the same parts of your script several times in several different locations so you can switch between them later.

✔ If you mess up a scene, don't worry. Instead, move to a new location, change your outfit, and then re-record. Later, you can cut to the secondary scene to hide the mistake.

✔ If you flub the audio, you can just re-record the sentence by starting at a natural place before the mistake. Then switch to a B-roll with the new audio. With this technique, people won't notice that your head position was slightly off in the middle of a paragraph, the way they may notice if you were to re-record both the audio and video.

Continuing your video education

If you really enjoy this video production stuff, then you'll love Dave Kaminski's "Web Video University" weekly tip series. Sign up for it here: `webvideouniversity.com/podcast`.

Every week Dave sends out a quick, two-minute video production tip. His material is quite helpful and makes this kind of work really interesting. I hope you enjoy it as much as I do!

✔ Find some visuals to represent part of your script. For example, if you want to emphasize your passion for creative marketing, you can show a sequence of your own creative portfolio flashing across the screen as you talk. You can also use key impact words on a simple black background or other silent video footage that adds meaning.

The best way to implement your B-roll is by following the instructions included with your video-editing software, but here's the general process:

1. **Separate the audio tracks from the video tracks.**

2. **Remove the video track that you want to replace with B-roll, leaving the audio behind.**

3. **On top of the remaining audio track, insert the B-roll video sequence.**

Making Your Video Available

I recommend you publish at least one version of your video résumé to as many video-sharing sites as possible. Create a general video résumé that isn't targeted at any specific position (think of this version as a personal commercial). The widespread adoption of social media opens up what I like to call *engineered serendipity*. That is, when you put yourself out there, you never know what amazing opportunities may come to you. In the following sections, I help you determine where to post your video and how to get it onto those sites.

Figuring out where to upload it

Instead of uploading your video to the 20-plus available video-sharing sites one at a time, you can use a content distribution system. I recommend OneLoad from TubeMogul (`www.tubemogul.com/about/oneload`).

After you create your free TubeMogul account, you can upload your video, description, and tags. From there, TubeMogul lets you choose which sites you want to syndicate to. Note that you need to have accounts with each of those sites. Then with one click, your video will be on 20 or so video-sharing sites. I suggest you take the time to create accounts on at least five different sharing sites, if not all of them.

YouTube is the second-largest search engine in the world. If you post your video on YouTube, engineer as many views and comments as you can. When hiring managers see that your résumé is watched and engages people, your social value increases. Send an e-mail to your friends and family, asking them to watch your video and leave a comment.

In addition to YouTube and generic video-sharing sites, consider uploading your video to résumé-specific sites. I've heard stories of recruiters trolling these sites for talent. Maybe they'll find you! Following are some recommendations:

- **BlazitResume:** This online résumé site (www.blazitresume.com) allows you to upload your video to its player.

- **Jobster:** Registered Jobster users can post YouTube-hosted videos by including a link to the YouTube version. Go to www.jobster.com to check it out.

- **MyWorkster:** MyWorkster (www.myworkster.com) users can link to a video résumé from their profile and share it with networking contacts and potential employers.

- **Resumebook.tv:** This site (www.resumebook.tv) gives you advice on making a video résumé and lets you upload your video résumé for free. The site's résumé management system helps you make your video résumé accessible to employers.

- **RezBuzz:** This site (www.rezbuzz.com) connects recruiters with talent and allows you to host your video.

- **uBoast:** uBoast (www.uboast.com) allows you to create a (free) professional page that includes an integrated video résumé.

- **Innovate CV:** Innovate CV (www.innovatecv.com) lets you upload your video directly into a slick-looking online résumé (more on this tool in Chapter 11).

- **VisualCV:** On VisualCV (www.visualcv.com), you can manage your entire professional portfolio via an easy-to-use interface and embed your YouTube video. (I go into detail on VisualCV in Chapter 11.)

- **WorkBlast:** At WorkBlast (www.workblast.com), you can upload up to three versions of your résumé (video or text) for free.

I know that all this uploading may seem like a lot of work, but after all you've done to produce a killer video résumé, you may as well take an hour to make sure as many people as possible see it. That's right: You can set up accounts and upload your video to all these sites in less than an hour. It's totally worth your time!

Discovering how to upload it

When uploading your video résumé to pretty much any site, remember to include very clear descriptions, categories, and tags. When you write the description of your film on a video-sharing site, start the description with `http://yoursite.com`, replacing `yoursite.com` with the domain name of your LinkedIn profile, résumé website, or blog. Adding `http://` tells the site to activate the link, making it clickable.

Make your description just one to two sentences long and include some of the keywords relevant to your target industry. Use your full name in the title of the video as well as in the description and tags. If people run a search on your name, you want them to find your work of art.

Chapter 11

Taking Advantage of Other Online Résumé Options

Although LinkedIn seems to have the highest leverage with recruiters and hiring managers, many job seekers still find it useful to publish several other online résumés so they can have full control over the look, feel, and flow of the content they present. After all, the more information you share, the better off you are. As a job seeker, your goal is to present a well-rounded version of yourself to the hiring manager. You want to get to an interview and have the recruiter say, "Geez, I feel like I already know you!"

In this chapter, I introduce you to some of the most innovative online résumé services available and reveal how to use them in a powerful way to better communicate your job application. Remember that the more of yourself you put out there in the Wild Wild West (otherwise known as the World Wide Web), the more likely you are to be found.

Why Bother with So Many Online Résumés?

Most recruiters I talk to say they're actively seeking candidates through keyword searches on LinkedIn. So why would a job seeker look anywhere else for online networking? In the next sections, I present four compelling reasons for having more than one online résumé and not limiting yourself to just LinkedIn.

I'm not saying you shouldn't use LinkedIn. In fact, I *love* LinkedIn and have used it for years. I'm simply saying that you should be aware that LinkedIn may not meet all your unique needs as a job seeker, so don't let it be the only tool you have in your tool belt.

LinkedIn gives you only one profile

When you apply for a job, you should customize your résumé to that position. Recruiters and hiring managers will look to see whether your résumé is generic or really addresses their organization's concerns.

But wait! LinkedIn gives you only one résumé. You can't customize it for multiple jobs. You may be testing the waters in two or more different industries, but LinkedIn doesn't allow you to cover all your bases. The online résumé options I show you later in this chapter give you a chance to create multiple versions of the same résumé.

LinkedIn is visually boring

People's profiles don't really differ on LinkedIn. And unless baby blue is your favorite color (it's apparently the favorite of the LinkedIn designers), you can't do much to improve the look and feel of your profile. What if you want to upload work samples, scan proof of a certification, or upload several videos?

With the online résumés available from tools such as VisualCV, DoYouBuzz, and Innovate CV (all of which I describe later in this chapter), you can change the color, the formatting, and even the type of information you share with great flexibility. This capability can unlock your personal brand and help communicate your personality to the hiring manager. (I help you develop your personal brand in Part II.)

Your information stays up-to-date

With online résumés, you can update your information once, and everyone with the link will always have the most recent version. You don't have to resend your résumé or worry about outdated info landing your name on a blacklist. If someone wants to share your info with a co-worker, the link he provides will automatically connect to your most recent online résumé.

You're building a web to catch opportunities

The more places you have a presence online, the better your chances of being found by the right employer. Having multiple online résumés helps you expand your social media presence. After you create your other online résumés, you can link them all together. LinkedIn allows you to share up to three outside links; I explain how to add these links to your profile in Chapter 9. And each of your other résumés can link to each other to create a web.

Getting Visual with VisualCV

A VisualCV is an Internet-based, multimedia résumé that gives prospective employers a three-dimensional picture of your career by allowing you to share video, images, links, and text. A VisualCV gives you the power to convey a huge amount of information in just a few seconds. (It's also a great marketing tool for professionals who aren't necessarily looking for a job and don't have their own website.)

Figure 11-1 shows you what a VisualCV can look like. To check out additional examples from a diverse number of professional fields, head to www.visual cv.com and click on the View Example VisualCVs link on the right side of the page. For details on how to create your own VisualCV, refer to the following sections.

Signing up for VisualCV

VisualCV is free and takes less than half an hour to set up, assuming you've already spent some time setting up a LinkedIn profile (I walk you through that process in Chapter 9).

To get started, click on the orange button on the main page of VisualCV and then fill out your name and other details. VisualCV verifies your e-mail address by sending an e-mail to the address you provide. Click on the link in the e-mail you receive to activate your account.

The first page you see after activating your account asks about your career interests — the professions and industries that interest you. Next, you select a privacy setting. You can choose to share your résumé with only people you select or make your résumé available to anyone.

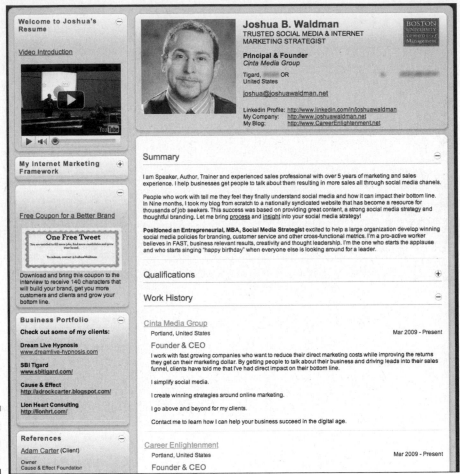

After you complete this basic signup, you actually have a bare-bones VisualCV that's ready to be dolled up and customized. At this point, your work with LinkedIn becomes useful. Just copy and paste your LinkedIn profile information into the new VisualCV you're setting up. You can customize the information later, but this strategy gives you a good foundation to start from.

Building your VisualCV for the best results

VisualCV lays out your résumé intuitively with a heading and two columns: a wide column and a narrow column. This setup makes laying out information highly manageable. Your basic résumé info goes in the wide main column, while highlighted, multimedia elements go in the narrow side column. Begin by choosing a Style — just click on the thumbnails across the top of the page to see your options, and choose the one you like best (see Figure 11-2). By default, the wide column appears on the left and the narrow column on the right, but you can make the columns trade places if you prefer; just click on the Swap Columns button next to the Style choices. Then proceed as explained in the following sections.

None of the fields are required. You can pick and choose which elements to fill in and which to leave out.

Figure 11-2:
Setting the look of your résumé in VisualCV.

The heading

In VisualCV, the heading appears at the top of the wide column and highlights essential information, such as your name and contact information. Info you entered previously — your name, city, state, country, and e-mail address — is plugged in for you. You have the option of adding your photo, an affiliate logo, links to other websites, and additional contact info.

The wide column

Beneath the heading, the wide column comprises three sections that VisualCV automatically adds to your profile: Summary, Work History, and Education. You can add more sections, such as Interests or Portfolio, by selecting the section you want from the ribbon at the top of the page.

You can change the color, typeface, and formatting of the text in any of the wide-column sections. Just click on the Need Help Formatting Your Text? link in the lower-right corner of the section's data-entry area for how-to info.

The narrow column

The multimedia aspect of VisualCV really comes into play in the narrow column. You can choose to add elements like an embedded video résumé or a portfolio of work samples worth highlighting. (I explain how to add such elements in the next section.)

VisualCV is *visual*. Where possible, supplement your written information with visual elements. For example, I used to work at Cisco, so I included an image of Cisco's logo on my CV. A client who was a project manager included scans of his PMP certification. What can you show visually from your résumé?

Creating your multimedia portfolio

One of the most unique features of VisualCV is the ability to integrate multimedia portfolios alongside a traditional résumé. Your portfolio is where you upload and store tangible evidence (in the form of documents, images, videos, or audio clips) of your capabilities and accomplishments. You can add items from your portfolio to each VisualCV you create, which is particularly great for professionals in creative industries such as design or advertising.

You need to upload items to your portfolio first before you can integrate them into your CV.

Think about work samples, videos, PDFs, images, and anything else you can use to tell your story to a potential employer. Make a list of such items for your reference and then follow these steps to upload them to your portfolio storage area:

1. **Click on the triangle next to the You link on any page, and then click on Your Portfolio.**

2. **On the Portfolio page, click the Upload New button.**

3. **On the Upload New file page, click on Browse to locate the file on your computer.**

4. **Type a title to help you organize the item in your portfolio, and then click on Upload.**

You can also link YouTube and Yahoo! videos as well as slides from SlideShare.

After you've uploaded work samples to your storage area, you can choose which items to include in the Portfolio sections of your VisualCV. You don't need to send all your work samples with every job application; considering the requirements of each position and customizing your portfolios accordingly are important. Here's how to add portfolio items to a VisualCV:

1. **Switch to the VisualCV you want to change or edit (if you're not there already) and click on Edit.**

2. **Add a portfolio section to the main column or sidebar by clicking on the Portfolio button at the top of the page.**

3. **Change the title of the portfolio section by clicking on the title.**

   Choose something like "Professional Work Sample"; then click on OK.

4. **Choose whether you want to display two, three, or four portfolio items in each row.**

5. **Click on Add a Portfolio Item; then click on the placeholder.**

6. **Select the portfolio item you want to add.**

7. **Choose a click-through behavior for images, documents, videos, or audio clips.**

   This action determines what happens when someone clicks. It may link somewhere, open up a lightbox to zoom in, and so on.

8. **Type a title and description for the item.**

9. **Click on Save.**

Innovate CV Can Innovate Your Résumé

Innovate CV (www.innovatecv.com) is an online, multimedia, résumé-building tool that's a great alternative to VisualCV. (Figure 11-3 shows you what an Innovate CV résumé looks like.) Its purpose is similar to VisualCV, but some considerable differences do exist between the two, such as the following:

✔ You can import your LinkedIn profile directly into your Innovate CV résumé. This feature saves a lot of time when building your profile.

✔ You have more design options that are cleaner and simpler than VisualCV.

✔ You can upload video directly into your CV rather than just linking to a YouTube video.

✔ Innovate CV offers many educational videos to help with writing your résumé and making it interactive.

✔ Innovate CV comes with a powerful Facebook application so you can leverage your personal network to share your résumé. (I tell you all about this application in Chapter 13.)

Consider creating both a VisualCV résumé and an Innovate CV résumé to increase your chances of getting found.

Figure 11-3:
A sample résumé created in Innovate CV.

Using DoYouBuzz and Emurse to Produce Your Résumé

Two other award-winning online résumé programs worth mentioning are DoYouBuzz and Emurse. DoYouBuzz is a great option if you want to have a personal website but don't want to deal with the hassle of starting one from scratch. Emurse is ideal if you want a digital résumé that looks just like a traditional paper one.

If you're already overwhelmed by having LinkedIn and VisualCV, you can bow out. However, if you want to double your impact and increase your possibilities of being found online, take a look at these options. Setting them up is even simpler than VisualCV, which I describe earlier in this chapter.

Designing a digital résumé on DoYouBuzz

Setting up your free online résumé with DoYouBuzz (www.doyoubuzz.com) is as simple as importing your LinkedIn profile. You're given this option when you first sign in. Just like with VisualCV, you can create a public résumé and then build customized résumés later.

DoYouBuzz gives you many more layout and color options than VisualCV and presents your résumé more like a web page than as a single document. The Home page in your DoYouBuzz résumé includes all the elements of your résumé on a single page. Then, each major heading of your résumé is made into a separate page. When you navigate to a subpage, your contact info remains visible on the sidebar. To see some examples of résumés built in DoYouBuzz, type "site:doyoubuzz.com resume" into a new Google search.

Some people prefer the layout of a DoYouBuzz résumé and use it as their primary web presence. The interface is clean and simple and allows you to see your traffic statistics, so you can see how many people view your résumé. DoYouBuzz can also export a professional-quality PDF version of your résumé, which you can take with you to the interview or attach to an e-mail.

Going the conventional résumé route on Emurse

Emurse (www.emurse.com) offers a more conservative-looking online résumé. In fact, you may say its résumés are just like traditional, hard-copy ones, only they're on a screen rather than paper. If you're uncomfortable with being visual or creative with VisualCV or Innovate CV, the advantage to using Emurse is that you can upload your profile information and make it look like a professionally formatted hard-copy résumé. For examples of what an Emurse résumé looks like, visit www.emurse.com and look at the bottom of the site for the Sample Entry Resumes link.

Emurse is a great option for recent college grads who may not have enough content to fill out a whole multimedia, online résumé like VisualCV or Innovate CV.

Five components make up an Emurse résumé:

- ✔ **Content:** In Content, you type in or copy and paste your résumé content into traditional buckets. Unfortunately, there's no LinkedIn import feature, so you have to do this part manually. Of course, if you already have a résumé or profile, copying and pasting it won't take you long.

- ✔ **Design:** Emurse doesn't have the flashy design options of VisualCV or DoYouBuzz. You will, however, find ten elegant formatting options. With these options, you won't need to hire a résumé writer again!

✔ **Distribute:** When you use the Emurse system to e-mail your résumé to a hiring manager, you can keep track of who you sent it to and set up reminders and events. Although this isn't the most robust organizing tool, it can come in handy if you want to know where your résumé has been and who has seen it (see Chapter 3 for additional tips on organizing your online job search).

✔ **Options:** Here, you can rename your résumé or delete a résumé.

✔ **Website:** Emurse gives you only one online résumé with a unique web address. The other résumés you create in Emurse are just for e-mailing to people or printing. The website allows you to specify how private or public you want your résumé to be. If you want Google to find your public online résumé, check the Allow Index setting. You can also see how many times your résumé has been viewed and downloaded.

Building a Résumé as a Website

Do you want complete control over your online résumé? Do semi-cookie-cutter templates like VisualCV, DoYouBuzz, and Emurse strike you as too limiting and unable to do your personal brand justice? If you answer yes to either question, you just may be the right candidate for a *website résumé,* which is a static site that simply displays your résumé elements visually on a set of web pages. It doesn't require the care and feeding that a blog does (see Chapter 6 for the scoop on running a blog), and it can be the central hub of your job search. Even better, because you design it, you control every element of its look and feel. The sections that follow explain what makes a website look like a unique résumé and walk you through the process of creating one and supplying it with content.

Buying the right domain

A *domain* is the website address you use to get to a site. Google looks at the domain name when calculating a website's relevance to a particular search. So if someone is searching your name and you've used your name as the domain name of your résumé website, the chances are quite high that your site will show up in the recruiter's search results.

You need to decide upfront what your domain name is going to be. Choose www.yourname.com, if possible. Another option is to choose the name of the position you want. If you go this route, an even better approach is to make your domain name www.positionlocation.com. Many recruiters search for job title and location when trying to fill a position. So if you choose a domain name like www.portlandCPA.com, you may start to rank in Google for those terms as well.

How to buy a domain

A new domain costs about $10 a year. To find one you want to buy, head on over to my domain name checker tool at `www.career enlightenment.com/jobseekers-website-setup`. Follow Step 1 to do a domain search for your chosen domain. If your chosen domain name is available, click on the link that appears to pick it up. ***Note:*** You'll need to host your domain somewhere, so be sure to pick up a year of hosting as well (see Step 2 on the website).

If you decide to use your name for your domain, be aware that someone may have already purchased it. This situation happened to me. Someone purchased the domain name `www.JoshuaWaldman.com` and did nothing with it, just waiting for a Joshua Waldman to make him an offer. Generally, domain speculators won't even consider selling you back your domain name until you start offering thousands of dollars. So here are some ways around burning a hole in your pocket while still taking advantage of Google's search algorithm:

✔ If `.com` is taken, consider buying `.net` or `.me`.

✔ Use your full name (Samuel) instead of a shortened version (Sam) or vice versa.

✔ Use your middle initial, but do this only if you're prepared to use your middle initial in every profile and domain you use as well.

✔ Add the word *résumé* to the domain, as in `www.joshuawaldman resume.com`

Employing easy website tools to create your personal design

You have literally thousands of options to choose from when building your own website, from premium HTML templates to developing in raw code. But the key to your job search is to spend as little time doing the back-end stuff and as much time networking as possible. The following sections present three easy solutions for building a custom website for your job search.

WordPress

WordPress is an open-source (read *free*) Content Management System, or CMS. This means your content is separated from your site's design, allowing you to post new content without worrying about layout. More than 60 percent of bloggers use WordPress. And literally thousands of people around the world develop *themes* (which control the look of a website) and *plug-ins* (which control the website's functionality). All you have to do is find the theme you like (they're usually free or less than $100) and fill in your content. Separating design from content makes it easy for you to focus on writing great web copy instead of fussing over code. Install your chosen theme on WordPress and then build the pages you need to show your résumé. (For details on how to install WordPress, flip to Chapter 6.)

The following are some of my favorite paid themes packages:

- **Elegant Themes:** `bit.ly/e_themes`
- **Templatic:** `bit.ly/templatic_themes`
- **ThemeForest:** `bit.ly/themes-forest`
- **WooThemes:** `bit.ly/w-themes`

Here are some premade résumé themes that look pretty good right out of the box. I recommend starting here for design options. In order to see the theme in action, click the Live Preview or Demo button on the following sites:

- `bit.ly/resume-theme1`
- `bit.ly/resume-theme2`
- `bit.ly/resume-theme3`

Weebly

Weebly (`bit.ly/weebly_website`) offers a free, visual, website-building platform. The paid upgrade opens up more advanced features for about $5 per month. But even with the free version, you're able to make a basic website. To see online résumés built in Weebly, enter "site:weebly.com resume" in your search engine. After you create a new website during setup, you're asked to choose a domain name. If you've purchased a domain, enter it here. Weebly gives you technical instructions on how to change your server records when you're ready to publish.

Creating a custom e-mail address for your website

Did you know that when you register your own domain, you get an e-mail address with it? With your domain registration service, you get an option to forward e-mail addresses. Set yours to `firstname@yourdomain.com`. Then forward that e-mail to your regular e-mail service such as Yahoo! or Gmail.

Tip: Gmail actually allows you to add an account. It receives e-mails addressed to your new domain address and even lets you send e-mails from Gmail that have your domain address in the From field. Just go to the gear icon at the top-right corner of your Gmail account and then click on Mail settings. Click on the Accounts and Import link and then select the Add Another Account link.

Choose the design template you prefer. Then, under the Elements tab, you can drag and drop images, text boxes, and even contact forms wherever you want them on the page.

When choosing a theme for your Weebly résumé, the simpler the better. Find simple themes by choosing Design. Then, on the left bar, pick All Themes. Finally, click on the link for Simple. These themes are the best ones for job seekers.

Squarespace

Squarespace (`bit.ly/sq-space`) offers the same service as Weebly, but Squarespace uses a different interface and does certain things better. Squarespace isn't free; it offers a 14-day free trial, after which you're asked to upgrade. As of writing this book, it's $12 per month to have a website with this service. However, the templates look more modern and unique than Weebly's. If you're a designer or have an eye for design, you may prefer Squarespace because the interface allows for more detailed customizations. To see some online résumés built in Squarespace, type in "site:squarespace.com resume" in your search engine.

If you don't change the domain name, *squarespace* will appear next to your name every time you share your link. It looks unprofessional, so you're better off avoiding it. To enter your own domain, go to Structure and then choose Custom Domain. You'll be given instructions on how to change your server records for the domain so that it points to the Squarespace page. Even though setting up your custom domain with this website seems like a pain, the advantage is huge. (*Note:* This same advice applies for Weebly.)

Writing the right content for your website résumé

After you've chosen a development platform for designing your online résumé (see the earlier section "Employing easy website tools to create your personal design"), you can get down to the business of figuring out what to write and what pages to include.

Your goal is to present a more rounded and colorful picture of your professional career than what can be found on paper. Don't just copy and paste your résumé text onto a website. Here are some guidelines for writing web copy:

- ✔ **Title every page.** When people land on your home page, they should know instantly that this is an online résumé.

- ✔ **Include headlines to help your reader scan your site quickly.** Use at least two levels of meaningful headers: a title (Level 1) and subheads (Level 2 or 3).

✔ **Link to other pages on your website.** For example, your professional summary may have the call to action, "Contact me." Link the words *contact me* directly to your Contact page.

✔ **Present one idea per paragraph.**

✔ **Use** bold **and** *italics* **on key phrases to make scanning easier.**

Your résumé website should summarize your résumé on the home page and then offer more detail in the subpages (much like DoYouBuzz does; see the earlier section "Designing a digital résumé on DoYouBuzz"). Following are the pages to include on your résumé website:

✔ **Home:** Use your home page to make clear that this site is a résumé and to punch up your key selling points. Think of this page as your extended professional summary. A hiring manager should take one glance at your home page and know what you're all about.

✔ **Résumé:** Here, outline the elements of your résumé with links to the corresponding subpages. The subpages can go into more detail. Example subpages include:

- Work History
- Education
- Skills
- Volunteerism

✔ **Social Networks:** If you haven't found a way to display links to your social networks in other locations — for example, via a static sidebar — you should have a page where people can connect with you.

✔ **Contact Me:** You can include your contact info as a footer or in a static sidebar throughout your site. However, having a contact page is nice as well. You can use a form that people can fill out directly on the page. Don't just put your e-mail address there or else you'll get spammed. Tell people what they can contact you about, such as job inquiries, consulting offers, or questions about your work. (I also include what *isn't* okay to contact me about, such as get-rich-quick schemes, link exchanges, and sending money to Africa scams.)

If you just drop your e-mail address on your website, you're likely to see an increase in spam. To avoid this, try an e-mail masking service like scr. im (www.scr.im). Scr.im forces viewers to verify that they're human and also gives you statistics about how many times your e-mail address has been viewed.

Part IV

Using Twitter, Facebook, and Other Sites to Find a Position

The 5th Wave   By Rich Tennant

"I'd respond to this person's comment on Twitter, but I'm a former Marine, Bernard, and a Marine never retweets."

In this part . . .

Don't be fooled by so-called experts who try to drown you in a plethora of social networking sites that are "guaranteed to help you find a job." The reality is that only a small handful of social networking sites have any value if you're just looking for your next career opportunity. They include Twitter, Facebook, and some other gems that I tell you all about in this part. Get ready to look at Twitter and Facebook in a new light!

Chapter 12

Uncovering the Hidden Job Market with Twitter

In This Chapter

▶ Demystifying Twitter for the job seeker

▶ Setting up a polished Twitter profile

▶ Using Twitter to grow your professional network

▶ Taking advantage of tools that make Twitter even more fun

*W*hat started as a joke among college dropouts at a failing startup has turned into one of the most influential technologies in the social media revolution. Twitter offers a forum for short messaging (all messages are 140 characters or less) among any of its members, from CEOs to mailroom clerks. This hierarchical flattening and instant communication make Twitter the most useful — albeit the most misunderstood — tool for a job seeker.

In this chapter, I demystify Twitter for you and explain why adding it to your job search doubles your effectiveness as a networker. I also cover important etiquette topics so you can rest easy knowing you look good to everyone in the Twitterverse and are using Twitter appropriately. Finally, I introduce you to some nifty tools you can use to speed up and organize what may become an overload of information and opportunities.

Your online reputation is as important to your job search as dressing well for an interview is. Having an active Twitter account means your name will rank in Google almost right away. And as employers discover more about you through your Twitter account, you can reinforce your personal brand to support your candidacy for a job. Because Twitter has so much potential to call attention to your personal brand, maintaining consistency of that brand in everything you do with Twitter is important. (For the full scoop on personal branding, see Chapter 4.)

The Whats and the Whys: Getting Up to Speed on Twitter

If you're not familiar with it, Twitter can seem intimidating (thanks to all the shorthand people use) or even unnecessarily time-consuming (who needs to read dozens of status updates, anyway?). But these perceptions couldn't be further from the truth. Twitter is actually pretty easy to follow after you know some of the basic terminology, and taking advantage of Twitter doesn't have to be time-consuming. Read on for a quick tutorial on Twitter vocabulary, common-sense responses to common Twitter-phobic objections, and a bit of insight into what makes Twitter stand out from the other major social media sites out there. (To find out about the latest updates to Twitter, visit www.careerenlightenment.com/fordummies.)

Presenting a Twitter vocabulary primer

Every social media outlet has a unique vocabulary, but Twitter has the most elaborate terminology of any network by far. Take a moment to familiarize yourself with the following jargon:

- ✔ **Tweet:** A tweet is a short (140 characters or less) message sent to your Twitter network from any device, phone, or computer.

- ✔ **Tweep:** A tweep is a single Twitter user.

- ✔ **Tweeple:** Multiple Twitter users are called tweeple.

- ✔ **Twetiquette:** Twitter etiquette; in other words, twetiquette is how to behave on Twitter.

- ✔ **Friend:** A friend is someone you follow on Twitter.

- ✔ **Follower:** A follower is someone who follows you on Twitter.

- ✔ **Retweet (RT):** To retweet is to send someone else's tweet to your own network, thus promoting that person on your network. A retweet is the biggest compliment you can pay another tweep and the highest compliment you can receive.

- ✔ **Timeline or Twitterstream:** This is the real-time display of tweets from other people in your Twitter network. As your network grows, your timeline moves faster and faster. When you post a tweet, it appears on your network's timeline. In essence, the timeline is the focal point of Twitter.

✔ **Lists:** Lists are groups of Twitter users (or tweeps) in your network. Classifying users in your network into lists allows you to see updates from specific individuals faster. Some groups are public; others are private. Getting featured on someone's list is a good way of getting promoted because that person's followers may look at that person's lists to find other interesting people (including you, if you're lucky).

✔ **Direct message (DM):** A DM is a private tweet to just one other person. To receive a DM, you must be a follower of the sender. Some people receive DMs directly to their phone via text messages.

✔ **@Reply:** An @reply is a public tweet wherein you mention someone specifically, thus bringing your tweet to a priority list on that person's timeline. You can use an @reply to alert someone to a tweet or carry on a public discussion. For example, you may use an @reply to thank someone specifically.

✔ **hashtag (#):** A hashtag is a subject (or *thread*) indicator you can include in a tweet for clarity. For example, using *#jobs* indicates that your tweet is about jobs; *#pdx #jobs* indicates that the tweet is about jobs in Portland. A hashtag can also tie a group of people together around a similar real-time experience. For example, if you attend a seminar, chances are that seminar has a hashtag. You can see — in real time — tweets from other attendees as they experience the same event as you.

✔ **Short URLs or shortened links:** Because the amount of space in a tweet is so limited, using *URL Shortening Services* allows you to shorten links to include in a tweet. For example, if you want to send a link about a *New York Times* article and still have some space in your tweet for a comment, you can shorten the link from `www.nytimes.com/ GreatArticleAboutTwitter` (40 characters) to `www.nyti.ms/ go11d4` (18 characters) by dropping the long link into `bit.ly`.

Tweeting for skeptics

By now, I've heard every misgiving about starting to use Twitter. Most excuses for not using it come from being misinformed, so many people miss out on one of the most powerful job-seeking tools ever invented. So before you write off Twitter, look at this section to see whether your reason holds any weight. Here are the most common objections to using Twitter and why those objections don't really stand up:

✔ **I don't like texting on my cellphone.** Although Twitter did evolve from a phone texting service, nowadays most people use a computer to interact with Twitter. Dozens of user interfaces and tools are available to make your experience even easier and more organized.

✔ **Twitter is a complete waste of productive time.** So was the Internet before it matured, but those who used it right found a great deal of value. Real-time technologies are in a very early stage of development, and Twitter is still evolving. And just like the Internet, whether the time you spend tweeting is useful or wasteful depends on how you use it. Believe it or not, you can use Twitter efficiently (not to mention effectively — hello, ranking on Google's first page!). I show you how in the later "Tweeting in ten minutes a day" section.

✔ **You can't communicate deep meaning in 140 characters or less.** If this were true, you'd have to say goodbye to every Haiku poem ever written. Twitter's length limit forces people (or *tweeple,* as Twitter users are called) to communicate in a very concise and efficient way. A system of abbreviations has been developed, and the process of boiling down your point can also help you clarify your thoughts.

✔ **I don't care what other people had for breakfast.** True, at one point, Twitter was mainly a network for personal updates, but that's not the case anymore. The world's top recruiters are posting jobs, CEOs of top companies are interacting with customers, and news is breaking in real-time.

Seeing what separates Twitter from the rest of the social media pack

If you're already on LinkedIn and Facebook, have multiple online résumés, and own your own domain name, you may wonder why on earth you should bother with another social network. I'm not saying that you *have* to use Twitter, but most people really enjoy using it after they get started. However, you can judge for yourself. Here are some of the key differences between Twitter and some other social networks:

✔ **Twitter is an open network.** Facebook and LinkedIn impose a mandatory mutual relationship. If you receive an invitation to join someone's network, you can either ignore the request, which severs the connection, or accept the invitation, which allows you to access each other's networks and updates. However, when people follow you on Twitter, you don't have to follow them back. They can see your posts, but you don't have to see theirs. This openness allows you to follow some very famous people even if they don't follow you back.

✔ **You can have conversations with anyone.** On Facebook and LinkedIn, only people who are directly connected to you can see your real-time updates. Likewise, if you want to follow the updates of a potential hiring manager, you have to get their permission first. With Twitter, you can see anyone's updates and, through @reply, you can even begin a conversation with anyone, whether you're connected or not.

✔ **Get instant access to the collective consciousness.** By posting a tweet to your network, you can get instant feedback, ideas, and help. And when your tweet is retweeted, your name, brand, and message are exposed to even more people, who can then start building relationships with you.

✔ **Twitter is like an empty canvas.** Because Twitter's use isn't clearly defined, people use the site for all sorts of reasons. Some people need more structure; others enjoy having full control. You can make your Twitter experience exactly what you want it to be. If you use Twitter to build your brand and expand your professional network, that's exactly what it will do for you.

Discovering How Twitter Can Help You Find a Job

When Twitter first became popular, the instructions for posting a tweet were simply to answer the question, "What are you doing?" Some people took this question literally, leading to such gems as "I'm taking a shower" or "I'm having coffee with breakfast." Fortunately, Twitter has since evolved from simple personal status updates into a place where people promote ideas, develop relationships, and break news as it happens in real time. This instant communication online is called *the real-time web,* and this concept is changing public relations and marketing on a global scale. As you can probably guess, the implications of the real-time web for a job seeker are enormous because when jobs are posted, you find out instantly. These implications are also precisely why Twitter is such a great tool for building your personal brand and developing key relationships at target companies.

Through my blog, I receive stories every month from people finding jobs through relationships they formed on Twitter. For example, one person in Australia moved to Melbourne from Brisbane and through a Twitter connection, she walked right into a job interview and on to her next job.

The following sections fill you in on why recruiters and hiring managers are turning to Twitter to announce jobs, as well as the ways Twitter can be beneficial for you as a job seeker.

Revealing how recruiters use Twitter

Hiring agents, internal HR staffers, headhunters, large human resource firms, and private recruiting professionals all use Twitter to actively fill open positions. Why? Because posting job openings on Twitter is not only free but also effective as a way to advertise positions to a small, yet highly qualified, pool of trusted professionals.

I'm confident that at least one major recruiter in your city is posting jobs daily to a Twitter feed (I show you how to find such recruiters in the later "Uncovering your city's underground Twitter job board" section). These recruiters hope to collect qualified résumés without having to spend $600 to post the opening on a major job board. Remember, recruiters get paid a fee if their candidate is chosen by the hiring company.

When a recruiter posts a job, he usually uses a *hashtag* to indicate that the tweet is about a job posting, for example, *#job, #career,* or *#hiring,* followed by a short description and a link to the position's online page. The link typically takes you to the job posting on the recruiter's website, where you can apply directly.

The use of Twitter for more than simply announcing jobs isn't common practice; however, I've heard of some creative companies asking candidates to apply for a job using Twitter directly. Applying for a job in just 140 characters is a lot harder than you think!

Tweeting as a job seeker

As a job seeker, you can use Twitter to find work in essentially two ways. First, Twitter allows you to create instant relationships within target organizations. Second, you can monitor job opportunities posted on your Twitter timeline like a real-time job board.

- ✔ **The Relationship Engine:** When you use Twitter to create, build, or strengthen relationships, you combine brand awareness and sales. Through your daily interactions, you raise awareness about who you are and the value you bring to the table. When you target specific people to engage with and try to bring those conversations to e-mail or phone, you use sales skills to sell your abilities to an organization.

- ✔ **The Real-Time Job Board:** Every day, thousands of jobs are posted on Twitter, often long before they wind up on more traditional job boards. With the proper setup (which I explain in the next section), your Twitter account delivers job opportunities to you as they become available in real-time.

Setting up Your Twitter Profile for Job Searching

After you decide to give Twitter a try for your job search, the easiest part is setting up your profile (unlike LinkedIn, where the hardest part is setting up the profile, but I help you figure all that out in Chapter 9). When you create a profile on Twitter, you first focus on picking a username and writing your *bio* — a brief self-description that appears on your Twitter home page. Then you can customize your profile further by selecting a background, adjusting your settings, and so on. Because you're creating this account for job-searching purposes rather than just for fun, I encourage you to make your personal brand a part of your Twitter account. I explain how in the next sections.

Choosing your name and username

Your name appears only in your Twitter profile, but your *username* (what you go by on Twitter; also called a *handle*) is attached to every tweet. Your username is also the domain name for your profile, as you can see in Figure 12-1.

Domain name   Title tag

Figure 12-1:
Your Twitter username appears in the domain name of your profile.

When picking a username, remember that its length eats away at your 140-character message. The longer your username is, the less space you have for your messages. If your name is long, consider abbreviating it, or use a keyword or description of your profession in a short and memorable way. Here are some examples of different name/@username combinations:

- ✔ **Twit Johnson (@TwitJohnson):** Your full name for both your name and username. This is the combination I use.
- ✔ **Twit Johnson (@TwitJPMP):** Your full name, then your abbreviated name plus a professional keyword. (PMP is a highly coveted project management certification.)
- ✔ **Twit Johnson (@SanFranPMP):** Your full name, then an abbreviated, differentiating professional keyword.
- ✔ **San Francisco Project Manager (@TwitJohnson):** A differentiating professional keyword, then your full name.

Picking a Twitter profile photo

Imagine trying to open Microsoft Word on your computer if the icon for the program were to change every day. You'd probably hesitate to click an icon you didn't recognize. The same is true with your Twitter photo. The photo you choose visually helps people to interact with you because they recognize you faster. To keep your personal brand consistent, post the same photo on Twitter and LinkedIn, and stick with it. (I offer tips on taking a good profile photo in Chapter 9.)

To set your name and username for the first time, simply head to www.twitter.com, click on the Sign Up button on the right-hand side of the screen, and fill in the required fields. If you already have a Twitter account and want to change your username, head to the top-right portion of the page, click on your current username, and then click on Settings. From there, you can make any desired adjustments to your username.

Changing your username often isn't wise because you want people to instantly recognize you, and your username helps accomplish that. Pick a username you can live with for a while; it's going to become a strong part of your personal brand (more on this in Chapter 4).

Your name and username form a *title tag* on your Twitter profile page; this title tag appears in the Internet browser's window (refer to Figure 12-1 to see what I mean). Google uses title tags as part of its search algorithm, which is a good reason to use your full name combined with your best keyword when choosing your Twitter name and username. Because Google indexes Twitter several times an hour, your chances of ranking on Google's first page for your name and keywords are quite high. (If you don't have a list of keywords yet, flip to Chapter 5 and make a list of ten or so.)

Writing your 160-character bio

Google uses your bio to index your Twitter account, so those 160 characters may be the first splash of information someone gets about you. For that reason, I recommend thinking of your Twitter bio as a sales pitch. People decide whether or not to follow you based on what they read in your bio. And because Twitter users are bombarded with thousands of followers and tweets every time they log in, your bio needs to grab their attention, make them curious, and cut through all the clutter.

Twitter isn't the same as LinkedIn: Whereas LinkedIn's etiquette is more formal and professional, in Twitter, you can show a bit more personality. A good way to describe yourself on Twitter is to imagine that you're at a networking event at a bowling alley and responding to someone's request to "Tell me about yourself." In Twitter, you can add a bit more personal color to your image as illustrated in the following examples:

> *Future focused finance executive. I know the weather & wear a rain jacket for changes in economic climate. Looking to fly a company above the storm clouds.* (155 characters)

> *IT Project Director specializing in web-based reporting. If it ain't broke, I'll make it even better. I want your systems working elegantly.* (140 characters)

> *Recent grad not looking forward to moving back in with parents. Love communications and creative problem solving. Amateur film critic with published reviews.* (157 characters)

> *Social media job-search coach. I once traveled the world with nothing more than LinkedIn & a bottle of gin. Let's trick the economy and get you hired.* (150 characters)

Testing different versions of your bio (unlike your profile photo) is a good idea. Over the course of a week, measure the number of new Twitter followers you get. Then change your bio slightly for the next week and compare the two numbers. If you get more followers, keep that change and try making an additional one. If you get fewer followers, revert to the previous version and try changing another detail instead. Good Internet marketers are always testing new copy for better performance.

Tweaking other Twitter settings

Spending a little time within the Settings panel is worthwhile when you're using Twitter to help you with your job search. Head over to the triangle drop-down menu next to your username on the top-right corner of the page and click on Settings.

Profile background

You can personalize the look of your Twitter account by uploading background images and collages. You want the colors, images, and words you use to be professional and consistent with your personal brand. (I cover personal branding in Chapter 4.)

Making your Twitter profile background consistent with your personal brand probably requires you to create a custom background instead of selecting one of Twitter's built-in backgrounds. To do this, go to the Settings page by clicking on the drop-down menu next to your username. Next, choose the

Design tab and then click on Change Background Image at the bottom of the page. There, you can upload an image file (smaller than 800 megabytes).

If you're savvy with any image-production or graphic-design software and want to build a custom background, check out these Twitter background guidelines: bit.ly/twitter-background-tips.

If you want a simple background that doesn't involve graphic design, following is a list of free online resources to try out. In most cases when you use these tools, your Twitter background is automatically updated when you finish with a design.

- **Free Twitter Designer:** www.freetwitterdesigner.com
- **Themeleon:** www.colourlovers.com/themeleon/twitter
- **Tweety Got Back:** www.tweetygotback.com
- **TwitBacks:** www.twitbacks.com

Choosing a link

You can share one clickable link in your Twitter profile for people to click on if they want to find out more about you. Choose your LinkedIn profile, another online résumé (like a VisualCV, which I cover in Chapter 11), or your own website or blog. Make sure this link takes people to a location that has more information about your job qualifications.

Preventing Twitter from becoming annoying

If you're not careful with your settings, Twitter can easily overrun your life. To keep Twitter under control, I suggest you make the following minor tweaks to your Account and Notifications settings in the Settings page:

- Don't let others find you from your e-mail address.
- Don't show photos and videos from everyone.
- Don't protect your tweets; doing so defeats the whole point of networking and building relationships.
- Don't tell Twitter to e-mail you if you get a new follower — unless of course you want to receive tons of pestering e-mails per day.
- Don't tell Twitter to e-mail you if you receive a direct message because DMs can be spammy.

Knowing What (And What Not) to Share

Google displays your last two tweets in search results for your name, and people often read these tweets before deciding to follow you. So what you do and don't tweet about (and how frequently you tweet) is extremely important. The sections that follow clue you in to what's worth tweeting and what's not.

As for how often you tweet, Twitter requires frequent interaction to be effective. Your followers' timelines are moving a mile a minute, which means your tweets don't just sit there waiting for someone to read them. The more often you tweet, the more likely your tweets are to be read. I suggest tweeting 5 to 20 times a day. This number may seem like a lot at first, but half of those tweets will be retweets and shared links, so you'll only be generating a few original tweets at a time. Trust me, the more you tweet, the easier it gets (and the more followers you wind up with).

Deciding what to tweet

Typically, the hardest step in getting started with Twitter is figuring out what on earth to say. When I train job seekers on Twitter during workshops, they frequently tell me that their biggest fear is not knowing where all that content is going to come from. Don't worry. Here are some ways to find content easily:

- ✔ **Follow industry blogs:** Compile a list of industry-relevant blogs to read weekly. Most blogs have a Tweet This feature that allows you to share the article directly via your Twitter account. Find industry blogs by checking out www.alltop.com or www.technorati.com.

   If you can't find enough industry-specific blogs in Alltop or Technorati, try entering this search string into Google:

   ```
   blogs + [industry name]
   ```

- ✔ **Monitor news sites:** One of Twitter's greatest strengths is how fast it can spread news. Participate in spreading breaking news by monitoring news sites. When you tweet about an article, add a quick opinion to the message, like "Great article" or "I wonder why this is."

- ✔ **Retweet good posts:** When you retweet what your fellow tweeps have to say, you pay them the highest compliment. So find a few companies you want to follow and spend a few days reading their tweets. Then help them spread their message by retweeting them.

Posting links to articles and retweeting are great ways to get started, but you'll want to get more personal after a while. After all, one of the main points of tweeting is to give hiring managers a chance to get to know you better. The following list gives you an idea of the kinds of personal information and experiences that may be worth sharing:

- **A quote:** Quotes are some of the most treasured tweets out there. Start collecting short quips to share on Twitter. If you hear a great one-liner in a movie or read something profound in a book, tweet it. Make sure you use the hashtag *#quote* to let your followers know you're being pithy.

- **A question:** After you have more followers, consider asking them questions. When Twitter was valued at $38 billion, I asked my followers why they thought that was, and I got back a slew of funny and interesting speculations. Questioning your network is a great way to build relationships.

- **Something special you do:** If you do something special or unusual, share it. I've shared accomplishments at the gym, classes I've enjoyed, and even noteworthy restaurants I've eaten at. Ask yourself, "Does sharing this allow someone else a chance to feel closer to me?"

- **Something you see:** If you see a killer sunset, snap a photo and share it with your followers. They may appreciate it, too.

- **An insight:** If you have an opinion, a pet peeve, or a flash of insight about a topic, why not let your followers know? Initiate conversations around industry-relevant topics that you feel you can contribute to in an intelligent way. Or perhaps just wax philosophical.

- **A recommendation:** Did you meet someone remarkable who helped you? Share your experience on Twitter and help promote your benefactor. Did you hire a résumé writer who rocked? Maybe you went to a networking group that was particularly worthwhile. All these topics make great recommendations to your network.

- **A direct communication:** If you find someone you want to talk to, why not start a conversation? Use @username in your tweet to alert the other person. As long as your post doesn't look like spam, chances are you'll get a reply.

- **An interruption:** Go to www.search.twitter.com to find a discussion that's happening right now and interrupt it. Butt in. Give your two cents worth. Every Thursday, human resource professionals have a Twitter chat. They use a special hashtag and welcome input from anyone listening in. Find a hashtag discussion about your industry to join.

With any of these tweet ideas, try to incorporate the word *you* rather than *I, me,* or *my*. For example, say something like "You'll love this new photo of the sunset from my weekend at Mt. Hood" or "What do you think of this new article on CNN?" *You* is a more retweeted word than *I*.

Ultimately, make sure your tweets are interesting and in line with your personal brand, and use your keywords occasionally. (I help you come up with keywords in Chapter 5.) As long as you're engaging and contributing to the collective conversation, you're fine! Also remember to tweet other people the same way you want to be tweeted. Avoid coming across as obnoxious or ordinary.

Discerning what not to tweet

Everything you tweet becomes public domain. Potentially thousands of people may read your tweets, and not all those people are kind, altruistic, social-media enthusiasts like me. Having some street smarts goes a long way.

Never share personal information that can be used against you or that can be used to impersonate you, such as the following:

- Your birth date
- Your phone number
- Your address
- Your mother's maiden name
- Details about your children
- When you're going on vacation or leaving your home
- Potentially damaging images or information about yourself

You're using Twitter to get a job. You don't have to be stuck-up, hidden away, or always on topic; however, keep in mind that a hiring manager may see your tweets, in which case getting too casual is a mistake. Be personal sometimes, but not all the time. I suggest you loosely adhere to the following breakdown of tweet types:

- **Retweets and shared links:** Rely on what others have to say 50 percent of the time. Any more than this, and people will think you have nothing original to say!

- **Industry/job-search topics:** Use your tweets to build your personal brand 40 percent of the time.

- **Personal topics:** Answer the questions "Who are you?" and "What motivates you?" 10 percent of the time.

- **Direct requests for job-search help or for a connection at a target company:** Don't ask questions of this nature more than once a week. You don't want to appear desperate. You can ask for help, but don't be that guy who shows up at a networking event expecting everyone to listen to him as he tries to sell his latest and greatest invention. Pay it forward and build some trust first.

Growing Your Followers and Friends

Ideally, you want as many people to follow you as you personally follow. This balance is called the *friends/followers* (or *FF*) *ratio*. The catch to achieving a 100 percent FF ratio is that the tweeple you follow don't necessarily follow you back. Prospective followers look at your most recent tweets, how long you've been on Twitter, and whether your profile seems legit. Likewise, you're not obligated to follow others just because they follow you. Be on the lookout for the telltale signs of a spammer and stay away! The following sections help you figure out who to follow on Twitter and who to avoid (like those annoying spammers).

Before you can build a Twitter network, you need to have at least ten interesting tweets in your timeline. You'll feel like you're talking to a wall at first. Just get those first tweets out of the way, and the people will come.

Finding people to follow

The best way to grow your Twitter network is to find other people with the same interests as you. After you post your Twitter profile, your bio, an image, and at least ten tweets, follow these steps weekly to grow your list:

✔ **Use Twitter's Find People features.** On your Twitter home page, click on the Who to Follow link to see who Twitter suggests you follow, browse by topics, and import your Gmail and LinkedIn contacts (see Figure 12-2). When you start off, invite people who know you. They're more likely to follow you back. And the more people you have following you, the more likely new people are to think you're legit.

Figure 12-2:
Twitter's
Who to
Follow page.

✔ **Follow the Twitter accounts of the companies or organizations you want to work for.** Watch their timelines for a week or so, paying attention to their topics, and then begin to participate in the conversation. Retweet a post. Send them an @reply with a question or reaction. After a while, the person (or people) managing the company's Twitter account will get to know you. After you establish this social credibility, you can ask for direct contacts to hiring managers within the company or note that you've just applied for a job there and are looking for the right person to follow up with.

✔ **Use Twitter's real-time search features to find conversations as they're happening.** Head on over to `search.twitter.com`, `www.twubs.com`, or `www.tagal.us` and type in a keyword related to your industry or field. The results reveal anyone who's tweeting that keyword in real-time. You can check people's profiles before following or just join in the conversation (retweet or @reply back, keeping any hashtags others use).

✔ **Look up interesting bios with Twitter directories.** Another way to find new people to follow is by looking at their 160-character bios. Either type in a keyword relevant to your job search or simply browse topics in the following directories:

- `www.twellow.com`

- `www.followfinder.googlelabs.com`

- `www.listorious.com`

- `www.twibes.com`

- `www.wefollow.com`

- `www.followerwonk.com`

✔ **Scan Lists from your favorite tweeps.** Review the profiles of your favorite (or just the most influential) people in your network; in particular, look at any lists they've put together. (I clue you in to what makes lists helpful in the earlier section "Presenting a Twitter vocabulary primer.") Adding those people to your network is a wise move. See Figure 12-3 for an example of what lists look like in Twitter.

You can follow up to 2,000 people. At that point, Twitter needs to see an FF ratio of less than 120 percent before it will allow you to follow any more. If, after a week, any of the people you chose to follow haven't bothered to follow you back, unfollow them. This action decreases your FF ratio and allows you to follow other people who may actually reciprocate. To find out exactly who didn't follow you back (and who you need to follow back), visit `www.friend orfollow.com`. Just type in your Twitter username and click on the Submit button to see your results.

Finding executives to network with

Created by Federated Media in partnership with Microsoft and Twitter, ExecTweets (www.exectweets.com) is a mini-network of over 200 executives on Twitter. The idea was to aggregate the most insightful people on Twitter so you can find and follow them. These people are highly recommended thought leaders whose messages are worth reading, and you can follow them and add them to your network with the click of a button. This is a great way to start building your Twitter account!

Figure 12-3: Looking at a person's lists in Twitter.

Knowing who to follow back and who to block

If someone follows you, you're not obligated to reciprocate. Indeed, every day more and more spammers and schemers are on Twitter. Some people @reply your username just to make sure your read their spam message. Others contact you directly with links you shouldn't click unless you want to welcome a hijacker into your Twitter account.

Here are some surefire signs you're being harassed by spammers:

- ✔ **They have a new Twitter account.** Anyone with an account younger than 30 days is suspect.

- ✔ **They're following *way* more people than are following them back.** Other people aren't following them back, meanwhile, they're on a tirade of following other people, which is fishy behavior.

- ✔ **More than 90 percent of their tweets are links.** These people are not good conversation partners.

- ✔ **They don't use @replies.** Obviously, they aren't interested in interacting, just broadcasting.

- ✔ **They repeat the same tweet over and over again.** Actually, this repetition is in violation of Twitter's user policy.

- ✔ **They've tweeted only five times in the last 30 days.** This person clearly isn't contributing to the collective conversation and probably has an automated tool that has followed you based on a keyword you've used. Lame!

If anyone ever really bothers you on Twitter, you can either just unfollow that person or — if it's really bad — you can block and report the tweep as spam. I report anyone who contacts me directly with lame marketing messages or who uses @replies to get me to click on unsolicited links. These people clutter up the Twitterverse and should be removed.

Seeking a Job, Tweeple-Style

Finding and following your target companies on Twitter can be a fun way of driving your job search. However, companies you may never have heard of are posting jobs and recruiting on Twitter as well. Setting up a *listening station,* a list of current tweets based on keywords you can view, helps you monitor and track all the important job-seeking activities going on around you. The following sections show you how-tos.

Uncovering your city's underground Twitter job board

Every major metropolitan city has a human resource industry wherein recruiters build a list of possible candidates to place into possible jobs. More and more, these recruiters are turning to Twitter to post jobs and recruit talent. Follow these steps to find your local recruiters so you can monitor real-time job postings:

1. **Go to any Twitter user directory and type the following into the search box: "recruiter, *[your city]*" or "executive search, *[your city]*."**

   I prefer www.twellow.com.

2. **Follow the firms who are active on Twitter.**

   Check their past few tweets to see whether or not they post regularly.

3. **Add your finds to a list called "Recruiters" so you can follow their posts easily.**

   I explain how to create a list in the later "Using lists to optimize your experience" section.

If you want to save yourself the hassle of trying to follow many recruiters all at once, add @microjobs to your list of people to follow. Recruiters from around the United States use this aggregation service. When a recruiter tweets a post to @microjobs, @microjobs automatically retweets the post to the thousands of people in the service's growing network. Although following @microjobs can be a time-saver, be aware that the job postings you see will be for opportunities throughout the country, not just in your local community.

Many cities have people who are so passionate about Twitter's job-networking ability that they maintain a Twitter account that aggregates job postings in your area. These Twitter accounts can be great resources for uncovering the hidden job market. To find them, follow these steps:

1. **Visit your preferred Twitter user directory and type "*[your city]* jobs" into the search box.**

2. **Find the Twitter accounts that are streams of job listings.**

   Often, these streams are broken down by industry, such as healthcare jobs or internships.

3. **Follow these streams and add them to a list called "Local Jobs."**

   I explain how to add lists in the later "Using lists to optimize your experience" section.

The final way to uncover the hidden job market on Twitter is to perform persistent searches for words and hashtags that contain the words *jobs, careers,* and so forth. As jobs are posted in your area, you'll be able to see them and apply for them in real-time. Just follow these steps:

1. **Create a new column for searching a keyword in your Twitter management software.**

   HootSuite and TweetDeck are two common types of Twitter management software. See the later section "Surveying Twitter management tools" for more info on these programs.

2. **Type in a job-related hashtag, such as** *#jobs,* *#careers,* **or** *#employment.*

3. **Further refine your search by using variations of your location.**

    For instance, Portland, Oregon — my city of residence — is often abbreviated PDX, so I have one search column labeled "PDX #jobs" and another labeled "Portland #jobs" in order to capture every possible way someone may post an opening.

Exploring other Twitter job-seeking tools

TweetMyJOBS (www.tweetmyjobs.com) is a great career-management company with plenty of traction in the U.S. employment marketplace. With more than 1 million job postings every month — including jobs from companies such as Starbucks, Kmart, and Comcast — TweetMyJOBS leads the way in tweetifying the job market. The site has been reviewed in the *Wall Street Journal,* on CNN, and in *Business Week.* I consider this tool to be the highest-leverage, Twitter job-searching platform available. Even if you don't plan to be very active on Twitter, taking a look at TweetMyJOBS to stay up-to-date is certainly worthwhile.

As a job seeker, you need to engage in three primary activities on TweetMyJOBS:

✔ **Subscribe to a job channel.** A *job channel* is simply a Twitter feed that's specific to your location and industry (see Figure 12-4). Job channels save you from having to review irrelevant tweets for jobs you don't care about in other locations. For example, you may subscribe to Boston Sales Jobs or Portland Writing Jobs.

   To subscribe to a channel, go to www.tweetmyjobs.com, create an account or log in, and then hover your mouse cursor over the Jobseeker Tools menu at the top of the page and choose JobChannels. Then you can sort by location, industry, or both (see Figure 12-4). When you find a channel you like, follow it the same way you'd follow any other Twitter user.

Figure 12-4: Sample Job Channels on TweetMyJOBS.

Available JobChannels™:
We have 9,956 JobChannels™. Use the drop-downs to filter and search the list.

	JobChannel™
	USA-CA-San Francisco Software Dev. - General/IT
	USA-CA-San Francisco Healthcare
	USA-CA-San Francisco Manufacturing
	USA-CA-San Francisco Banking
	USA-CA-San Francisco Sales

TweetMyJOBS is a registered trademark of ARC International Group, LLC. All Rights Reserved.

✔ **Upload your résumé and then tweet a link to download your résumé to TweetMyJOBS's exclusive @TweetAResume account.** @TweetAResume has more than 10,000 followers who are instantly alerted every time a new résumé is posted, which translates into terrific exposure for you!

To get started, simply fill out your profile in TweetMyJOBS (you can access your profile from the home page or the Jobseeker Tools menu). Then click on the Tweet My Resume button at the top of your profile page. Doing so sends a link to your public-facing profile to thousands of followers.

✔ **Create a social profile.** Companies that post jobs through TweetMyJOBS can view social profiles, so creating your own profile is like getting added to a company's database of viable candidates. To fill out your profile, just hover over Jobseeker Tools at the top of any page and click on Social Profile/Tweet Resume. Then simply fill out the form and click on Save.

Understanding hashtags

Hashtags, which are preceded by the # symbol in Twitter, are subject markers. Hashtags are used to create continuity within the chaos of the thousands of tweets being posted every second. Recruiters post jobs by using several different hashtags. Here are some hashtags worth searching for in www.search. twitter.com or in the search column of your Twitter management tool:

#career

#careers

#employment

#hire

#hireme

#hiring

#job

#jobhunt

#jobhunting

#jobinterview

#jobpostings

#jobs

#jobsearch

#jobseeker

#jobseekers

#laidoff

#recruiters

#recruiting

#work

Another useful job-search tool for Twitter users is TwitterJobcast.com (www. twitterjobcast.com), which was created by a laid-off software developer from Michigan. Rather than feeling bad for himself, he decided to build a tool that would be helpful for other job seekers. TwitterJobcast.com allows people to post jobs for free as well as display job-related tweets. The site uses a search algorithm to figure out which tweets are job postings and which ones are just people complaining about their jobs. You can browse by your city and see job postings appear in real time; just type in the required information at the top of the page and click on the Search button. This tool is worth keeping live in your browser!

Time-Saving Secrets for Using Twitter Efficiently

Twitter's interface can be somewhat confusing. Seeing whether your name has been mentioned, setting up persistent searches, and organizing all the stuff going on are hard tasks to accomplish. Essentially, Twitter wants you to spend as much time on its web page as possible. However, your primary goal as a job seeker is to get in and out quickly. I encourage you to use Twitter but limit your time by being very efficient. The next sections help you figure out how to do just that.

Surveying Twitter management tools

The three Twitter management tools I recommend are HootSuite (www. hootsuite.com), TweetDeck (www.tweetdeck.com), and Seesmic (www. seesmic.com). You can use any of them because, essentially, they all offer the same functionality (with minor differences in user interface and price). Table 12-1 gives you a quick summary of what each tool offers. I suggest trying all of them and then choosing just one to serve as your primary interface with Twitter.

Table 12-1 Comparing HootSuite, TweetDeck, and Seesmic

	HootSuite	TweetDeck	Seesmic
Price	Free with $5.99/ month upgrade to get it ad-free	Free	Free

continued

Table 12-1 *(continued)*

	HootSuite	*TweetDeck*	*Seesmic*
Supported Platforms	Any web browser	Desktop application and Google Chrome only	Both desktop and web browser versions available for all browsers
Mobile Versions	iPhone, Droid, Keitai, and BlackBerry	iPhone, iPad, and Droid	iPhone, Droid, BlackBerry, and Windows Phone 7
Tabbed Interface?	Yes	No	No
Clear Statistics	Very easy to see your Twitter performance: how often you're retweeted or your links are clicked	No	No
Built-in URL-Shortening	Yes, but uses only its own proprietary shorteners	Yes, you can pick from bitly, tinyURL, and more	Yes

Personally, I prefer HootSuite because it resides in my web browser rather than on my desktop, and I like its tabular user interface, which you can see for yourself in Figure 12-5.

Figure 12-5: HootSuite's tabbed interface is easy to navigate.

Tweeting in ten minutes a day

Twitter may possibly become one of your favorite online activities, posing the danger that you may spend way too much time on Twitter to the detriment of other important job-seeking activities. So I developed the following simple, ten-minute checklist to keep your Twitter activities on task while maximizing your time online. Feel free to modify the list as you see fit.

1. **Respond to any @replies in your Mentions column.**

2. **Respond to any DMs (direct messages) in your Messages Inbox.**

3. **Write an original tweet and share it with your network.**

4. **Read through your timeline and lists, retweet what resonates with you, and @reply to engage in conversation.**

5. **Add new, strategic people to your network and add them to an appropriate list.**

    Use a Twitter directory and a hashtag search to help; I explain how to use these tools earlier in this chapter.

6. **Occasionally, unfollow people who haven't followed you back. Likewise, make sure you follow back people who are worth your time.**

    Use www.friendorfollow.com to analyze your network.

7. **Occasionally, DM strategic people you want to deepen your engagement with.**

    Strategic people may be contacts at a company you're targeting, a key influencer in your industry, or an author you admire.

Using lists to optimize your experience

As your Twitter connections grow, your timeline moves faster and faster, increasing your chances of missing critical pieces of information, job postings, and relevant industry news. That's where lists come in. With the lists feature on Twitter, you can drag-and-drop certain Twitter friends into categories. Each list only displays tweets from its members.

Each of the three Twitter-management tools I describe earlier in this chapter takes advantage of this concept and very easily allows you to create, add to, and read lists. Twitter's own native interface also allows you to create and manage list members.

Creating a list is easy. Simply go to www.twitter.com, click on Lists, and then choose Create a List. You can title your list, write a short description, and mark it Public or Private. If the list is sensitive, like a list of hiring managers at target companies, then you may want to make it private. If the list is topical, like a list of thought leaders in your field, then why not make it public.

You're allotted 20 lists per Twitter account, and lists can't begin with a number. I suggest creating the following lists:

- **Local recruiters:** You may name this list "Michigan Recruiters" or "Dallas Recruiters."

- **Local job boards:** Try to locate Twitter accounts that post job openings in your area, like @CAjobs or @RIjobsbot.

- **Personal friends:** This list, which allows you to follow personal friends in your network, may be private.

- **Great companies:** Having top-notch companies in a single list — especially the ones you're targeting in your job search — can significantly simplify your research.

- **Top tens:** You may want to list the best tweeps about a certain category, such as "Best job search advice" or "Best nonprofit tweets."

Chapter 13

Using Facebook as a Job Hunter

Facebook is a social networking site that was originally intended just for college students within the United States but has expanded into a global phenomenon. It has literally defined a generation, changed general perceptions regarding privacy, and inspired an army of entrepreneurs. But dangers still lurk around the corner for the average Facebook user in the form of dumb posts that have bad consequences. Job seekers who don't take ownership of their Facebook accounts may pay the highest price.

I used to advise people to keep their Facebook profiles totally separate from their professional aspirations. But thanks to Facebook's dominance as the leading social network combined with the changes in how recruiters are using Facebook to find and filter talent, it's become clear that people simply can't avoid Facebook. If you're serious about finding work — and people really are finding jobs through Facebook — you need to have a presence on this site. The question is how to have fun on Facebook while simultaneously satiating the curiosity of HR professionals and hiring managers.

This chapter helps you figure that out by explaining exactly why Facebook is essential for your job search as well as how to protect your privacy, update (or create) your profile strategically, and post politely and effectively. It also introduces you to some great new apps that can potentially cut your job search in half and reveals how a simple Facebook ad may help you land your dream job. (For the scoop on the latest updates to Facebook, check out www.careerenlightenment.com/fordummies.)

Getting the 411 on How Facebook Works

Facebook has become one of a job seeker's most valuable tools, thanks to *engineered serendipity*. To understand what engineered serendipity is, think about that moment when you bumped into someone you knew from high school or that friend who just happened to know of an open position that was perfect for you at the exact time you needed it. These moments are moments of serendipity; in other words, they're happy accidents.

The magic of Facebook is that it manifests happy accidents by running your profile information through a fancy algorithm and then showing you the names and pictures of some people you may know.

After you complete your profile, Facebook suggests friends for you. You grow a little network by sending and accepting friend requests, and then you're ready to participate in the main way people use Facebook: writing on your or other people's *Walls* — an area where friends can leave or comment on short messages, links, or even videos. The way your Facebook Wall works is also a key part of engineered serendipity. Good use of the Wall helps you spread the word about your professional aspirations faster than anything you can imagine.

When you post something to your Wall, that post may show up on your friend's home page. (I say *may* because whether it does is actually determined by a fancy algorithm.) And your friend's friends may see your post if you set your privacy settings right. Also when you post comments on your friends' Wall posts, their friends can see those comments. So your communications can spread to people you may not even know yet.

All of this is great news! It means your personal brand and your messages can quickly spread to new people within a trusted referral network. Of course, that means you need to be careful of the messages you post. Don't worry, though. I fill you in on what you can say in your Wall posts and comments in order to get people calling you about job openings in the later "Practicing good Wall etiquette" section.

Discovering Why Facebook Needs to Be a Component of Your Job Search

At first, Facebook was used almost exclusively for personal reasons among college students. Soon, complications arose: What if my mom wants to connect with me on Facebook and sees my party pictures? If my ex-girlfriend wants to connect, what will my wife say? Will my boss be upset if I don't accept his friend request?

Then companies started to exploit the rich profiles of Facebook users to market their products and services. And companies looking for talent used Facebook to show off how cool they were to work for. In short order, Facebook has become the largest social network in the world. Other networks try to copy its technology, business strategy, and company culture. And because of its size and importance in society today, Facebook can no longer be ignored in your job search.

Following are the reasons Facebook is so essential when you're looking for a job in today's social media–focused world, from the most important reason to the least important one:

- ✔ **Facebook is the size of a large country.** No exaggeration here. As of this writing, Facebook has more users than the United States has citizens. The number of interconnections, relationships, and interactions between people in the network are infinitely complex, which presents a wonderful opportunity to meet new connections who may be helpful. It also means that your personal brand (see Chapter 4) can be exposed to more people and accelerate your career.

- ✔ **Potential employers are using Facebook to check you out.** And I don't mean they're gauging your attractiveness in order to ask you out on a hot date. Hiring managers are using Facebook to check out who you are outside of work — for example, does the person described in your profile match up with the person described in your résumé? They're also trying to decipher whether you'd be a good fit for their company, personality-wise. Not being present on Facebook can raise red flags and cause hiring managers to ask questions, such as "What is he hiding?" or "Does she really have no social life?"

- ✔ **You can use Facebook to find out more about a company.** Just as companies can get the inside scoop on you and your personality by looking at your Facebook profile, so too can you discover the facts about and vibe of a company by "liking" its Facebook *Page* — a public Facebook account designed for organizations to interact with customers who "like" them. You can also conduct your research about the company from its Page because all the links to the company's blogs and websites are right there, as well as information about benefits, culture, and other important HR information.

Not only can you find out a lot about the personality of organizations based on what they post and how they interact with consumers online, but you can also (in some cases) find out about job opportunities. Many companies today are using their Facebook Pages to attract new talent and interact with possible job candidates. So if you haven't "liked" your target company's Page yet, your competition may have already beaten you to it. Find out whether your target company has a Page by simply entering its name into the search bar at the top of your Facebook account. If a page pops up, navigate to it and click on the Like button.

Why aren't they talking to me?

Recruiters may not want to interact with you at all on Facebook. They may ask to be your friend, and they may take a look at your profile and your pictures, but they may not be totally comfortable talking to you there. Some recruiters may still, somehow, feel uneasy about nosing into your private life on Facebook. They know you've only accepted their friend request because you're hoping they'll hire you. And that interaction probably seems ingenuous on a network of friends. So unless you already know the person, expect to conduct your interactions elsewhere.

Tip: If you want to interact with recruiters directly, I suggest you do that via LinkedIn. LinkedIn's purpose is to facilitate the interaction between professionals, so people engage with each other much more professionally there.

Protecting Your Private Life

The social norms regarding what's considered private versus public have changed. Whether or not you're comfortable with it, people are going to find out information about you online sooner or later. Whether you want to be in control of what they find is up to you.

I can't tell you how many stories I hear where some smarty pants says the wrong thing on his Facebook Wall and winds up jobless and looking dumb the next day. Only *you* are responsible for the content you post to Facebook; the powers-that-be at Facebook can't be held responsible for you posting a picture of yourself frolicking on the beach when you told your boss you were deathly ill.

The privacy settings Facebook gives you by default are not necessarily the ones you want to maintain during a job search. If you don't want to learn this lesson the hard way, then you need to make some adjustments. The next sections walk you through how to properly manage your Facebook privacy settings so your profile always looks its best in case a hiring manager's eye comes upon it.

Facebook privacy basics

Once upon a time, the complexity of Facebook's privacy settings was enough to make you want to bang your head against a wall. Nowadays, they're much simpler to use. To access the privacy settings page, click on the Account button at the top of any page and select Privacy Settings from the drop-down menu that appears (see Figure 13-1). You can then change settings in any of the following categories:

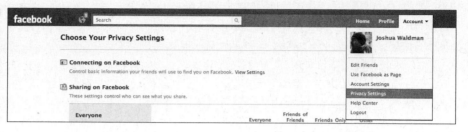

Figure 13-1:
Where
to find
Facebook's
privacy
settings.

✔ Connecting on Facebook

✔ Sharing on Facebook

✔ Apps and websites (as in the ones connected to your profile)

✔ Lists of blocked users and applications

Note: I don't actually cover privacy settings for apps and websites in this chapter, so feel free to explore them on your own.

The first two categories, Connecting on Facebook and Sharing on Facebook, offer a few different levels of privacy that you can select from. Here they are, in order of least private to most private:

✔ **Everyone:** Content you deem safe for everyone is indexed by Google and appears on your public profile (so hiring managers can see it). I always set my bio and links to be viewed by Everyone because they're a part of my personal brand; for the ins and outs of personal branding, flip to Chapter 4.

✔ **Friends and Networks:** This setting is for content that can be seen by second-degree connections and anyone who belongs to the same networks you do. (A *network* in Facebook land refers to a school or a company.)

✔ **Friends of Friends:** Any content marked with this label can be seen by second-degree connections.

✔ **Friends Only:** Only first-degree connections can view content with this label.

In the following sections, I go into detail about how to customize your privacy settings for connecting and sharing on Facebook. I also provide some recommendations for what to share (and who to share with) in each category of your Facebook profile.

The generational divide

In a study conducted by Pew Research, members of Generation X (people born between 1965 and 1980) and baby boomers (people born between 1946 and 1964) were far more careless with their online privacy than the Millennials (people born between 1981 and 2000). Shocked? I was. I expected to hear stories of twenty-somethings sharing photos of their beer bong toga party and getting canned for it. But actually, the opposite is true. Gen Xers and boomers are more likely to say something careless online, and because of their status in life, suffer far worse consequences.

Millennials, on the other hand, grew up with Facebook, e-mail, and texting. They've learned, either the hard way or vicariously, the real consequences of their online actions (perhaps what they said online last night came back to haunt them the next day at school). Meanwhile, many Gen Xers and older generations first started using e-mail when in college or at a new job and only recently started using Facebook. They're simply not used to understanding the new norms of online privacy and how to manage it.

Think of communicating online like speaking another language. Millennials grew up speaking the language of Facebook; Gen Xers and boomers learned it later in life.

Connecting on Facebook

As a job seeker, you want to be found. But you also want to control what information people can find about you. That's where the "Connecting on Facebook" category comes into play; it allows you to restrict what people see and who can contact you.

Facebook automatically makes your name, profile picture, gender, and networks visible to anyone and everyone. Sure, you can limit the number of people who can search for you and actually find you, but that's a little counterintuitive when you're looking for a job. After all, as I note earlier in this chapter, hiring managers are likely to search for your Facebook profile to scope you out. You want to be as open as possible to connecting without violating your own sense of privacy. Everyone has different comfort levels. So ask yourself, "How much am I willing to open up?" Personally, I'm okay with letting everyone be able to send me messages or friend requests (even if I don't accept all of them). However, I do like to keep my Friends list, likes, activities, and location private by setting them to be viewed by Friends Only, as shown in Figure 13-2. These pieces of information simply add nothing to my personal brand but have some meaning to my friends.

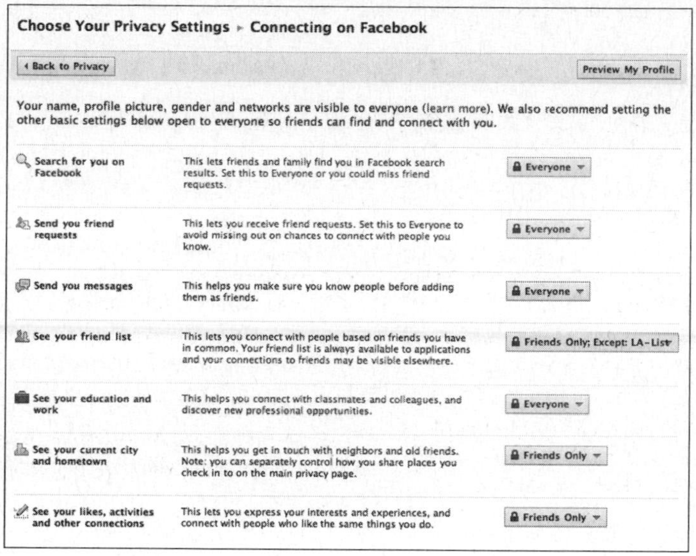

Figure 13-2:
Suggested
privacy
settings
for con-
necting on
Facebook.

Sharing on Facebook

Sharing settings relate to how you interact with Facebook. In other words, this category allows you to control who can view (and comment on) the various tidbits you decide to reveal about yourself. It also allows you to restrict who can see the comments other people post on your Wall and what they tag you in. *Remember:* You can't always control what your friends post, so you want to be extra careful with these settings.

Facebook offers a Recommended setting so users who don't want to spend much time on managing each and every privacy setting can simply choose their comfort level and be done. However, opting for Facebook's generic Recommended setting isn't good enough. As a serious job seeker, you want to understand every detail of what's being shared and with who. From the Choose Your Privacy Settings page, I strongly encourage you to click on the Customize Settings link under the Sharing on Facebook category. Tables 13-1 and 13-2 provide the necessary recommendations to help you own your personal Facebook privacy settings.

Table 13-1	Customizing What You Share	
The What	*The Recommended Setting*	*The Why*
Posts by you	Friends and Networks	If your post is seen by a friend's friend and members of any Page you "like," you want your personal brand to be communicated widely, so make sure your Wall posts are appropriate and that they communicate your brand. (Remember that you can always adjust the privacy of each individual Wall post later.)
Family	Friends Only	You don't need recruiters knowing the names of your parents, siblings, and other relatives.
Relationships	Friends Only	Who you're dating and whether you're married is too much information for non-friends, in my opinion.
Interested in	Friends Only	Whether you're interested in boys or girls has little bearing on your employability. Too bad you can't choose "I'm interested in a job."
Bio and favorite quotations	Everyone	Your bio and quotes can be keyword-rich value propositions that you want associated with your brand. No reason to hold this one back from the masses.
Website	Everyone	Include your LinkedIn profile and any other websites associated with you, such as your blog or online résumé. Doing so gives recruiters a chance to learn more about you.
Religious and political views	Friends Only	Always avoid religion and politics in professional settings.
Birthday	Friends Only	You want to be really careful with your birth date. It's one of those pieces of info that's often used to verify identity, which means it's one of the few things an identity thief needs in order to steal from you. So guard this with your life.
Places you check into	Friends Only	Facebook Places is an app that allows you to *check in* to a location to share with your friends where you are. Some places even give coupons for checking in there. Either way, it's too much information for a recruiter.

Table 13-2   Customizing What Others Can Share about You

The What	The Recommended Setting	The Why
Photos and videos you're tagged in	Friends Only	Because you can't exactly control what your friends tag you in, keeping photos and videos away from the curious eyes of hiring managers is the safer option.
Permission to comment on your posts	Friends Only	Your friends are your friends because you like them. Unless you're inviting strangers to comment on your posts, keep this setting controlled.
Suggest photos of you to friends	Enabled	Without this, Facebook just wouldn't be fun!
Friends can post on your Wall	Enabled or Disabled	You have to decide this setting on your own. I enable it because I know my friends won't say anything stupid, and I like giving them the option to interact with me this way. Even if they do post something stupid, I can always remove it. So the question here is this: Do you trust your friends?
Can see Wall posts by friends	Friends Only	Although having your friends comment on your Wall is a lot of fun, you can't control what they say, so I advise restricting this one just in case.
Friends can check you into Places	Disabled	That's just wrong!

If someone posts something on your Wall that you don't want others to see, you can always remove it. When you hover your mouse cursor over the post, a little X appears in the top-right corner. Clicking on it deletes the offending post from your Wall.

When you customize your "Sharing on Facebook" privacy settings, you can also control the level of privacy each individual photo album is set to. For example, you may want to share your New Year's Eve party photos with Friends Only but share your job fair photos with Everyone. You can set these options whenever you create new albums. If you already have some photo albums that you want to retroactively change privacy settings for, just click on the Edit Privacy Settings for Existing Photo Albums and Videos link on the Customize Settings page.

Tag, you're it!

In Facebook, people can tag you in Wall posts or in photos. A *tag* essentially associates your name with your friend's post or photo. If the photo is inappropriate, you need to untag yourself right away because that photo is subject to the privacy settings of the person who posted it, not yours. So even if you're very careful about what you post and you strategically manage your own privacy settings, you may still be caught in an embarrassing photo simply because your friend decided to share it on Facebook. ***Remember:*** Always pay attention to what you're tagged in.

While you're at it, you may want to do some house cleaning and check any past photos you've been tagged in and remove yourself if you don't like what you see. After all, you don't want to lose control of any images that may present you in a less than professional light.

Creating Block Lists

Perhaps you have one of those best friends who makes you laugh uncontrollably at his completely inappropriate jokes. Well, this buddy may become an annoying liability during your job search if he insists on posting those jokes to your Wall. Or maybe you keep getting invited to join someone's mafia gang or grow some cats on a cat ranch. Frankly, I find these games, as well as their invitations, annoying.

So what's the cure for ridding yourself of problem posters or immature games? Block 'em. Just navigate to the Privacy Settings page, look for the "Block Lists" category on the bottom of the page, and click on the Edit Your Lists of Blocked People and Apps link (see Figure 13-3). Follow any instructions, including where to type the people's names who need to be brought under control.

Lesser-known privacy features

Facebook constantly changes its user interface. Many of those changes go unnoticed but can seriously affect your privacy. Of course, the most visible changes get the most media attention, but what about those minor feature updates that not many people discuss? Some of the features I cover in the following sections are mostly unknown but can have a huge impact on how you use Facebook.

Wall post privacy

Many people don't know this, but you can choose the privacy level for each individual post you write on your Wall. At the bottom right of the post's text box, next to the Share button, click on the small padlock button to open up privacy settings for the text, link, picture, or video you're about to post (see

Figure 13-4). If you don't set this manually, the post defaults to your global privacy settings (see the previous section).

Figure 13-3:
Finding the
Facebook
Block Lists
link.

The Block Lists link

If you're smart, you'll post personal branding messages (any text, links, images, or videos that reinforce your professional image and talk to why you're different) to be viewed by Everyone and keep the rest of your messages to the default. So every couple of days, you may try a new version of your *value statement* — a statement that summarizes who you are and what makes you unique — and strategically leak it out to the public. (I help you craft a value statement in Chapter 5.)

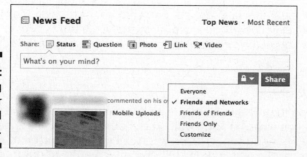

Figure 13-4:
Setting
privacy for
each Wall
post.

Limited Access lists

Using lists in Facebook is one of the most misunderstood yet powerful tools for the modern networker. By grouping certain friends together into a list, you can assign specific privacy settings to only that list.

As a job seeker, creating lists is your best defense against recruiters, bosses, or other professionals who want to friend you on Facebook but who you don't really know personally. Talk about an awkward situation! If you ignore their request, you may either offend them or signify that you have something to hide. If you accept their request, they now have penetrated all the work you've done with your privacy settings to make sure only your friends get access to your personal life.

I advise accepting such friend requests (so they don't get offended) but with a caveat: Create a "Limited Access" list of individuals and put recruiters and other professionals you don't know personally on this list so they can't see everything in your profile. Here's how:

1. **Click on the Account tab at the top of the page.**

2. **Click on Edit Friends from the drop-down menu.**

3. **Click on the Create a List button and name the new list "Limited Access," as shown in Figure 13-5.**

Figure 13-5:
Creating a Limited Access list.

4. **Scroll through your Friends list and add anyone to your Limited Access list who you may want to restrict certain information from.**

5. **Return to your Privacy Settings page and click on Customize Settings.**

6. **Go through the list of Things You Share, pick the Customize option from the drop-down menu, and add your Limited Access list under the "Hide this from" section, as shown in Figure 13-6.**

   This step allows you to pick and choose what you want to exclude these people from. For example, I don't want recruiters and other strangers to know who my friends are, what my religious views are, or when my birthday is.

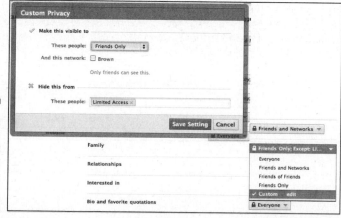

Figure 13-6: Excluding a specific list of people from select information.

When you have to add someone to your Facebook network that you really don't want to add, simply drop them into your Limited Access list. This way you avoid offending the person while still protecting your private information.

Facebook's secure browser

Facebook now offers secure browser settings (SSL) so no one can snoop on your connection to Facebook. SSL is a security feature used by bank websites, e-commerce checkout screens, and e-mail applications.

You have to manually turn on the SSL in your Facebook account. First, look at your browser window to see whether the address says http or https. If it says http, then navigate to Account Settings from the Account drop-down menu, click on the Change link next to Account Security, and then check the box for Secure Browsing (https).

Presenting the Missing Facebook Manual for Earnest Job Seekers

When you have your privacy settings under control, which I help you with earlier in this chapter, Facebook can be a very valuable resource for your job search and your career. You can communicate your personal brand, or unique message, through strategic parts of your profile. And you're able to take advantage of your trusted network to spread the news about what you're looking for and the value you bring to the table. After all, most jobs come from people you know through your network.

Whenever you invite new people to join your network, I encourage you to always include a customized message in addition to the standard message Facebook sends. After you click on the Add as Friend button, a box appears that allows you to add a personal message at the bottom of the friend request. Be sure to provide your new connection with some context on how you know each other and why you should connect.

When you first set up your Facebook account, I'm sure you didn't have professional networking in mind, so now's the time to revisit your profile and make some changes. If you're brand-new to Facebook, that's perfect. Nothing quite compares with starting from a clean slate. Either way, the following sections get you in tune with how to maximize your Facebook presence for the benefit of your job search.

Editing your profile for hiring managers' eyes

Your Facebook profile can be made visible to people who haven't joined your network yet. If you spend time and fill it in, then nosy hiring managers and recruiters can learn more about you. Your profile info also helps Facebook find new people to suggest you add to your network. The more accurate you are in your profile, the more accurate Facebook's suggestions are for who else you can connect with. Making sure your profile is filled out is worth the extra five or ten minutes.

In order to make updates to your profile, click the Edit Profile button on the top-right side of your profile page (see Figure 13-7).

The following sections cover the elements of your Facebook profile that are worth spending time on.

Figure 13-7:
Where to
click in
order to
edit your
Facebook
profile.

Click here

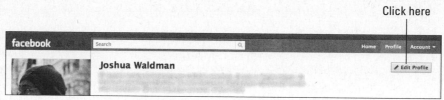

Your profile photo

In Facebook, your profile photo is attached to every communication you send and is considered basic information in your privacy settings. The reason is that Facebook is first and foremost a visual platform.

If you're actively seeking employment, use your LinkedIn photo as your Facebook profile image. Why? Because unless you're interviewing for a position at a nightclub as a dancer, you want your first impression on Facebook to be as professional as possible. For tips on taking a good profile photo, flip to Chapter 9.

Your About Me section

When you click on the Edit Profile button and scroll to the bottom of the page that appears (in the Basic Information page), you find a box called About Me that's just waiting for information about you. Your About Me section should serve a very similar function as your LinkedIn profile summary, in that it communicates who you are professionally and what makes you unique. The text you enter in this section appears publicly and may be the only prose a hiring manager conducting some preliminary screening may read about you on Facebook.

If you're actively seeking work, I recommend pasting a copy of your value statement in the About Me section of your profile (see Chapter 5 for guidance on creating a value statement). If you want to add a little bit more personality or personal information as well, lead with a professional statement of who you are and then conclude with a more personal statement, perhaps even mention some interests or hobbies.

Your Education and Work

Be sure to completely fill out your education and work history within your profile. Hiring managers are looking for inconsistencies (after all, some people lie on their résumés), so if they see that you're consistent with your résumé in several places, they're more likely to believe you.

Your Philosophy

I don't recommend that you fill in your religion or your political views in this section. However, sharing who inspires you and what your favorite quotes are can be powerful ways of differentiating yourself.

Spend time thinking about your role models and quotes that stick with you. (If you prefer to go the role model route, turn to Chapter 4 for an exercise that gets you thinking about who you admire most.)

All the other profile settings

Your Facebook profile also allows you to enter information about the types of music, books, movies, and TV shows you like, as well as your favorite sports teams, activities, and interests. Don't be afraid to fill in this information. Sharing it helps round out your personality in the eyes of a hiring manager. Just keep in mind that your selections should be appropriate; use the "Would I talk about it in the office?" test to be sure. Revisit these parts of your profile with your career in mind.

Practicing good Wall etiquette

The Facebook Wall is your venue for communicating with your network and letting people know who you are and what you're looking for. The Wall is an amazing platform for expressing yourself, but you need to use it wisely. The sections that follow offer some general guidance on Wall etiquette.

Don't be desperate

Avoid posts like, "Help! I need a job. Can you pass my résumé on?" You don't want to come across as desperate. And you don't want people's help out of pity. Remember, your goal is to provide value and be upbeat.

Start conversations

Unless you're a celebrity, posting about yourself all the time won't get you many comments. You may have to start conversations from time to time. Ask questions, post an article and share your opinion of it, bring up something from current events — all of these ideas can kick-start a conversation with members of your network.

You can also turn other people's posts into more interesting conversations by commenting and getting the conversation ball rolling.

You may be filtered out: The importance of interaction and the two-week rule

A new feature in Facebook's *News Feed* (the home page that shows you what your network is doing) is now automatically set to show posts of only people you've recently interacted with. So if you aren't interacting with the most important people in your network on a regular basis, they may stop receiving your updates, and you may miss out on important interactions and connections.

Facebook users speculate that you have two weeks after a person has joined your network before they become blind to your Wall posts if you don't interact. If you consider people in your network to be important in your job search (for example, they're well connected or willing to help), be sure you comment on their Wall posts, include them in your own Wall posts with tags, poke them, or interact with them every two weeks. Doing so ensures that they continue to see your newest Wall posts.

Share industry-related content

At least once a week, post something related to your industry and set the privacy to Everyone (I explain how to manage the privacy settings of your Wall posts in the earlier "Wall post privacy" section). Sharing your opinion about professional issues can help position you as an expert.

Following are some ways to include industry-related content on your Facebook Wall:

- ✔ Link to articles about your target industry.

- ✔ Share your comments about a particular article. Your Wall shows your (hopefully) intelligent comment and a link to the article.

- ✔ Run competitions where you can be the judge of the winner. For example, you can ask your network for the best idea to solve some industry-related problem.

- ✔ Share a story from your professional life that shows you in a good light.

- ✔ Post an "Ask Me" post where people can ask you questions about your industry and you answer them. For example, "Are you working in a hospital and have no idea why things are done a certain way? Ask me and I can help explain."

Ask for introductions

Nothing's wrong with asking your network for a little help sometimes. Because the power of your network is in who the people in it know, the best thing you can do to help yourself is to ask for introductions.

Be specific when asking for a referral. For example, don't ask, "Does anyone have connections at a CPG company in marketing?" Instead, say something like, "I'm looking for work as a business analyst at a CPG company. Do you know of anyone in marketing at Purina?" You inevitably get much better results if you can say the name of the company and the exact role of the person you want to meet.

Pitch your value (statement)

A great way to let people know who you are and what you're all about is to post your value statement on your Wall. (I help you create a value statement in Chapter 5.) An added bonus of posting your value statement on your Wall is that you can ask for direct feedback about it regarding what works and what doesn't. As long as you don't overdo it — meaning don't post your value statement every day — your friends will give you feedback and help you make your value statement better.

If you're confident about posting your value statement on your Facebook Wall, you can set the post privacy to Everyone so that Google and unconnected people can see your statement.

Journal your job-search journey

Use Facebook as a platform to share your job-seeking progress with friends and family. Let them know what steps you took that week to find work. Share interesting insights about yourself or about job seeking in general. Celebrate your successes, like having finished your résumé or getting a callback from a target hiring manager.

Tracking your Wall's appropriateness with Reppler

Reppler (www.reppler.com) is a simple Facebook Wall scanning tool that monitors your pictures and Wall posts for tone, appropriateness, and any telltale signs of someone hacking your account. To use this tool, simply log in with your Facebook account and give it a few minutes to scan your Wall. Using Reppler is a great way to keep your Wall clean during your job search. Also be sure to sign up for weekly e-mails to make sure any new posts you accumulate aren't harmful to your reputation during your job search.

Don't get pulled in!

This chapter was the hardest one for me to write. Why? Because every time I visited Facebook to capture a screen for my figures, I was inevitably distracted by someone's Wall post. "Oh! Look at what Meri is doing in Hawaii!" And before I knew it, I was deep inside Facebook's comfortable labyrinth and struggling to find my way back to writing this chapter.

I'm not the only one who experiences this draw to Facebook. Sociologists are busy conducting studies about how Facebook is changing our behavior. Neurologists are busy discovering dopamine connections with Facebook and Twitter use. So if you find yourself getting pulled in, it may not be completely your fault. It may be changes in collective behavior as well as the facts of our neurochemistry. Just do your best to stay focused.

Ironically, sometimes the people closest to you are more reluctant to help. But if you post about your job-seeking journey so that friends and family can see how committed you are to finding a better position, then they may be more serious about offering to support you and make introductions for you. That's exactly what happened for a client of mine who had a history of job-hopping on Wall Street. His behavior wasn't a problem before the market crashed. But when the job market got very competitive with many brokers out of work, his reputation caught up with him. His friends and family had been disappointed with his inability to settle down, and so they were unwilling to risk their own reputations to help him out. He used Facebook to start journaling his progress and through targeted Wall posts he was able to reinforce his commitment. Slowly, his friends' and family's resistance wore down and they began to see him in a better light. In the end, it was an introduction on Facebook that landed him his next position.

Perusing Facebook Job Apps

Unlike LinkedIn, which I tell you all about in Chapter 9, Facebook wasn't designed for professional networking. Consequently, seeing what companies are in your network and what opportunities your connections may know about isn't that easy. That's why several companies have developed Facebook applications designed to fill this need. I highlight the best ones in the next sections.

BranchOut

In early 2010, Facebook acquired a small startup called BranchOut. BranchOut does one thing: It offers LinkedIn-style functionality to your Facebook network. Because of Facebook's official endorsement of this app, every job seeker should take a serious look at BranchOut.

After you install BranchOut by visiting www.branchout.com and connecting the app to your Facebook account, you're offered a chance to import your LinkedIn profile in order to populate your BranchOut profile. This means you don't have to rewrite your entire résumé again. After you're in, you can make further edits to your new Facebook résumé.

The most powerful feature BranchOut provides is allowing you to see what companies are in your Facebook network and what people in your network you can ask for an introduction to. Because your BranchOut profile is essentially the same as your LinkedIn profile and is viewable by second-degree connections, finding people to get introductions to on Facebook is much easier. If you want to meet someone at a company, just use the "Ask for Introduction" feature.

Simply Hired

Simply Hired is the world's largest job aggregation service. I'm a big fan of it as a job board because the Simply Hired folks were early adopters of a LinkedIn integration that let you see who was in your LinkedIn network for each job posting. This feature allows you to network with people who work at the hiring company rather than just blindly apply to it. They've taken this a step further and now offer powerful connections with a Facebook integration.

After you've integrated Simply Hired with your Facebook account by visiting www.simplyhired.com and clicking the Login with Facebook button at the bottom of the page, you can use Simply Hired not only as a normal job board but also as a list of your Facebook friends to see who works or used to work at the companies you're searching for.

When you find someone you know who works at a company you may want to target, Simply Hired lets you send that person a private Facebook message. You can also see your list of friends organized by company. My favorite part is the Where Your Friends Work page, where you can see interesting statistics about your network as well as Simply Hired's suggestions for a good search.

I think Simply Hired is one of the best services available for job seekers because it's been willing to adopt social media early on and it doesn't assume that everyone wants to simply apply to every job on its site. Simply Hired makes networking easier.

Innovate CV

Based out of the U.K., Innovate CV (www.innovatecv.com) started as an online résumé service. Now it offers job-search related courses, web video TV, and help in producing video résumés. With Innovate CV, you can import your LinkedIn profile content and then design a nice-looking online résumé. With the Innovate CV Facebook app, you can then manage this online résumé right from your Facebook account. You can also post to your Wall, ask for feedback, send your CV to anyone via Facebook, and even enter a CV competition to win a prize.

To set up your own Innovate CV app, search for "Innovate CV" in the Facebook search bar and choose The App, not the Fan Page.

Innovate CV really adopted Facebook early as its primary medium for networking and sharing. Innovate CV's designs are attractive, and it's growing as a company. I think it offers a valuable service and would suggest any job seeker use it regularly.

Jibe

Jibe (www.jibe.com) is an experimental job board and recruiting tool empowered by social media. First, you connect your LinkedIn and Facebook accounts to your Jibe account; then you can see job listings based on who you know. Jibe is different from traditional job boards in that you can actually apply to the job on Jibe without having to leave the site. Jibe sends the hiring manager your résumé and a filled-out application that includes your social media profiles with who you know.

Jibe also shows you some interesting tidbits about your network, including which industries are represented, what the most common job titles are amongst your friends, and even the unemployment rate of your network as it compares with the national average. I highly recommend using Jibe as a launching-off point for discovering opportunities and for leveraging your network to find out more about target companies.

CareerAmp

CareerAmp is a very simple career plug-in for your Facebook Page. All it asks you to do is identify three industries you're targeting for your career. After you install it, you can search for opportunities within those industries and share those opportunities to your Wall or network. (This can be a great way to pay it forward, especially if you find an opening that someone you know may qualify for.) You can also see your friend network and look at what companies your friends work for.

To get CareerAmp, type it into the search bar at the top of your Facebook screen, click on the results page, and then click on the Go to App button.

CareerAmp is still in Beta, and I haven't seen any new features in a while. So although seeing your friends based on where they work is interesting, this app may be useful to only some people. I think CareerAmp is worth checking out, but you can be the judge of whether the information it gives you is useful.

InTheDoor

InTheDoor (www.inthedoor.com) is a job-opportunity search tool that cross-references your Facebook friends and where they work with job listings on Indeed (www.indeed.com). When you first log in using your Facebook account, you see a list of the top companies represented by your network and how many jobs they've posted. So instead of searching for jobs based on location or industry, InTheDoor searches for jobs based on who you know.

InTheDoor is a cool way to use a job board because it gives you results based on who's in your network. At the very least, if you use this tool, you can visualize just how powerful Facebook is for your career.

Buying Targeted Ads to Promote Yourself

Facebook ads appear on the right side of a user's Facebook Page. Everyone sees different ads because the ads are targeted to you based on your demographic and your interests. Why do you need to care about ads on Facebook? Because if you take out an ad for yourself, that ad may just lead to a connection that in turn leads to a job.

Read about what marketing professional Marian Schembari did to jump-start her career. She'd heard about other people targeting ads at employees of certain companies on Facebook, so she decided to do it herself. Marian took out an ad (see Figure 13-8) for each of her target companies and made many powerful connections. In fact, one of the connections introduced her to the person who soon became her next employer. For $100 over just two weeks, I'd say the ad was well worth her time and money.

The following sections fill you in on the points to consider about Facebook ads and walk you through the process of creating one.

Figure 13-8:
Marian
Schembari's
successful
Facebook
ad.

What to keep in mind

Taking out an ad costs money. You actually pay per 1,000 impressions, also known as *CPM* (M is the Roman numeral for 1,000, thus *Click per 1,000*). Sometimes you can pay per click, or *CPC*. Facebook recommends the best option for you based on your selections.

Following are some additional tidbits to keep in mind if you're considering buying a Facebook ad to promote yourself:

- ✔ The most successful ads target specific companies and use the company's name in the headline text.

- ✔ *Location targeting* — where you can limit which area the ad is shown — doesn't return good results alone. You also have to limit demographics, interests, and so on to focus your audience.

- ✔ The more money you're willing to spend on an ad, the more results you're likely to get. (The standard budget for a job-seeking Facebook ad is about $50 per week.)

- ✔ Using Facebook ads really only works for larger companies that have many employees currently using Facebook. I don't suggest trying to use an ad to get the attention of a small business.

- ✔ Don't expect a straight shoot. You'll still have to use your networking skills to work your way to the right person. Your first contact may only be the first step.

How to create an ad

Setting up your very own Facebook ad campaign for networking and for job seeking is actually pretty simple. Just follow these steps:

1. **Scroll to the bottom of any page on Facebook and click the Advertising link.**

2. **Click on the green Create an Ad button.**

3. **Enter the domain name (URL) of where you want your ad to direct people when they click on it.**

   You may choose to link your ad to your LinkedIn profile, VisualCV, Innovate CV, personal blog, or a landing page that captures visitors' information and tracks who downloads your résumé.

4. **Type in the Title and Body of your ad and select the image you want to use, as shown in Figure 13-9.**

   I suggest you spend some time crafting your title and body copy in a word processor before logging into Facebook. Think about what you can say to get the attention of your ideal person. Remember that you aren't selling yourself yet, you're just selling the click. Your goal with the ad copy is to get the person to click.

   Use a version of your LinkedIn profile picture for the image. Doing so gives your brand a sense of consistency and professionalism.

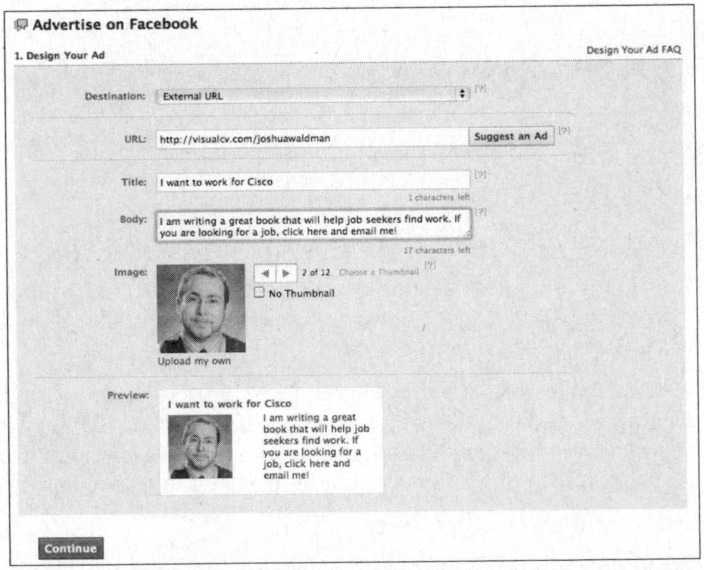

Figure 13-9:
Creating a
Facebook
ad.

5. **Click on Continue and enter your demographic information.**

   This step is where you filter it down so that only people who work in your target company see the ad, as shown in Figure 13-10. I recommend being as specific as you can with your selections. Even if your ad is shown to only 1,000 people, that's okay. Note that you have to click on Show Advanced Targeting Options in order to choose the workplace.

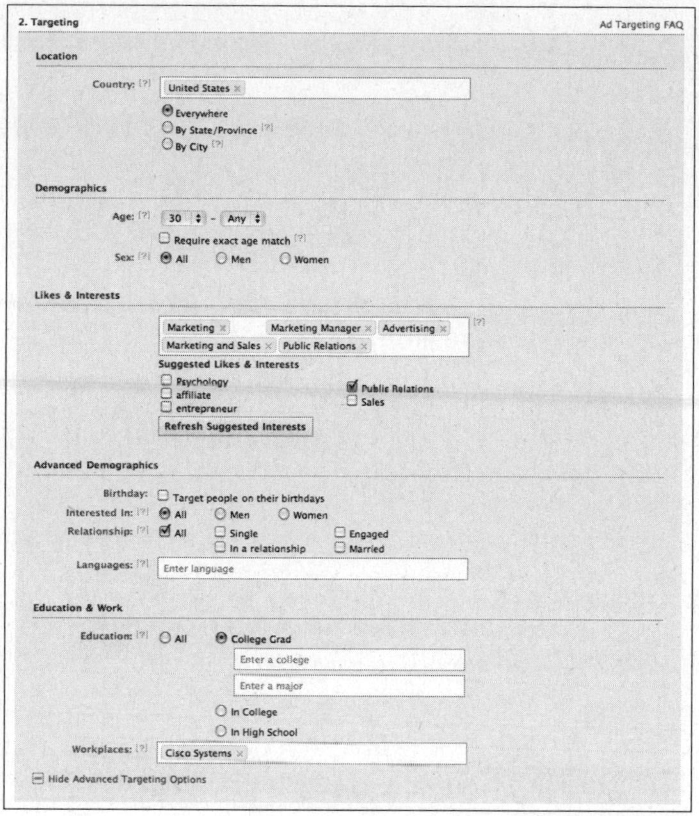

Figure 13-10:
Targeting
your ad to
a specific
company
or demo-
graphic.

6. **Choose your budget and time frame (see Figure 13-11).**

The more you spend, the more your ad shows up. Think about spending about $10 per day. This doesn't mean you will pay $10 a day, it just means your charges won't exceed that amount.

Run your ad for one-week intervals. Each week, change something in your campaign. Then compare each week's results. If your change increased the number of people clicking, then it was an improvement. Continue the campaign until you feel you've made progress in your job search.

7. **Review and place your order.**

You're prompted to enter your credit card information at this point. Before you do, take several moments to look over all your ad information very carefully. Make sure everything's correct and that the ad looks the way you want it to.

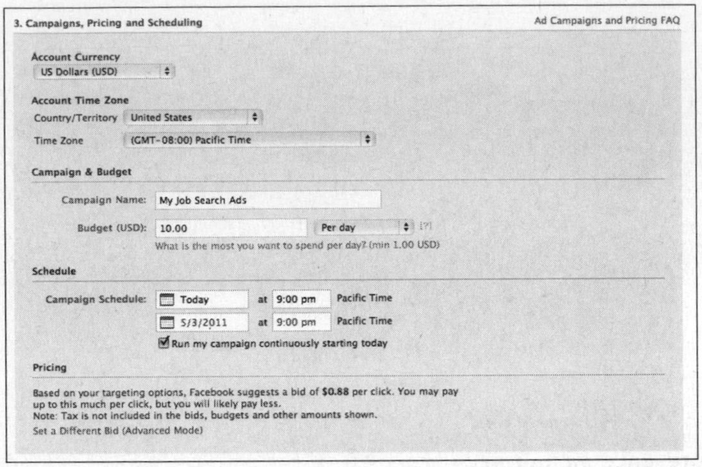

3. Campaigns, Pricing and Scheduling   Ad Campaigns and Pricing FAQ

Account Currency
US Dollars (USD)

Account Time Zone
Country/Territory   United States
Time Zone   (GMT-08:00) Pacific Time

Campaign & Budget
Campaign Name: My Job Search Ads
Budget (USD):   10.00   Per day   [?]
                 What is the most you want to spend per day? (min 1.00 USD)

Schedule
Campaign Schedule: ☐ Today   at 9:00 pm   Pacific Time
                     ☐ 5/3/2011   at 9:00 pm   Pacific Time
                     ☑ Run my campaign continuously starting today

Pricing
Based on your targeting options, Facebook suggests a bid of **$0.88** per click. You may pay
up to this much per click, but you will likely pay less.
Note: Tax is not included in the bids, budgets and other amounts shown.
Set a Different Bid (Advanced Mode)

Figure 13-11:
Selecting
your budget
and time
frame.

Tracking your campaign in real time is important so that you can make small adjustments to improve it. With Facebook's ad analytics, you can see how many clicks you're receiving and how much money you're spending. You can then widen your demographic filters if you aren't getting enough clicks to expand how many people see the ad. Or you can make small changes to the ad copy if you think it can be more effective.

Respond to e-mails and requests from your ad campaign right away. You're spending good money to make these connections, so don't delay when someone shows interest in your ad.

Taking out a Facebook ad isn't for everyone. If you feel that you can't pull this off, then you probably better not try it. Advertising your employability takes a certain type of brashness, and not everyone can pull it off. In fact, there are more failed attempts than successes. So be sure you're really comfortable putting yourself out there before trying.

Chapter 14

Getting Familiar with Lesser-Known Sites for Job Hunters

In This Chapter

▶ Joining additional social networking sites to benefit your job-search strategy

▶ Managing your presence on multiple networks

▶ Surveying a variety of professional networks, from the general to the niche

*Y*ou may think that using one social networking site during your job search is good enough. For the average person, this may be true. But if you're trying to separate yourself from your job-seeking competition, then what's good enough for most people shouldn't be good enough for you. (After all, even LinkedIn isn't free from certain limitations, such as having weak visual portfolio elements, language limitations for international networking, and poor contact management features.)

In this chapter, I spell out why having membership in multiple online networks is beneficial for you as a job seeker. I also introduce you to several online networking sites to join (*other* than LinkedIn, Twitter, and Facebook). Choose a few that make sense for your career.

Casting a Wide Net for Success

LinkedIn is the highest-leverage tool for any professional at any stage in his or her career. However, LinkedIn doesn't hold a monopoly on professional networking, and other sites have emerged as key players. Ultimately, the more online profiles you have, the better your chances are of getting found. Think of using online profiles like casting a net to catch fish. You want to facilitate the possibility of a recruiter finding you and reaching out to you. Although you can't control who finds you, every profile you create increases your chances, the same way casting a net rather than using a line ups your odds of catching multiple fish.

The question is, with so many networks to manage, won't you just be wasting your time? Although that's a possible risk, following these tips can help make managing multiple networks much easier:

- **Establish a weekly routine or checklist with each of your networks and visit them at least once per week.** Using a checklist for your weekly routine is a great tool because you don't have to rethink about the same things each week.

- **Use the same username/password combination on every network.** Doing so lowers the physiological barrier to using them. If the annoyance of having to remember a password is the first experience you have with a website, chances are you won't go there much.

Change your password every six months. Although the chance that someone will hack into a social networking site and steal data from the actual network itself is always present, updating your password twice a year can be useful in helping you avoid these hackers.

If you happen to use any kind of Google service (such as Gmail or Picasa), then you have an easy way of consolidating all the various social networks you participate in, thanks to your Google Profile (which you already have because you use a Google application — if you don't have a Google account yet, setting one up is easy and free and I highly recommend it). Think of your Google Profile as the way Google displays information about you online. (Don't worry: Your profile doesn't display any private information unless you explicitly tell it to.) You can use your Google Profile as a holding account for all the networks you're active in by simply adding links to each of your social networks, which can help you keep track of where you have profiles.

Follow these steps to claim and customize your Google Profile:

1. **Visit www.google.com/profiles and click on the Sign In link on the top-right corner to see your profile link.**

   Remember that if you already use any type of Google application, you shouldn't have to create a Google Profile from scratch.

2. **Upload a photo.**

   I suggest using the same one from your LinkedIn Profile.

3. **Copy in your value statement in the Introduction area.**

   Flip to Chapter 5 for help creating a value statement if you don't already have one.

4. **Add links to sites containing more information about you, such as your LinkedIn profile and website.**

!K09g1ga9ak#: Setting a secure but easily memorable password

If you struggle with remembering passwords, here's a little trick to help you generate a very strong password that's still easy to remember and difficult for anyone to hack:

1. **Think of something in your life that's easy to remember but has a longer name.**

   For example, say you visited Alaska and you toured a small town called Kongiganak.

2. **Substitute some of the letters with numbers.**

For example, an *o* can be a 0, an *n* can be a 9, an *i* can be a 1, an *e* can be a 3, and so forth. In the Alaska example, I would do this: K09g1ga9ak.

3. **Augment the transformed work with some expletives, such as !, @, or #.**

So the example password becomes !K09g1ga9ak#.

Choosing the Right Networks to Join

Keep in mind that you're not expected to join every single networking site that comes your way. Before joining a site, think about what you're trying to accomplish and what your strategy is. For example, if you're looking for an international job, then consider some of the more internationally focused networks. If you're a creative professional and want to display your work and get found by specialized recruiters, then consider joining one or two networks for professional creatives. (I share some lesser-known networking sites for international jobs and creative types later in this chapter.)

The trick to social networking is simple: Join the networks that have the highest leverage to get you where you need to go. The big three (LinkedIn, Facebook and Twitter) should be low-hanging fruit for you. They have, by far, the largest number of members. But some other, more niche networks may help you achieve your goals as well. So consider joining one or two lesser-known networks in addition to the big three.

The only downside to joining several networks is not having the time to stay active on them. If you find yourself not able to keep up with all your networks, delete the one you're the least active in. Deleting your account is much better than letting a forgotten profile languish in obscurity. Whatever you do, don't let inactive profiles hang around forever. As your personal brand changes over time, these forgotten profiles can be red flags for hiring managers if they stumble across them. Your online profiles should be your assets; manage them accordingly.

Taking a Look at Professional Networking Sites besides LinkedIn

Many creative people are starting networking sites. Some of them are simply variations on existing ideas, like LinkedIn look-alikes, and others are unique combinations of ideas, like what happens when you mash Facebook with LinkedIn. Even though the sites in this section aren't as popular as Facebook or LinkedIn, they may still have some benefit. Not only do they help you cast a wider net, but also they help facilitate interactions that may turn out to be valuable some day. So whatever your motivation for expanding beyond LinkedIn, try these networking sites out and see whether you like how they work.

Brazen Careerist

Brazen Careerist is a social network designed to provide a platform for young professionals to express their ideas and interact with one another. On the Brazen Careerist site (www.brazencareerist.com), Facebook meets LinkedIn in the sense that most discussions are about professional topics, but there's no shyness around talking with new people — in fact, members are encouraged to comment and interact with one another. The site's founders, Penelope Trunk and Ryan Pough, believe that "your ideas are your résumé" — meaning you don't have to fill out your past work, school, or anything else to complete your profile. Instead, the ideas you bring to the collective discussion are more important.

Every day, Brazen Careerist features blog posts from active members. These blogs can help grow your professional exposure. (In fact, many of my articles from www.careerenlightenment.com have been featured on Brazen Careerist and have sparked a lot of interesting discussions.) Brazen Careerist also encourages local, face-to-face networking. I've attended Portland's Brazen Careerist happy hour several times and met some key people in my professional network.

One of Brazen Careerist's most innovative contributions to the world of social networking is called *Networking Roulette*. It takes the basic idea of being thrust into a random video chat but with professional networking as the main focus. When you participate in Networking Roulette, you have three minutes to talk with the other person and choose whether they can help your network. Each month, Brazen Careerist changes the theme. One month it may be on mentorship; another month it may be on leadership.

I highly recommend joining Brazen Careerist for a couple of reasons. First, major companies look for fresh new talent here. Because they totally get that "ideas are your résumé," the fact that you're showing what you *can* do, not what you *did,* makes it easy to move into new job roles. Second, most of the people on Brazen Careerist want to expand their network and typically show genuine interest in helping others.

Biznik

Biznik (`www.biznik.com`) is a community of small business professionals looking to network their services by fostering in-person interactions. I take some risk mentioning Biznik here because its main focus isn't for job seekers; however, if your job search is primarily focused on finding work at a small business or if you have aspirations of starting your own business, then Biznik is a very active community to join.

Apart from offering face-to-face networking events in most cities and towns, Biznik boasts of being Google friendly. In fact, users can update their tags and Google Summary on their profile in order to better control how they appear on search results. This summary connects to every article they publish in the Biznik community, so a user's reward for participation is possible higher Google rankings.

Biznik really is focused on small business, so don't expect to find glaringly obvious job opportunities. Use it, instead, to research small businesses in your community that you can network with and provide some value to.

Focusing on International Networking Forums

LinkedIn isn't the only game in town. Non-English-speaking countries have adopted other professional networks, and in some cases, professionals in some countries use only these networks. If you're pursuing a career overseas, then make sure you sign up for at least one of the networks I mention in this section. All these networks use a *freemium model,* which means they allow you to sign up and use basic features for free. Advanced features cost a nominal amount of money.

Viadeo

Viadeo (`www.viadeo.com`) is an up-and-coming networking site in Europe. It has 35 million professionals in its network from around the world with fast-growing adoption in Asia. For job seekers looking for work in Europe, China, and India, joining Viadeo is a must. Indeed, one of its major sources of revenue comes from offering professional recruiters selective access to their database.

Similar to LinkedIn, Viadeo offers users the following features:

- ✔ A clean and simple user interface
- ✔ Status updates
- ✔ Job postings and events
- ✔ Interest groups called *Communities*
- ✔ Professional recommendations

Finding other professionals with Viadeo's search feature is easy. You don't have to be connected to anyone in order to send messages, which opens up a lot of possibilities for reaching out and communicating with new people. Viadeo is robust enough that any strategy you use in LinkedIn (like the ones I note in Chapter 9) would work here as well. It took me only ten minutes to set up an account and complete my profile. Creating a profile is worth the time just for a chance to use the search feature and see who you may be able to connect with.

One issue that Viadeo struggles with, and something LinkedIn handles quite nicely, is that many people don't fill out their profiles completely, which makes it difficult to get a feeling for who you're connecting with. Part of the issue is that Viadeo doesn't tell you that your profile is only 80 percent complete (as LinkedIn does). So without an incentive to fill everything out, members tend to just enter a minimal amount of data. Of course, if you add more complete information, you can really stand out.

XING

XING (www.xing.com) is an international version of LinkedIn. Over the last several years, XING has acquired social networks in various European countries, including Italy and Turkey. According to the site, XING operates in more than 17 different languages, and its more than 10 million users come from over 200 different countries. Clearly, XING is the network to consider joining if you're looking for a job in Europe.

Functionally, XING differs from LinkedIn in that e-mailing someone despite your degree of connection is much easier. The user interface is also considerably different than LinkedIn, which alone has won over many fans in the U.S. who are frustrated with LinkedIn's ever-changing and increasingly confusing interface. One of my favorite features is the integration with Google Maps that allows you to see your contacts based on where they live. For those job seekers looking to relocate for work, this feature may be really handy.

If you're on LinkedIn, some of XING's features may seem familiar to you, including the following:

- ✔ A list of connections and options to import your address book
- ✔ Events, jobs, and groups
- ✔ A long list of applications you can plug in to your account for functions that range from personal productivity, carpooling, team management, and document management
- ✔ An option to go Ad Free for premium members
- ✔ Low-cost premium membership options ($5 to $10 a month)

Because XING is a German company, it really is most useful in Germany. Despite its concerted efforts to expand to other countries, as of the writing of this book, the vast majority of users are still German.

Ecademy

Ecademy (www.ecademy.com) was founded in 1998 by two British IT professionals (Penny Power and Thomas Power) to provide an online social networking forum focused on small business owners and solo business owners. Several hundred thousand people from 200 countries use Ecademy. This social network is particularly valuable to join if you're a European small business professional (especially if you're looking for work in the U.K.).

One of the more interesting features of Ecademy is the ability to set up an automatic e-mail to anyone who's visited your profile. For a job seeker, that may be an opportunity to follow up with more info or links about you, such as your LinkedIn profile or online résumé.

When it comes to user interface, I find the navigation of Ecademy to be frustrating, and I'm interrupted with a pop-up to upgrade every time I go to a new page. Furthermore, I was bombarded with e-mails from Ecademy until I figured out that I needed to opt out of them in the contact settings.

Browsing Networking Sites for Visual Creative Professionals

If you're an illustrator, photographer, or some other type of creative professional, then you're probably frustrated at how limited LinkedIn can be. Not only does every LinkedIn profile look the same, but LinkedIn's profiles don't allow for the exhibition of a creative portfolio — a fact that can be quite off-putting if the quality of your work is one of the key factors in what makes you unique in the market. Following are some networking sites designed with you, the creative professional, in mind. Join at least one that shows your talents in the way you want them seen.

Behance

Behance is rapidly becoming the most powerful authority for creative professionals online. (Even global organizations, such as AIGA, Adobe, and MTV, have used Behance's technology to create portfolios for their work.) Much more than a portfolio generation website, Behance (www.behance.com) offers project management software, industry-specific job boards, award-winning blogs with advice for creative professionals, and a LinkedIn plug-in.

The Behance network of sites has four main categories:

- **The Behance Network:** This site (www.behance.net), shown in Figure 14-1, is the portfolio creation platform. Besides allowing users to set up an online gallery of their work, this network also hosts job postings, runs creative competitions, serves recruiters, and allows networking opportunities through interest groups. (And thanks to a new partnership with LinkedIn, you can now display your Behance portfolio directly inside your LinkedIn profile.)

- **Served Sites:** As content uploads into the Behance Network, it streams into industry-specific sites called *Served sites* (www.theserved.com), which include the following:

  - Branding Served
  - Digital Art Served
  - Fashion Served
  - Illustration Served
  - Industrial Design Served
  - Motion Graphics Served
  - Photography Served
  - Toy Design Served
  - Typography Served
  - Web Design Served

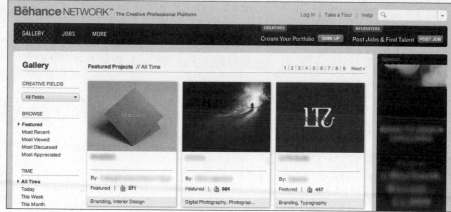

Figure 14-1:
Behance is
a network
for creative
professionals.

✔ **The 99Percent:** This site is the brainchild of Behance's CEO, Scott Belsky, and is the name of a blog, creative consulting service, and annual conference. The website, www.the99percent.com, contains great articles and resources for creative professionals of all kinds. Topics include playlists to listen to for better creativity, productivity tips, and video lectures from leading creative professionals around the world.

✔ **The Action Method:** Behance used its unique position of having access to thousands of top creative professionals worldwide to figure out what makes successful creatives productive. Through this research, Behance devised what it calls the *Action Method,* which is a project management philosophy that claims to "make ideas happen." The Action Method includes an online tool, iPhone app, and paper planners. Check it out at www.actionmethod.com.

Carbonmade

Creative professionals often struggle with finding ways of demonstrating their past work online. After all, you can't e-mail a physical portfolio or stumble across one through an Internet search. Setting up a website can take many hours of tinkering, and a lot of online portfolio sites charge monthly subscriptions. Carbonmade (www.carbonmade.com), on the other hand, is a free, easy-to-use portfolio builder that supports Google indexing and public facing profiles, which means there's a greater chance of someone finding your portfolio during a Google search of your name.

Your Carbonmade account gives you two main pages, one displaying your work and another with information about you. (Click the Examples button at the top of the home page and then select a sample portfolio to see what I mean.) The more content you include, the better your chances are of appearing on someone's list of search results.

Although Carbonmade isn't a community site, you can browse other people's creative portfolios; generally speaking, if they've included their contact info, they want people to contact them. Find other creative professionals on Carbonmade by entering your industry or keywords (see Chapter 5 for info on keywords) with the following code in a fresh Google search:

```
Site: carbonmade.com "[your keyword]"
```

For your keyword, try these search terms:

- ✔ Branding
- ✔ Copywriting
- ✔ Creative
- ✔ Designer
- ✔ Graphic Design
- ✔ Interactive
- ✔ Packaging

Carbonmade's free version only has a few designs and limits the number of pieces you can upload, so you have to be a bit picky about which items you display. Although it claims to be Google-search friendly, I haven't seen evidence of this. So be sure to link to your portfolio from LinkedIn.

FigDig

FigDig (www.figdig.com) is an online portfolio tool that allows you to upload images and PDFs to display in high-definition. It also has a job-posting section worth taking a look at. Although membership is free, FigDig displays ads to subsidize its revenue, which can make the site look a bit cluttered.

One distinction FigDig has from other online creative networking sites is that people can rate and leave comments on portfolios. Having this type of peer review may help you foster more engagement with your work and motivate you to post your best work. To see other professional portfolios on FigDig, just use its keyword search tool and type in related keywords.

Part V
Executing Your Proactive Social Media Job Hunt Strategies

The 5th Wave   By Rich Tennant

It was on the WhaleNet site one night that Capt. Ahab caught up with his obsession.

In this part . . .

You may know how to use the various social media tools at your disposal. You may even have the nicest looking LinkedIn profile on the block. But if you aren't proactively networking and looking for job opportunities with key decision makers, then all those tools are wasted.

In this part, I share a four-step method for a proactive job hunt online: *finding* the right people, *understanding* a hiring manager's issues, info *interviewing,* and then finally, *reaching out* to hiring managers. Follow these steps, and you'll find yourself months ahead of where most job seekers would be otherwise.

Chapter 15

Tracking Down Opportunities, Companies, and People to Target

Companies don't hire people. People hire people. Consequently, developing direct relationships with the people who have a hand in hiring is a better use of your time than trolling job boards and applying to the positions you find through them.

But how exactly should you go about developing those direct relationships? Consider this chapter your guide. In it, I explain how to identify the companies you want to work for and the people you need to connect with online and offline to get your name added to the employee roster.

First, I help you discover some new, social media–powered ways of finding hidden job openings — the kind you wouldn't know about otherwise. Then I help you peel back those opportunities to reveal the very people making the decisions about them. I guarantee you'll walk away from this chapter with a top ten list of companies and hiring managers that can help you begin focusing your social media job-search strategy.

Taking Advantage of Niche Job Boards to Find Opportunities

I'm sure you didn't buy this book to discover how to use job boards. In fact, I'm willing to bet you're already quite comfortable visiting one of the major job boards, like Monster, Indeed, or Simply Hired, finding possible fits, and then applying online. But because you still haven't found a suitable job, you've probably discovered that applying on these huge websites isn't always the best use of your time. Only a very small percentage — about 2 or 3 percent — of available jobs appear on job boards.

Don't get me wrong: Checking out the major boards can be helpful, but one of the better ways to find out who's hiring is to search the postings on *niche job boards,* which have smaller, regional or industry-specific listings. Niche boards generally have less traffic than the big ones, which means you have less competition to some jobs that appear only there. Employers who don't want to spend big money for a major board and who want to advertise the opening to only a narrow segment of the population, generally post jobs on niche boards. The following sections introduce you to three such boards. Happy browsing!

Using niche job boards to build a list of companies you want to target with your social media strategy is a terrific tactic. Just make sure you don't jump the gun and start applying to those companies immediately after identifying them. Before you apply anywhere, you want to be sure to research your target companies and their hiring managers in order to identify their real needs; I help you do just that in Chapter 16.

Using Google search strings to ID hidden job boards

Because more than 4,000 niche job boards are available on the Internet, many job seekers don't even bother trying to find them. The task just seems too daunting. Yet, very often, these niche boards hold the key to the best job postings.

Why do these boards offer the cream of the crop? Think of it this way: If a fresh, young company must choose between paying $600 to a major job board only to get tons of spammy résumés or paying a cheaper $60 to niche boards to get targeted résumés, it will likely choose the second option. The problem with these industry-specific boards is that they're smaller and often harder to find.

Here's the quick-and-easy way to find these smaller, hyper-focused, industry-specific job listings: Enter either of the following search strings, just as you see them here, in a fresh Google search, replacing *[your field]* with the name of the industry or field in which you hope to find a job. Be sure to keep the quotation marks intact as shown.

```
"[Your field]" Careers intitle: "job board"
```

```
"[Your field]" Careers intitle: "job listing"
```

Here's an example search string that I entered:

```
"Nonprofit" Careers intitle: "job board"
```

Then I entered this string:

```
"Nonprofit" Careers intitle: "job listings"
```

Try entering these search strings with marketing, accounting, teaching, design, or whatever your industry happens to be.

The International Association of Employment Web Sites (IAEWS) is an international association just for niche job boards. It has thousands of members from every field imaginable around the world. Its site is an amazing resource for finding a local or focused job board in your area. Go to www.employmentweb sites.org, click on Members, and then click on Browse by Industry/Area to see a listing of boards by industry and location.

Discovering the hidden uses of traditional job boards

Traditional job boards can actually be useful in ways that aren't so obvious. For instance, you can use them to

✔ Find out which companies are growing.

✔ Study what language is being used to describe what you want to do.

✔ Prepare your job interview skills by determining what's expected of you in similar positions.

✔ Analyze which industries and fields seem to be hiring more than others.

✔ Build a list of target companies to focus your strategy on.

Tip: If a company is hiring, take a look at its competitor. You can identify competition by using Hoover's (www.hoovers.com). The free version gives you the top three competitors for almost any organization. Looking at the competition is a great way to expand your list of target organizations. Even if the competition isn't posting jobs on any job boards, the company may still be hiring.

Automating craigslist for fast job-posting alerts

Despite the craziness of craigslist (www.craigslist.org), it's still a marvelous place to find up-to-the-minute job postings. (If you've ever tried to sell something on craigslist, you know that some people are nut cases!) In fact, if you were to walk into a business and ask the hiring manager about the first place he would post an ad for a new job, without much thought he'd likely say, "Oh, I'll just drop it on craigslist to get some résumés in the door." Craigslist is a great resource for part-time jobs, temp jobs, and entry-level jobs. Typically, jobs posted on craigslist are filled at a fast pace and can be a real solution for someone not interested in spending (or not in a position to spend) a lot of time on strategy or networking.

Although I typically recommend you spend time researching a company before applying for a job, listings on craigslist don't always allow for that. You want to apply when you can and as soon as you can, before someone else snatches the job right from under you.

Follow these steps to guarantee you're the first person to know about any new job postings in your area of interest without camping out on craigslist all day:

1. **Visit www.craigslist.org and go to the Jobs section you're interested in.**

2. **Type in all the necessary filters in the search field so you see specific jobs that interest you.**

   For example, if you're an educator, click on the Education link in the Jobs section and filter with the keyword "ESL." The results should be a list of jobs you could do pretty well at.

3. **Click the small, orange RSS button at the bottom of your results page (see Figure 15-1).**

4. **Copy the entire web address that appears on the RSS feed page's browser window.**

   (It'll be long and ugly, so use copy and paste for this one.)

5. **Open a new browser tab or window, head to the Feed My Inbox website (www.feedmyinbox.com), paste in that long web address and your e-mail address, and then click on the green Submit button.**

   You'll soon receive an e-mail asking you to confirm your feed by clicking a link.

6. **Click on the link that appears in your confirmation e-mail.**

   After you confirm the feed, craigslist sends you daily e-mails, providing information on any new job postings that match your criteria.

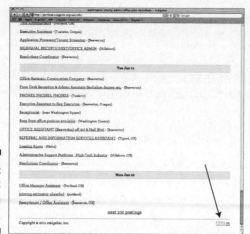

Figure 15-1:
The RSS
button on
craigslist.

The faster you respond to a craigslist posting, the more likely it is that some-one will read your résumé. So while daily e-mails are helpful, they may not help you beat the competition. You need more instantaneous information. For about $5 per month, you can upgrade your Feed My Inbox account so you receive updates the instant a company posts a new job matching your criteria to craigslist. Consider this small investment to improve your chances of get-ting hired and speeding up your job search.

As you find job opportunities on craigslist, remember to jot down the names of the companies. You need these names later when you search out people on LinkedIn to talk to. (I explain how to use LinkedIn as part of your job search in Chapter 9.)

Following Twitter for job postings

Almost every city has an entire hidden job market that's accessible only through Twitter. Even if you never send a single tweet, you can still take advantage of this underground market. Here are the four ways people post jobs on Twitter:

✔ **Local recruiters often post their job openings on Twitter first in order to test the level of interest and determine whether to post them to a job board later.** You can take advantage of this trend by finding recruiters on Twitter and following their tweets. Type in the keywords "recruiter" or "executive placement" at Twellow (www.twellow.com) and Listorious (www.listorious.com). (These two websites allow you to look up interesting Twitter bios based on keyword searches.)

✔ **Volunteer Twitter accounts aggregate and stream jobs posted in specific locations.** As a result of these volunteer accounts, local job-search channels are emerging in almost every city. You can find and follow them by searching for "*[your city]* jobs" at Twellow or Listorious.

✔ **Companies sometimes use their Twitter accounts to post jobs.** Some companies also have Twitter accounts specifically designed for recruiting. You can find these corporate Twitter accounts either by locating a link on the company's home page or by searching it out on Twellow.

✔ **Many leading brands use TweetMyJOBS (www.tweetmyjobs.com) to find talent.** TweetMyJOBS is a job board that's unique because it posts jobs only through a specific Twitter account for your industry and location.

Flip to Chapter 12 for more details on how to use Twitter to access the hidden job market in your area.

Preparing your résumé to respond to a craigslist job posting

Employers in your city post hundreds of new jobs on craigslist every day, and thousands of job seekers troll the site for chances to e-mail their résumés to a number of different companies. On average, a company's hiring manager stops reading résumés after the first hour of posting the job to craigslist. The manager gets so many that he could never read them all. So you have 30 to 60 minutes to send a somewhat untargeted résumé regarding a new opportunity.

Tip: If you plan to regularly respond to craigslist jobs, prepare three or four versions of your résumé that you can shoot off at any given moment. (Preparing just as many cover letters is a good idea, too.) Having some choices ensures that your résumé blast doesn't seem so generic to the hiring company. Here's how to make your résumé appear more targeted for speedy posting:

1. Identify three or four types of positions you typically want to apply to.

2. Look at the general duties and requirements for each.

3. Customize several versions of your résumé to address each of those requirements in turn.

4. In the "Professional Summary" section of each résumé, leave a field open so you can mention the hiring company by name.

   For example, you can say something like, "I'm very excited for the opportunity to work for *[fill in company name]* because . . ."

With this preparation, you can impress the hiring company by showing how fast you can tailor a résumé to the job posting.

Hello, Hiring Manager! Finding Decision Makers through Key Social Sites

Chances are that the people you need to talk to about future employment — the many hiring managers in the job market — are online. And lucky for you, a considerable amount of information is available about them. Just like in sales prospecting, knowing your key decision makers helps create your strategy and puts you in a competitive position during interviews.

In the following sections, I walk you through the steps for using two key social media sites (LinkedIn and Twitter) to track down hiring managers for the companies you're interested in.

Looking to LinkedIn for information

Ten years ago, you would have had to pay hundreds of dollars for the information that's freely available about companies on LinkedIn today. Every year, LinkedIn augments its features in the direction of turning company profiles into rich sources of information.

Using LinkedIn, you can follow changes in a company and be alerted to promotions, layoffs, and new hires. Companies also use this social media to display products, make status updates, and address the public. What's even more useful about LinkedIn is your ability to uncover great places to work and then find the exact people you need to talk to about employment.

To access LinkedIn's hidden list of recognized industries (shown in Figure 15-2), go to `linkd.in/browse-industries`. (Note that you need to be signed in to follow the link to the page.) From there, follow these steps to start building your list of companies and their hiring managers:

1. **Click on the industry that's most closely related to the field you want to work in, and then filter down your choices by location and company size.**

   Play with your filters until you get a list of about ten possible places to work.

2. **Follow each of the companies that appeal to you.**

3. **Click on the Employees tab at the top of the company's page and then again on the See More Employees link.**

   This link brings you to a people-search results page that allows you to filter that company's employees.

4. **Filter your search by location and add a keyword that's related to the role your hiring manager may have.**

For example, if you're hoping for a marketing job, type "marketing." If you're going for operations, type "operations." The keyword opens the search to contacts beyond your current network.

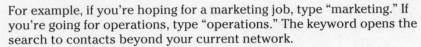

If you have a paid version of LinkedIn, you can also filter by seniority level to make sure you're viewing directors and managers.

After you pick out some hiring managers, you're ready to start gathering some information about them. Check out the later section "Picking up relevant information from LinkedIn profiles" for details.

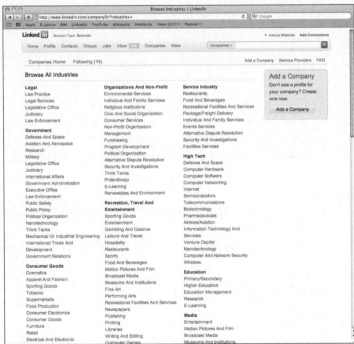

Figure 15-2:
You can browse industries on LinkedIn.

Seeking out key folks on Twitter

Many hiring managers maintain Twitter accounts. Following these managers on Twitter, reading what they have to say, and then ultimately interacting with them can put you ahead of the other candidates for a job.

When people have Twitter accounts, they often link those accounts to their LinkedIn accounts. So you're smart to check the profile of any hiring managers you find on LinkedIn (I explain how to find them in the preceding section). Also pay careful attention to the blue-shaded area at the top of their LinkedIn profile. If a hiring manager has linked a Twitter account to his or her LinkedIn profile, you can see it there in the blue box. Just look for the Twitter line to access a link to that person's Twitter account; this line is usually located just before the Public Profile line.

You also have the option of seeking out hiring managers directly from one of the many Twitter user directories. (Of course, if the person doesn't mention that she works at a particular company, you won't be able to find her unless you search for her name.) I recommend using a Twitter directory service like Twellow (www.twellow.com), Listorious (www.listorious.com), or Followerwonk (www.followerwonk.com). Check out Chapter 12 for tips on using these services.

With these services, you enter the name of the company, and then the directory tells you about any profile in which that company name was used. You can also check to see whether your target hiring manager is on Twitter by searching for her name directly. I suggest following this person and reading her tweets for a week before trying to engage with her. Listen first, talk second. Her bio or picture should clue you in on whether she's the right person. See Chapter 12 for tips on engaging with hiring managers through Twitter.

As you find and follow hiring managers, drop their Twitter username into a Twitter List called "Hiring Managers" and make that list private. This list allows you to track their tweets easily. (For details on how to create a Twitter List, see Chapter 12.)

Spying on Hiring Managers before They Spy on You

When you apply for a job, especially if you qualify and make it into the final group of ten applicants, chances are very high that the hiring manager will research you online. He'll look you up on Google, study your LinkedIn profile, and analyze your Twitter feed for any red flags. In essence, he's going to spy on you (cue the James Bond theme song).

Now that you know this, why not spy on the hiring manager first? You have the advantage because he'll be on your radar long before you're on his. After you complete the research I describe in the earlier "Hello, Hiring Manager! Finding Decision Makers through Key Social Sites" section and have uncovered the names of the very people who will be making a decision about your future, start your spy mission by using the methods I describe in the following sections.

Setting up Google Alerts with managers' names

Google Alerts is a service from Google that sends you e-mail notifications whenever a topic you've specified gets picked up online. Here's how this feature works: Google's robots scour the web at an incredibly quick pace finding new content, analyzing it, and indexing it. Google then sends the newly indexed web pages to your e-mail however frequently you choose to be notified. When Google alerts you, you get fresh content in near real time. Essentially, you get an e-mail when something new appears online related to the keyword you've set up.

Now that you know what a cool tool Google Alerts is, you can set up alerts for information on potential hiring managers. I walk you through the steps of setting up a Google Alert for yourself in Chapter 7. To modify those instructions for the purpose of getting the scoop on a potential hiring manager, just type the name of your targeted hiring manager in quotation marks rather than your own name.

Create a folder in your e-mail system to keep track of your Google Alerts about each specific hiring manager.

When analyzing the results of your alerts, look for the following information:

✔ News items you can mention during an interview or in an e-mail

✔ Similarities that you can lead with when you reach out to the person

✔ Articles the person has written or was mentioned in so you can congratulate her

✔ Red flags so you can determine whether the company is truly a match for you

Picking up relevant information from LinkedIn profiles

Earlier in this chapter, I show you how to use LinkedIn to find the hiring managers that you want to follow and, well, spy on. After finding these key folks, you can begin gathering information about them that you can use to connect on a more personal level. When looking at a hiring manager's profile on LinkedIn, pay careful attention to the following elements:

✔ **The school he went to:** School spirit can be a great topic to break the ice. USC grads are nuts about the Trojans. Boston school grads worship the Red Sox. Find out whether a manager's school has a strong school team or is noteworthy in some way. Then use this information to connect with him.

✔ **Similarities you share:** As you glance through a manager's profile, pay close attention to anything you have in common. Look at his interests, schools, and past jobs. When you reach out to him later, lead with a similarity.

✔ **The LinkedIn Groups he belongs to:** At the very bottom of a manager's profile, you often can find a list of groups he's joined. Look for industry-specific groups and then join them.

When you join the same LinkedIn Groups as a potential hiring manager, you gain access to the same stream of information he's getting. As you participate in that group, the hiring manager may see your name for the first time. Later, when he sees your job application, he may recognize you. (For advice on participating in groups, see Chapter 9.)

Some LinkedIn profiles are full of rich information about a person; other profiles are barely filled out. What does this imbalance mean for you? Simply that you're at the mercy of how much information a particular hiring manager decides to disclose. If one hiring manager doesn't give you much to go on in his profile, find his equivalent at a competing company. After all, you want to gain access to the most content-rich profile possible in order to further your job search.

Asking Your Social Media Network for Help

As you begin interacting with people on social media, becoming a valuable source of information to them, you grow what's called *social equity.* Social equity is like having money in the relationship bank. You keep depositing to that bank every time you do a good deed in the eyes of your network, such as retweeting, commenting on blogs, or helping someone make a valuable connection on Facebook. After you have enough relationship money, and only once in a while, you can make a withdrawal (in other words, you can ask your network to return the favor). Who knows when you may need to ask for an introduction or request a referral so your résumé gets to the top of the pile.

A common mistake people make is asking for help without building up any social equity. I had a client who rarely used LinkedIn when he was working. In fact, his profile wasn't even complete. Then he got laid off and e-mailed everyone in his network asking for help. Not surprisingly, no one jumped to his aid.

In contrast, I've interviewed many successful job seekers for my blog who were enabled to succeed through the generous help of their networks. The difference? The successful job seekers built up strong relationships over many months before making a social equity withdrawal in the form of asking for assistance.

The trick to asking your network for help is to never appear desperate or needy. If you're looking for general information about a company or an industry, sending out an unfocused, untargeted message is appropriate. However, if you're specifically asking people to step up and pass on your résumé or any other thing that would put their neck on the line, then ask on a one-on-one basis. Never send a mass e-mail to your contacts, asking whether anyone can pass on your résumé because you have nothing else to go on. Doing so may be perceived as offensive.

I've spoken with many people who were introduced to the person who hired them because they asked their network for help. One blog reader simply changed his LinkedIn headline to say, "Recently Unemployed." In a day, someone in his network made an introduction that got him hired two weeks later. This client was a very outgoing fellow who never hesitated to help people in his network and who spent years adding value. And frankly, he also got pretty lucky. Don't expect this to happen to you — but if it does, don't be surprised either!

Here are some effective ways you can ask your network for help.

- ✔ **Send mass e-mail updates to your connections every once in a while.** First, make sure you BCC people on the e-mail addresses so people aren't receiving the e-mail addresses of everyone else in your network. Also, if you haven't e-mailed these people in a while, you better build some equity first by giving them an update about your life and asking about theirs.

  For example, I receive a newsletter from a job-seeking friend of mine once a month. In the newsletter, she tells me some cool things she's doing in her life, shares some fun links, and then asks for a connection to a specific company. I enjoy reading about her journey, and because she uses a specific company by name, I can easily think about my own network and see whether I can help.

- ✔ **Always be very specific about what you need people to do for you.** Never say, "I just got laid off; does anyone know of any jobs out there?" Instead, say, "I'm looking for my next career opportunity, and I'm very passionate about optimizing supply chain processes. Do you have connections at an import/export firm in town that I can call on for advice?"

✔ **Make your mass messages (think e-mail blasts, discussions on a LinkedIn Group, or tweets to your whole audience) positive and undemanding.** These messages aren't the place to ask people to stick their neck out for you. Instead, use large groups of people for what they're good at: general info. Ask about industry trends, cool companies to look out for, what skills you may need to master, and so forth.

✔ **Ask for more specific help in one-on-one interactions.** For example, you may ask for someone to pass on your résumé, give you the name of the hiring manager associated with a specific job opening, or even just have informal conversations about an industry. This is where LinkedIn InMails, Twitter DMs, and personal e-mails — all of which are forms of direct, one-on-one contact — come in. You're calling in a favor, so find a way to make it easy and rewarding for someone to help you.

For the most part, people really do want to help you. Being helpful makes people feel good, especially if they can make a difference and their efforts are properly appreciated. If someone lends you a hand, always tell him exactly what his help has done for you by sending a short thank-you note.

Organizing All the Data You Gather

After about a week of researching target companies and the hiring managers within those companies, you may find that you have way too much information to keep in your head. Ultimately, you need some kind of system for organizing all the data you accumulate about people.

I recommend creating dossiers of important people in your network. (A *dossier* is a file or collection of information about someone.) Here are three services I like to use; pick the one you like best:

✔ **Gist:** Gist (www.gist.com) is an innovative, young startup company that has set a trend for social media–based customer relationship management (CRM) systems. Your Gist account collects all your contacts and presents them in a single interface. It also integrates all the social media profiles together. Visiting LinkedIn to find someone only tells you what that person says on LinkedIn, but Gist tells you what one person has said across multiple networks.

Gist also allows you to make notes about people. The program runs an automatic Google News report to tell you whether your targeted people have been in the news. When you print a dossier, all this information is available on a single page. (I explain how to use Gist in Chapter 3.)

- **JobKatch:** JobKatch (www.jobkatch.com) is a job-search organizing platform that keeps records of the opportunities, companies, and people you're targeting in your campaign. Each contact has a notes section where you can record similarities with yourself, groups joined, and any other data points you need to remember.

- **Becomed:** Becomed (www.becomed.com) is similar to JobKatch, but it looks and feels a bit different. It allows you to rank contacts and categorize them as friends, recruiters, or company contacts. You also can associate web links and documents with each person. As you find companies that are hiring and identify their possible hiring managers, enter them into Becomed to organize your notes.

You may feel like you're overdoing things by keeping so many notes, but believe me, your work will pay off. To avoid kicking yourself for not remembering a crucial fact about a hiring manager that you discovered weeks earlier, make sure you're organized from the very beginning. Use the techniques I present earlier in this chapter to find opportunities, companies, and people to target, and then keep track of them in one of these organizing tools.

Chapter 16

It's About What I Can Do for You: Discovering a Company's Needs

Thanks to basic brain chemistry, every person on the face of this planet is walking around thinking about his or her problems and aspirations — and your future boss is no exception.

If you can find out what this potential employer is concerned with — meaning her needs, problems, and desires — then your job search will be more effective. Out of all the hundreds of job candidates a hiring manager sorts through, she'll pay particular attention to you because by using the info provided in this chapter, you'll be able to show her that you're the solution to her company's problems.

The trick to finding out what a company (and, therefore, that company's hiring manager) is concerned with is to do a little research. Thanks to social media and its real-time applications, you can easily find out what's likely at the top of a hiring manager's mind right now. This chapter shows you how to use social media sites to keep up with what's going on in your industry (and companies) of choice. It also reveals how to draw conclusions based on the wealth of information you're sure to find so you can make it clear that you can help the company with whatever it needs.

Staying on Top of Industry News with the Help of Social Media

In the old job-search paradigm, figuring out what a hiring manager cared about without conducting extensive info interviews was particularly difficult. Now with social media resources, you can pretty much determine what people care about, what goals they're trying to achieve, and what industry problems they're trying to overcome. Find out for yourself by checking out the social media websites and tools I describe in the next sections.

The key to any social media campaign is to make sure you're listening. Professionals are always talking; they're just hoping you're actually listening to what they have to say.

Finding the top news websites for your industry

As you begin your listening campaign to figure out what your target hiring managers care about, make sure you're up-to-speed on industry trends by reviewing the latest industry news. (This advice is particularly helpful if you've been laid off for a while.)

The news industry has shifted away from quarterly trade rags to real-time, user-generated content and research online. Find the top ten, industry-relevant, news sites and blogs, and then make a habit of reading them daily. The following sources are great for finding industry information:

- **Alltop:** This site is like an online magazine rack in that it serves as a directory of the web's top blogs and news sources based on category. Go to www.alltop.com and type your field or industry in the search bar at the top. Alltop then recommends categories for you to choose from.

  Create a MyAlltop account to customize your online magazine rack. You can add and reorganize news feeds from any category you choose. Then, when you're looking for news, just visit your customized MyAlltop account and get a fast overview of the top five articles from news sources you've already deemed important.

- **Technorati:** Technorati is one of the most well-known blog directories. After navigating to the site at www.technorati.com, click on the Tags link (located just below the list of drop-down menus on the home page) to see a list of topics listed in the directory.

- **Helium:** Helium (www.helium.com) is a user-generated content news website. Its articles aren't as time bound as other news sites but are very well written. In the Channels column on the left-hand side of the web page is a list of topics that may be relevant to your target industry.

✔ **Examiner.com:** Examiner.com is also a user-generated news site. Although topics tend to be less polished, they're more time relevant. Go to `www.examiner.com` and move your mouse cursor over the News & Info drop-down menu (found on the far right just below the examiner. com banner) to find industry-related categories.

Examiner.com delivers news items specific to a location. Each major city has its own Examiner.com site with different people writing for each location. So this is a great source for getting local trends and industry news.

✔ **MarketWatch:** This site is a great starting point for more quantifiable information about your target industry. Is it trending up or down, grow-ing or shrinking? Check it out at `www.marketwatch.com/industries` and click on the Analyze by Industry link (below the Industries header) to see the market index for the sector you're trying to get a job in.

✔ **Social Edge:** Social Edge (`www.socialedge.org`) is a great site for following trends in the nonprofit world with expert authors on various topics, such as philanthropy, business models, social entrepreneurship, and so on. Type the topic you're interested in into the search box at the top of the home page.

Getting news delivered to you with RSS feeds

Really Simple Syndication (or *RSS*) *feeds* are a way of pulling the news from multiple websites into a single *feed reader* (the application that displays your feeds). RSS feeds allow you to read all your news sites in one spot. Essentially, instead of exploring different sites for the news, the news comes to you.

Many news websites and blogs have an RSS link, which looks like the symbol in Figure 16-1. Clicking on this link connects your reader with the feed so that your reader displays the latest posts as they're published. After you start accumulating tens to hundreds of valuable news sources, having a single place to read them all can be a huge timesaver.

Before you can put RSS feeds to work, you have to decide which RSS reader you want to use. The following two RSS readers are easy to set up and use:

✔ **Google Reader:** Google Reader is a simple RSS reader, and anyone with a Google account can access it. (Basically, if you have a Gmail account, you can use Google Reader.) Simply visit `www.reader.google.com` to see your reader. Google suggests a couple of popular feeds to get you started. As long as you're logged into Google, you can subscribe to any feed you come across on the web by clicking on the RSS link (refer to Figure 16-1).

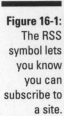

Figure 16-1:
The RSS symbol lets you know you can subscribe to a site.

TIP

✔ **Feedly:** Feedly is my personal favorite RSS reader because it transforms your feeds into a beautiful magazine interface, as you can see in Figure 16-2. You can view highlights on an automatically generated cover page and view and share full articles easily. Feedly is also very easy to configure. To access it, go to www.feedly.com.

Feedly is compatible only with Firefox, Chrome, and Safari browsers.

Figure 16-2:
Feedly's cover page.

After you choose the feed reader you want to use, build your subscriptions by using the resources for valuable news sites on your industry covered in the preceding section. Then follow these steps to add the subscriptions to your feed reader:

TIP

1. **Click the RSS link in either the address bar of your browser or on the web page itself.**

   The RSS link appears differently from page to page. Sometimes it simply says RSS; other times it has some fancy variation of the icon.

2. **Designate which reader you want to use to view the feed.**

   If you aren't using Feedly, then you'll be prompted to choose your reader from a drop-down list. Simply pick the one you want to use.

3. **Add the feed to the appropriate folder or category.**

   In Feedly, you can assign categories to your feeds. Doing so helps you navigate your feeds when you accumulate many news sources. If you're using Feedly, set up your categories so when you subscribe to a site, you just have to pick the proper category. If you aren't using Feedly, put the new feed in some kind of folder for easy retrieval later.

Joining industry groups on LinkedIn for news

If you've already joined the LinkedIn Groups that your targeted hiring managers belong to, as I show you how to do in Chapter 15, then you're probably aware of how being part of such industry groups helps you stay informed of topics your targeted hiring managers are concerned with.

Another way to find industry-related LinkedIn Groups worth joining is to do a group search. Simply click on Groups from the drop-down menu next to the search bar and type in your industry or field. When the results pop up, focus on active groups, which usually have more than 150 members. (Typically, the largest groups appear at the top of a search-results list; they're the ones worth joining.)

 Every industry has a professional organization, such as the National Association of Colleges and Employers, and typically these professional organizations have LinkedIn Groups. Type in the abbreviation or whole name of some professional organizations in your target industry and join their groups.

 The trick with using LinkedIn Groups for industry trends is to look for patterns and levels of interest. *Patterns* are similar topics between two or more groups. For example, you may see wind turbine real estate issues coming up in several green energy groups. Chances are something is going on there. Also the group's page lets you see the most popular topics. Make note of these popular topics because they're most likely on people's minds.

 Fellow members of professional groups on LinkedIn are often eager to help. I've seen people post requests for advice about starting in a certain field and receive more than 50 replies from good-hearted Samaritans. So don't be afraid to leverage these groups to learn as much as you can.

Mining Twitter for real-time feedback on industry issues

Because Twitter offers a real-time look at the popular topics and issues, you can use Twitter to uncover current industry trends. Use the following techniques to get started (for additional tips on using Twitter to further your job search, see Chapter 12):

- ✔ **Find industry-specific conferences.** Conferences usually have a *hashtag* (a way of tagging tweets around a similar topic) associated with them. If the conference had a session that resonated with many people, then you should know about it. Use `search.twitter.com/advanced` and type in the name of the conference. You may have to change the dates of your search to match when the event happened.

- ✔ **Search for trends on Trendistic.** Go to `www.trendistic.com` and type in your industry in the top search box to see what people are saying.

- ✔ **Find out where the trends are happening with Trendsmap.** This tool allows you to search topics based on geography. It shows you a huge map of tweets coming from different locations so you can figure out what's going on in your area (or in the area you're hoping to move to). Check it out at `www.trendsmap.com`.

- ✔ **Use BuzzTracker to find articles most blogged about based on category.** This service (`www.buzztracker.com`) highlights online trends based on what articles are popular on Twitter. It covers current events as well as more than 2,000 topics.

Following Companies through Their Social Networking Sites

Although seeing a broad view of the industry is a great start, sooner or later you need to understand the needs of a specific company and a specific person in that company. Sure, you can read annual reports and browse the About Us sections of your target companies' websites, but both of those options have their downsides.

An annual report takes months of production to get published, and corporate websites can take weeks to get updated, which means the intel you have on that company may already be outdated.

The best places for real-time information about a company are its social media sites because news appears instantly on these sites. Start looking for your target companies on the following social media outlets:

✔ **LinkedIn:** Following a company means that you're alerted anytime anything changes about that company on LinkedIn. If someone was fired, newly hired, or promoted, you'll know. If the company has new products or made a status update, you'll know. Make sure you're following *all* your target companies and checking their updates weekly.

To follow a company on LinkedIn, find the company's profile page and click on the blue Follow Company button at the top-right corner of the page.

✔ **The blogosphere:** These days, most organizations have a blog. Corporate blogs can vary in the type of articles they publish: Sometimes they're thought leaders, other times they're self-promoting. Either way, a corporate blog can give you important insights about an organization's strategic initiatives and market positioning. Either subscribe to the blogs of your target companies or visit them on a weekly basis.

When reading the blog of a target company, feel free to comment on or tweet an article. Companies find running a successful blog difficult and often hire consultants to help get more traffic to it. Help them out by leaving the first comment, which can help inspire more comments. Also, tweeting a link to your followers can help drive more traffic to a company's blog. At the very least, the person in charge of social media will be grateful to you. Later, you can call in that favor to get an introduction to a hiring manager.

✔ **Twitter:** Make sure you're following your target company's Twitter account. Whether you have little interest in tweeting and doing other Twitter things, watching your target company's Twitter posts can be insightful. Drop your target company into a private Twitter List so you can read all its updates at once without getting distracted. (A Twitter list is a folder you can create to put your contacts in; I explain how to create one in Chapter 12.) Pay close attention to topics the company repeats, articles it links to, and people it retweets. All these activities are clues to what's important to the company right now.

Drawing Conclusions about a Company's Needs and Your Fit

After you have a clear picture of industry trends and what's going on with your target company, turn that research into a clear list of issues you think said company's hiring manager cares about and how you can help address them. (If you still need to target the right hiring manager, see Chapter 15.) I recommend creating a chart like the one in Table 16-1.

Table 16-1			Charting Company Trends and Issues			
Company	Position	Hiring Manager	Similarities	Goals/ Initiatives	Problems (Business & Personal)	How You Can Help

The first three columns are pretty self-explanatory. Here's a breakdown of what to put in the next several columns:

- ✔ **Similarities:** Jot down anything you find out about the hiring manager, either from LinkedIn or Twitter, that aligns with your own interests or experiences. Mentioning friends and schools in common is a great start for when you reach out.

- ✔ **Goals/Initiatives:** As you read industry blogs and company tweets and look at recent hires in the organization, you get a sense of a company's strategic direction (what it's trying to achieve in the market this year). Take a guess at what you think this hiring manager is trying to accomplish. It may be raising funds from investors, cutting operations expenditures, or filling a recent vacancy.

- ✔ **Problems (Business and Personal):** Note the top three issues that this hiring manager is likely struggling to overcome based on your industry and company research.

- ✔ **How You Can Help:** Just knowing and then naming a company's problems isn't enough. You need to offer to help solve them. Think about your skill set. Which of the company's problems do you think you can address? List any specific skills or experiences you have that specifically address the problems.

After you call out these skills in this table, refer back to them when customizing your cover letter or résumé. These skills or experiences should form the foundation of the main points you try to communicate in your application. You also need these points in Chapter 18 when I show you how to reach out to hiring managers through social media.

Chapter 17

Embracing the Informational Interview for an Insider Advantage

In This Chapter

▶ Looking at innovative new ways to discover people who can give you the inside scoop

▶ Walking through the proper etiquette for asking strangers to a meeting

▶ Managing the interview so all the participants benefit

*B*eing a master of social media and conducting expert research on an organization is one thing, but validating that research with real people who work at that organization is another. In fact, any research you do on a target company without validating it with primary sources is just based on assumptions.

That's where the informational interview comes in. An *informational interview* is your chance to get a feeling for what working at a particular company or in a specific industry is like by having a brief conversation with someone who works at that company or in that field and can give you the inside scoop. An informational interview, or *info interview* for short, is strictly for obtaining information, not for scoring a job offer. It can be the very thing that allows you to know deep in your bones that you're a fit for an organization or industry. These types of interviews can also help when changing careers by providing valuable insight on whether the new field is right for you.

In this chapter, I explain how to find people to speak with from the company or industry you desire, how to arrange an info interview, and how to run the interview so (A) your contact feels excited to advocate for you, and (B) you get the info you need to have a conversation with a hiring manager later on.

Tracking Down the People with the Information You Want

As you grow your social networks, you may find that many of your second- and third-degree connections can be useful to you. For example, your sister's college roommate may know someone working at your dream company. With social media tools, you'll know of the connection and can then figure out whether that person is able to give you more information about your industry or company of choice. The following sections reveal how to track down these potential information goldmines through two of the top social networking sites: LinkedIn and Twitter. They also highlight how you can find industry and company contacts simply by staying on top of related news.

Just because I specifically call out LinkedIn and Twitter here doesn't mean you can't also apply the same strategy to Facebook and other networks as well.

Finding info sources with LinkedIn

After you grow your LinkedIn network to about 150 connections, which is roughly the tipping point for a powerful network, and complete your online profile (I show you how to do both in Chapter 9), LinkedIn can be an extremely powerful tool for finding people with whom you can conduct informational interviews. I've found two groups in particular to be useful for my clients: new and former employees of your target company and your alumni network.

Don't try reaching out to new people until you've completed your profile. If you contact people and your profile doesn't look amazing, they may decide not to get back to you. Also you find access to more people if you can grow your network to about 150 contacts.

New and former employees

Generally, many professionals, particularly new hires, enjoy talking about their positions and their industry. Let's face it: New hires have accomplished something extraordinary. They demonstrated the qualities necessary to beat many others to the position they now occupy. They're probably quite proud of their accomplishments, and they can share valuable lessons with you about getting into the industry or company.

Former employees tend to have something to say as well, although what they have to offer may be less enthusiastic than what a new hire has to offer. Former employees are likely to tell you about the skeletons in the closet, the hard questions to ask during an interview, and any insight into the future of the company.

Don't forget about seasoned employees or industry vets

Some people who have worked in an industry or at a company for a while may feel a sense of responsibility to help others trying to enter their field. Although not all industry experts are willing or have the time to take you under their wing, you may as well try to connect with them.

To find current employees to connect with, start by entering your target company in the search bar at the top right of LinkedIn's page (be sure to select Companies from the drop-down menu). Visit the company page and then click the Employees tab. At the bottom of the Employees

section, click on See More Employees. Here, LinkedIn generates a people search filtered by that company. If it's a large company, you may need to filter by keyword to pare down your list.

To find seasoned veterans in your industry, start with a simple people search on LinkedIn by entering the name of your field in the search bar at the top right of the page. LinkedIn displays a list of people who use that word in their profile. Then you can use the filters to narrow your list.

Here's how to find new hires and former employees in LinkedIn:

1. **Visit the company profile page for your target company.**

   To conduct a company search, click on Companies from the drop-down menu next to the search bar in the top-right corner, and then type in the name of your target company.

2. **Click on the New Hires tab.**

   Does anyone on this list seem like they're in a position to offer you advice? Perhaps they're new to the department or business unit you're going for. Or maybe they just look friendly.

3. **Scroll to the bottom of the New Hires section and click on See All Activity.**

4. **Click on the Filter By drop-down menu and then click on New Hires for one search and Recent Departures for another search.**

   Up to 25 names can be listed at a time, and depending on the size of the company, the search can go back as far as three months or just one day.

Your school's alumni network

Nothing is stronger than the connection you have with fellow alumni. Your school's alumni counsel and career center have high hopes for the LinkedIn Group they started. Not only are schools encouraging alumni to join their alumni group, but also they're promoting participation in events, discussions, and networking with other members. In fact, I've been specifically instructed to show students how to fully use their alumni LinkedIn Group in almost every webinar and training I do.

To access your school's alumni network for info interviews, just follow these simple steps. (But first, make sure that you're in fact a member of your school's group on LinkedIn by reviewing the list of groups that appears when you click on the Groups tab in the top ribbon of your LinkedIn page.)

1. **Click on the Advanced link next to the search bar at the top right of the page (see Figure 17-1).**

   Make sure the search field is set to People and not something else, like Jobs or Answers.

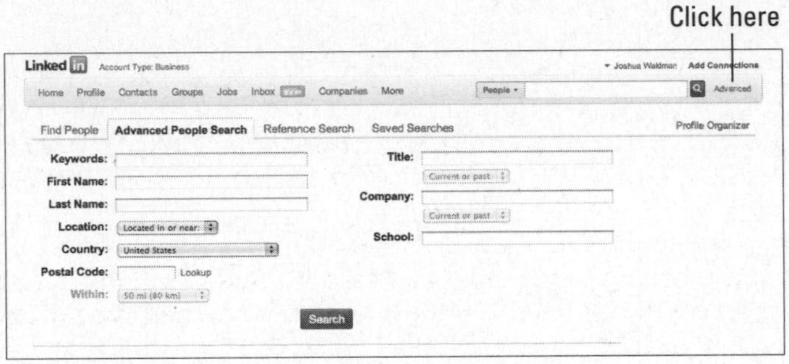

Click here

Figure 17-1:
Using the
Advanced
People
search in
LinkedIn.

2. **Type in the name of your school in the School field.**

3. **Scroll down to Relationship and click on Group Members.**

   Make sure no other box is checked in the Relationship area.

4. **Click on the Search button at the bottom of the page.**

5. **Scan the additional filters on the results page and make sure your school is checked and not another school with a similar name.**

   For example, LinkedIn delivers results for Boston College in addition to Boston University when I do this search.

6. **Enter a keyword to expand the search beyond your network.**

   Using a keyword, like your industry or field, tells LinkedIn to look beyond your second- and third-degree network for results. If you use a good keyword to expand your search, then you'll have a very strong list of potential sources for information. Of course, you can also further refine your list by searching only the specific companies or industries you're targeting.

   Scan these results to find out what groups you share with these people. Most of the results on this page are fellow alumni as well as fellow members of the alumni group. Without the previous steps, you're not able to identify alumni to network with.

When I did this search, I filtered the results by zip code and found 20 alumni living in Portland who I don't know yet. Even though I'm not looking for a job, I'll probably reach out to them just to network.

If you pay for a more advanced LinkedIn account, you can do a people search and filter the results by a particular group, such as your alumni network.

Using Twitter to find info sources

Finding info sources on Twitter isn't that different from finding news about a company on Twitter. (I explain how to do the latter in Chapter 16.) After all, if someone is talking about your target company, chances are that person has a deep connection there as well.

Large companies tend to have multiple Twitter accounts, and many of their executives tweet. To find them, go to any Twitter directory, like Twellow (www.twellow.com), and type in the name of the company you're targeting. The results show people who've used the company's name in their profile.

Often, employees of a company don't mention their employer in their profile but may occasionally mention it in a tweet. To find mentions of your target company in real time, go to search.twitter.com and type the company's name in the search bar.

Social media managers (the people who run a company's Twitter account) are often willing to direct you to the right person. Send a Direct Message to a company's Twitter account and ask for help finding an info source. (Remember that you can use only 140 characters in your message.) You may say something like, "Hi, I'm looking to speak w/ someone in marketing abt an opening I saw. Just info interview. Can you put me in touch?"

Looking at the news to find info sources

Thanks to social media tools, the people mentioned in articles about your target industry or company are all accessible to you. Stay on top of the news relating to your targets by setting up *RSS feeds,* which pull news from multiple websites into a single one for your browsing convenience. (I show you how to manage RSS feeds in Chapter 16.)

If you find someone mentioned in a blog post, press release, or other news source (like a local business journal's website) who you feel would be a great connection, don't hesitate to reach out to them. They're just people. They may be busy, but they still read e-mail and are likely to (A) be on LinkedIn and Twitter and (B) be flattered by the fact that you read about them in the news.

Having read their article, either written by them or written about them, you now have something to congratulate them on. Lead with telling them you read their article in any communication you send out.

I've had great luck getting in touch with industry leaders and authors by retweeting their articles and then asking them questions on Twitter. If you read an article or blog post you particularly like, jump on Twitter and see whether you can follow the writer or source's tweets. Engaging with someone on Twitter is a great way to get that person's attention. Later, when you e-mail that person through LinkedIn, he or she will recognize you.

Asking for a Meeting the Right Way

After you find people who you think can provide you with some insight into an industry, company, or opportunity, you're ready to take the next step: contacting them to ask for an informational interview. However, reaching out to someone without first thinking about your messaging is a mistake.

Between LinkedIn and Twitter, LinkedIn is the better way to reach out to potential info interview contacts because you can be more detailed in your request, thanks to LinkedIn's lengthier messaging format. If you use Twitter, you're confined to 140 characters, which doesn't help you make a compelling case about why the person should talk to you. So use Twitter to get a person's attention, but use LinkedIn to request the call.

I've received frequent info interview requests through LinkedIn since I began using it in 2006. And I enjoy analyzing how people structure their messages to me and my clients. Over the years, I've compiled a list of attributes of a successful info interview request on LinkedIn. Keep the following pointers in mind the next time you reach out to someone to secure an informational interview:

- ✔ **Lead with something in common.** If you have nothing in common, then mention how you found the other person. Chances are you found that person on LinkedIn during your research. Although what you have in common may be obvious, leading with it really works to contextualize the conversation.

- ✔ **Get to your point fast.** Don't beat around the bush. Tell the person exactly what your intentions are for the communication. In the context of an info interview, the purpose of the call or visit is so you can ask questions about a company or industry.

- ✔ **Reassure the person that you're not asking for a favor.** No one likes being put on the spot. If people suspect that you're going to ask them for a job, they may anticipate having to turn you down. Saying no isn't fun and most people try to avoid it. Be firm in your intention that this isn't a job solicitation.

✔ **Talk about what makes you qualified.** A lot of desperate people are looking for work. Most of them don't qualify for the positions they apply to, and many people desperately ping others for favors out of a sense of entitlement. Show your contact that you're not one of these people. You're uniquely qualified based on your skills and background. You are, in short, very seriously pursuing your career.

✔ **End with a strong call to action with a time limit.** I urge clients to put a fence around how long the conversation will last. Mention that you need only 10 to 15 minutes of their time. Make sure you end the conversation with a clear next step. Are you going to call them? Are you asking them to pick a time next week? Are you asking them to coffee?

✔ **Show appreciation for their time.** Professional appreciation can go a long way and help you look more assertive. It sounds something like this, "I'd really appreciate it if you would . . ." or "I understand that things may be busy for you, but I'd really appreciate just a few minutes to . . ."

Using these building blocks, I've constructed the perfect info interview communication. Feel free to use it as a template for your own search for information.

> Dear *(name of the person you're contacting)*,
>
> I found your profile through the *(name the common LinkedIn Group or network)* on LinkedIn. I have been working as a *(name last position)* at *(name last company)*, and I am in the process of making a career transition.
>
> It would be helpful for me to find out about your experiences as a(n) *(name role)* for *(target company)*. I promise not to take more than 15 minutes of your time.
>
> I am not expecting to discuss a particular job opening, but I would appreciate being able to talk with you on an informational basis.
>
> What is the best way to reach you this week? I have Thursday at 9 a.m. and Friday at 2 p.m. available. If these times conflict with your schedule, I am happy to meet with you at your convenience. I thank you in advance.
>
> Regards,
>
> *(your name)*

If someone doesn't get back to you within a week, you can try sending another request. Assume that this person is simply busy. After the second try, however, assume the answer is no, and stop pursuing this contact. The last thing you want to be is a pest.

A real-life example of a great info interview request

As if reading my mind, the person in this example sent me an e-mail that fit almost exactly into my ideal interview request template. I thought it was too much of a coincidence that I received this e-mail the same week I wrote this chapter, so I feel I should share it with you. He did a *very* nice job getting my attention. See whether you can spot each of the elements I bulleted in the "Asking for a Meeting the Right Way" section. What works in his e-mail? What would you do differently?

Hi Joshua,

I noticed that we are both connected to M. F. — how do you know M.? I first met her at Sally's Pillow, and she actually photographed my wedding. Small world.

I wanted to touch base with you because I saw an open position at J.R. that I thought would be a great fit for me. I'm located in Portland now (after being in Massachusetts and N.C. for many years) and do social media strategy for a digital marketing agency here in town.

It's a fun role, but you know how agencies are — fingers in a lot of different businesses but no ability to truly own a marketing program. It looks like I would be able to do that with the Marketing Communications Manager role that is posted.

Would you mind if I called you sometime this week to hear about your experience at J.R. and your perspective on the marketing organization there? I'd really appreciate it.

Conducting an Informational Interview That's a Win-Win for Everyone

Even though an informational interview is a lower stakes conversation with non-decision makers, your info sources may be able to help you in ways you can't anticipate, so you should be prepared to respect their time. Walking into an interview without first preparing is a big mistake. I help you get ready for an info interview in the next sections by illustrating the discussion framework you should use and the types of questions you should ask.

Think of an info interview as a regular, yet casual, job interview, but instead of looking down at your résumé or answering a lot of questions, you get to ask the questions. Aside from these differences, all other job interview rules apply: Be on time, dress appropriately, and be prepared with questions. If you're conducting this info interview over the phone, be sure to sit in a quiet place where you won't be disturbed. Either way, resist the temptation to ask for a job. Your sole goal is to obtain information.

Leading the discussion in your info interview

Ultimately, you want the informational interview to be a fun, relaxed experience for you *and* the person you're talking to — which means you may not want to have a list of ten questions ready to fire off. Instead, you may want to shoot from the hip and just enjoy the conversation. Although that's a great strategy, you still need to round all the bases and get the info you set out to get. In my experience, the best way to enjoy a fresh conversation with someone new and interesting (while still making sure I get what I need from the interaction) is to keep a discussion framework in my head.

If you're searching for the next question to ask, or if you find yourself asking follow-up questions and directing the conversation, think about how to drape your questions to find out what's working, what isn't working, and who else you can talk to about the industry, company, and personal experience. I outline a few questions for each category in the following list:

- ✔ **What's working well?** I like to start info interviews on a positive note. Break the ice by asking your info source how he or she chose this career or job. Why is your info source happy with the current role? Is the industry in a state of growth or decay? Perhaps you discovered something exciting in your research that you want an opinion about. On a personal level, what parts of the job role does your info source enjoy most? Is the company growing? What does the company do particularly well? Are there job openings in certain areas that you should know about? What are skills, talents, and personal qualities that help people succeed in this work?

- ✔ **What isn't working well?** Here is where you can ask about the problems facing the industry and the company. On a personal level, you can ask what the person may improve about the job. If you researched the problems facing the company (as I show you how to do in Chapter 16), now's your chance to validate your findings. Where were you off the mark? Did you nail it dead on? Are the issues you thought were important really important at this company?

- ✔ **Who else can I talk to?** End every conversation with this question. You spent hours on LinkedIn finding a valuable source of information, someone who's already agreed to talk to you. When this interview finishes, don't go back to LinkedIn! You have, in front of you, someone with first-hand knowledge of the organization. Perhaps this person's colleagues can also answer some questions. Finally, make sure to ask about the hiring manager. Is the person you found on LinkedIn really the right person to talk to? If not, who is? What are the hiring manager's initiatives right now?

In-person meetings *always* turn out better than phone calls. If your contact insists on a phone call, keep it short and find a way to invite your info source to coffee. In-person meetings have a tendency to go longer, which allows you to develop chemistry and form a deeper relationship.

Knowing what questions to ask about a specific company

If you're quite advanced in your job search, then you probably already have a masterful grasp of your industry. That means your primary focus is finding just which company you should work for.

In *Job Hunting For Dummies,* 2nd Edition (John Wiley & Sons, Inc.), author Max Messmer presents five dimensions of a job and a company that you need to know about before making a decision. Although a lot has changed in the job-seeking world since that list was written in 1999, it can still apply to your job search. I lay out the list for you, with my own (social media) twists, in the following sections.

Lifestyle at work and away from work

With at-will employment, declining loyalties, and the average job lasting two years or less, lifestyle has become the most important deciding factor in finding new work. I use the term *lifestyle* to include the lifestyle both at work and outside of work because there isn't much distinction between the two anymore. These days, most people agree that if you're going to spend 9 to 14 hours of your waking day devoted to a job, you'd better enjoy it. Life doesn't start at retirement. People want to enjoy who they work with. People want autonomy to make their own decisions about their time and how they do things on the job.

If you're like me, then you want to know about the lifestyle of someone in your desired role at a company. If I have to turn in a tardy slip if I get stuck in traffic, then that's not the place for me.

Be sure to ask the following questions to determine whether the lifestyle the company offers is what you want:

- ✔ What's it like to work there?
- ✔ What's life like outside the office?
- ✔ How much autonomy do you have?

The work itself

Sometimes a job posting doesn't give you much info about what you'll actually be doing on a day-to-day basis. Marketing Coordinator may actually mean Copy Writer. Account Executive may actually mean Telephone Rep.

You want to understand what the daily tasks are. How much teamwork will you have and what are the dynamics of those teams? Will you travel? If so, how much? A really great question to ask your info source is, "What's your typical day like?"

Available opportunities

Many recruiters agree that most job opportunities aren't posted to job boards. And sometimes, it takes weeks to get a job posted on a company's own website. Your best bet to find out about opportunities at your target company is to talk with people who work there — hence the beauty of the informational interview. The info interview is your chance to get behind-the-scenes information about where to focus your job search.

During your interview, find out what areas the company is growing in. Which departments are hiring? If a job opens up, is it pretty competitive? Ask whether employees receive a referral bonus for bringing in new talent. Many companies give monetary rewards to employees whose referrals stay in the job for at least three months. This means that your contacts at the company (should they like you) may have an incentive to push your résumé to the top of the pile.

Advancement

When I worked at Cisco, my managers consistently asked me, "Where do you want to take your career, and how can I help you get there?" They saw their role in my professional life as coach and facilitator. A good job is a job that offers you the chance to grow and develop mastery in your skills.

Find out from your contact how that company supports advancement, mastery, and success, including professional development opportunities to take courses, training, or attend conferences. If you get bored with your job, will you be asked to leave? Or will the company find you a parallel role in another department? How will the company feel if you spend 20 percent of your time doing something other than your immediate job role?

Compensation

Naturally, compensation (including pay and any other benefits) is going to be of interest, but instead of asking the person you're interviewing how much she makes a year, try a less personal question, such as "Compared to other companies, do you think the salary is higher or lower than average?" If the salary seems low, you may inquire about the typical job path. Find out how your contact got where she is and how long it took.

Make absolutely sure you ask about healthcare and other non-monetary rewards for employment. When it comes time to negotiate an offer, you want information about other perks. This info gives you more leverage to ask for more than just a higher salary.

Thanking Your Contact, Social Media Style

You don't need to read a book about social media to know that you should always thank someone for his time after a meeting. Showing your appreciation via social media is a great way to add value back to your contact. Consider offering your info source a Twitter recommendation (assuming he has a Twitter account). After the meeting, tweet a message like this to your followers:

> Just met with *@infosource* and was super impressed with his knowledge about the future of Agile Project Metrics. Thanks for the chat!

Because you used his @twitter username, he'll see that you thanked him. And because you tweeted about him to your followers, you help him open up his network even more. This is a great way to return the favor of the person sharing his or her time with you.

You can also use LinkedIn to show your gratitude. First, check to see whether you're connected to this person by finding him on LinkedIn through a people search. If you aren't connected, you can write your thank-you note in the body of your LinkedIn connection request.

This approach ensures you a first-degree connection inside the organization you're targeting. And you'll be more likely to have a second-degree connection to a potential hiring manager.

What's the best way to send a thank-you note?

There's no hard and fast rule on the best way to follow up with contacts. Generally speaking, you want to move that contact closer to you. So if you're not connected to your contact on LinkedIn, use the follow-up to add her to your network. If you're already connected on LinkedIn, use personal e-mail to follow up. Each step brings her closer into your network.

If your contact is on Twitter, helping her grow her network by tweeting about her is always a good add-on to a lengthier thank-you. The only thing I advise against is using Facebook to follow up. Unless the person is a close personal friend, adding her to your Facebook network isn't appropriate.

Chapter 18

Engaging with Hiring Managers through Social Media

In This Chapter

▶ Using the right online etiquette when contacting decision makers

▶ Knowing when to follow the rules and how to use them to your advantage

▶ Figuring out what to do after you apply for a position

▶ Learning from a failed online approach to make sure you win the job the next time

As the saying goes, "You never have a second chance to make a first impression." So make your first interactions with a hiring manager you want to impress count big-time by demonstrating your value without being pesky. In this chapter, I get you up-to-speed on proper online etiquette for communicating with a hiring manager, even if no jobs are open.

If you're applying to a job, or if a hiring manager won't talk to you until after you've formally submitted a résumé, then you can try several social media tricks to remain top of mind and relevant. In this chapter, I reveal these tricks and how to improve your online approach after experiencing a rejection.

Reaching Out to the People with the Power to Hire You

In this day and age, using social media to reach out to hiring managers, specifically those people who can make a decision about bringing you onboard at an organization, gives you a better chance of having your message heard. Contacting a hiring manager through, say, Twitter rather than by phone gives her more time to respond to you. Because you're not sitting on the other end of the telephone line waiting for an immediate reaction, the decision maker has less pressure on her, which ultimately helps her let her guard down. You also give her a chance to check you out first.

Hiring managers can browse your online profiles, Google your name, or do a background check before deciding that you're not wasting their time. As long as you spent time polishing off your profiles and improving your online reputation, you'll improve your odds of hearing back.

The following sections help you make contact with your target hiring managers by following the proper online etiquette so you don't wind up sounding like a pest. (*Note:* I'm presuming you've already created a list of hiring managers to contact. If you haven't, flip to Chapter 15 before trying to apply the following advice.)

Getting introduced on LinkedIn

When using LinkedIn to make your first contact with a hiring manager (and chances are you'll use LinkedIn to do this), never ever, ever (did I say ever yet?) invite a hiring manager to connect with you as your first communication. Many professionals guard their first-degree connections on LinkedIn very carefully. If a stranger comes around looking not only for a job but also for access to their network, they may get defensive. Restrain yourself from connecting with a hiring manager on LinkedIn until *after* you've met in person and you've asked whether it's okay to connect (unless of course the hiring manager invites you to connect with him first).

The best way to contact a hiring manager via LinkedIn is through an introduction. A LinkedIn Introduction has two parts to it: a note to the person you're targeting and a note to whoever's introducing you to that person. Figure 18-1 shows you what a typical LinkedIn Introduction looks like.

If you've done a good job conducting informational interviews, as described in Chapter 17, then you'll have met with and made connections with people at your target organization. Adding these folks to your LinkedIn network increases the odds that you'll become the second- or third-degree contact of your targeted hiring manager, which means you can ask for an introduction to that person through your first-degree contact.

You can request a limited number of introductions per month depending on your level of subscription on LinkedIn. To ask for an introduction, follow these steps:

1. **Navigate to the profile of the hiring manager you want to speak to.**

2. **Click on the Get Introduced through a Connection link on the right side of the page.**

   If you have more than one common contact, choose which of your connections you'd like to make the introduction. Then put your note to the target person and the introducer in the two-part form that appears.

3. **Under the Category drop-down menu, choose Job Inquiry.**

Figure 18-1:
A sample
LinkedIn
Intro-
duction.

4. **Include the name of the person introducing you in the Subject line, such as, "Friend of Ian Troducer looking to connect about a potential fit."**

   According to Neal Schaffer, a friend and fellow LinkedIn trainer, this approach to introduction subject lines adds credibility to the note and increases the likelihood that the person will respond.

Before filling out your message to the hiring manager, focus on your message to your first-degree contact first. By asking this person to pass on your introduction, you're asking her to put her reputation on the line for you, meaning she's taking on some risk if you monkey things up.

Pay as much attention to your request for an introduction as you do to your message to the hiring manager. When asking a contact for an introduction, make sure to follow these guidelines:

- ✔ **Tell the introducer why you want to talk to the target person.** Reassure your contact that you're not planning to ask the hiring manager for a job. Instead, you're simply exploring the possibility of a fit between you and the hiring manager's employer. Say how this introduction will help you with your professional goals.

- ✔ **Specify what the conversation will be about.** Share the types of questions you plan to ask. Reassure the introducer that you won't pester her contact.

> ✔ **Offer to answer additional questions about yourself and your intentions on the phone with the introducer.** It helps to throw this option out there, but leave the final decision up to your contact. Don't start calling her every day to find out whether she's passed your introduction along. Just one call or reminder e-mail is sufficient.

> ✔ **Show appreciation for the impact this person may have on your career.** Be professionally assertive, not casually apologetic. Say something like, "I would very much appreciate it if you would . . ."

Here's an example of a note you may send to a contact asking for an introduction:

> Hi *(name of your contact)*,
>
> I am interested in setting up an informational interview with *(name of hiring manager)*, one of your connections on LinkedIn.
>
> I want to ask her about open positions she may have at *(target company)* and see if I may be a fit for the organization.
>
> If you are more comfortable passing on this introduction after a phone call, I am happy to chat with you about my intentions. You can decide whether to pass my name on from there.
>
> Otherwise, I would very much appreciate it if you would forward my message to *(name of hiring manager)*.
>
> Thanks for your help,
>
> *(your name)*

After you have your message to your contact drafted, you can start writing your message to the hiring manager. Because you're not yet sure of your fit with the organization and, in some cases, you may not even know whether a position is open, don't be overconfident in your message to the hiring manager. I've spoken with quite a few hiring managers who are turned off by candidates who insist they're perfect for an organization when clearly they have no clue. So instead of making this faux pas, be clear that you're just looking to explore the possibility of a fit. After all, *thinking* you're a fit and admitting that you're curious to find out whether that's true is perfectly okay.

Follow these guidelines when crafting your message to your target hiring managers:

> ✔ **Lead with something in common or how you found them.** A common group, school, or interest is a great way to show that you've done your homework and helps hiring managers put their guard down. Pending that, context also helps open them up. For example, tell them you found them when researching your interest in XYZ Company.

- ✔ **Respect their time by getting to the point fast.** If you think you're a fit for the job, say, "I think I'm a fit." You're looking to explore the possibility of employment, so say so. There's no shame in admitting that.

- ✔ **Show your value.** This introduction may be your first impression, so do what you need to do to separate yourself from the crowd within the structure of your personal brand. (I help you craft this brand in Chapter 4.) Repurpose your value statement based on all the research you've done on the needs of the company and the hiring manager. (If you haven't yet done this research, turn to Chapter 16 for some pointers on conducting it.)

- ✔ **Establish credibility.** Use social proof, such as recommendations, blog traffic, and other evidence, that shows people respect you. Doing so reduces perceived risk about you as a candidate. How so? Well, if a hiring manager sees that other people are willing to vouch for you, then he knows that you must be all right.

- ✔ **Talk about how you can help them solve their problems or reach their goals.** Remember that the job search is about the employer. The company has many choices about who it can hire, and you have lots of competition. The company is ultimately going to hire the person who seems like he'll benefit the company the most.

- ✔ **Invite them to learn more about you before deciding.** Take some of the pressure off by inviting hiring managers to see your blog, an online résumé that's different from your LinkedIn profile, or other link. Inviting them to learn more about you also helps establish credibility. (For guidance on creating a blog, see Chapter 6; for the scoop on other online résumés, see Chapter 11.)

- ✔ **End with a request to move the conversation offline.** Ask for a meeting and put a time limit around it. Be sure to be professionally assertive, not pushy or needy. You can take the conversation offline by meeting for coffee or meeting at the hiring manager's office. For out-of-towners, you can simply request a phone call.

The sections that follow show you how to put all these elements together to craft your message to your target hiring manager based on whether that person's company has an opening you're interested in.

Example letter to a hiring manager if the company has an open position you want

When writing to a hiring manager who is actively trying to fill a position, you can approach your letter to them more directly. I suggest naming the position in the first sentence, as I do in the following example. Be sure to jump into some credibility-building statements derived from both your personal branding work and your research. End with a call to meet.

Hi Mary,

I found your listing for an Assistant Supply Chain Manager and think I may be a good fit for the position based on the job description. Before I apply, I want to be sure that I'm not wasting your time or mine, so I'd love a chance to chat with you about a potential fit.

For the last nine months, I've volunteered at a local food distribution center that serves area homeless shelters. I've helped it increase throughput by 10 percent while simplifying the delivery routes and boosting participation. Prior to volunteering, I was supply chain manager at Home Improvement, Inc., for five years.

You can view my VisualCV with some work samples at `www.visualcv.com/ILoveSupplyChain`, and I also blog about my views on supply chain at `www.ILoveSupplyChain.com`.

Do you have 10 to 15 minutes for a chat sometime this Thursday after 10 a.m. or Monday morning?

I look forward to speaking with you.

Thanks,

Gitta Kwainted

Example letter to a hiring manager if the company has no obvious openings in your field of interest

If you can't find an open position, don't worry. Most jobs never make it to job boards anyway. Plus a good hiring manager goes out of his way to meet potential candidates in the event something opens up. When writing to a hiring manager with no obvious positions open, you can lead with something you have in common instead of a specific opening. Because you're not sure whether the hiring manager is currently looking to fill a position, be sure to say that you understand his situation. Check out the following example letter:

Hi Mary,

I found your name when researching fast-growing import/export businesses in town, and we are both in the Supply Chain LinkedIn Group. I'm not sure whether you're hiring, but I'm impressed with what I've learned about your company so far. I'd love a chance to chat with you to see whether you have a place for my skills on your team.

For the last nine months, I've volunteered at a local food distribution center that serves area homeless shelters. I've helped it increase throughput by 10 percent while simplifying the delivery routes and boosting participation. Prior to volunteering, I was supply chain manager at Home Improvement, Inc., for five years.

You can view my VisualCV with some work samples at `www.visualcv.com/ILoveSupplyChain`, and I also blog about my views on supply chain at `www.ILoveSupplyChain.com`.

I understand that you may not have any job openings now, but I would really appreciate 10 minutes of your time to learn more about the company and any potential fit in the future.

Do you have 10 to 15 minutes for a chat sometime this Thursday after 10 a.m. or Monday morning?

I look forward to speaking with you.

Thanks,

Gitta Kwainted

Generating curiosity with Twitter

Twitter is a great tool for generating a hiring manager's curiosity about you. The short bursts of interesting content directed at your target company can leave people wanting more and with the impression that you really know what you're talking about. (However, Twitter isn't good for asking for an in-person meeting because you have such a limited amount of space — just 140 characters — to get your message across.)

A great way to generate some curiosity is to send a hiring manager an @reply message. An *@reply* is any tweet that includes the Twitter username of someone with the @sign in front, like @name. An @reply is a public tweet that the hiring manger is alerted to. But because you don't want to keep this conversation in the public domain, try asking for a DM reply. A *DM,* or *Direct Message,* is a private tweet. Try something like, "I have some ideas that may help you with improving supply chain costs. DM me back with an e-mail."

Knowing what's relevant to hiring managers separates you from all the other job seekers they interact with on a daily basis. Take the time to research any problems that the company — and consequently the hiring manager — may be facing. If you do, you'll automatically know what to say to get a hiring manager's attention. Head to Chapter 16 for guidance on conducting your company-related research.

Sparing everyone's sanity by following up the right way

What do you do if you haven't heard back from a hiring manager after a week? Keep in mind that a non-response or a slow response may have nothing to do with you. Before you jump to any conclusions, consider some of these possibilities:

- ✔ The person may be very busy.
- ✔ You may have picked the wrong person to talk to about the opportunity.
- ✔ The person may not check his LinkedIn messages very often.
- ✔ The job position may be very competitive and the person has chosen not to respond.
- ✔ The person's HR department may forbid her from responding.

I knew a hiring manager who was very busy and also very clear in setting expectations with candidates. One time, he told a candidate that he'd get back to her in about five days. But this candidate called the next morning, then e-mailed, then called again the day after that. Her persistence turned into peskiness and showed the hiring manager that she couldn't take direction.

If you don't hear back after your first attempt to get a hiring manager's attention, hold off a week before trying again. When you do try again, it's better to assume that he's busy, not that he thinks you're inadequate. For example, your second communication may start off with, "It seems like things must be really busy for you right now. I can appreciate that, which is why I'd be even more appreciative of just a few minutes of your time at your convenience to discuss . . ."

After making three attempts to follow up with the same hiring manager, with at least a week between each attempt, give up and try someone else.

"Apply First": Dealing with HR's Insistence on Following the Rules

If you're reaching out to a hiring manager who has a position open that you want to fill, you may find this person unwilling to talk with you until after you've followed company procedure and actually applied to a job posting. Either the company is strict about its internal processes or the job opening is so competitive that employees are overwhelmed by people asking them for advice. In either case, following the rules is a wise choice.

The following four-step strategy has worked for many people in situations where a hiring manager has asked them to follow standard procedure:

1. **Do your research about the job opening and the company.**

   Be sure you tailor your résumé and value statements appropriately.

2. **Apply to the job according to the company's instructions.**

   The company has either an applicant system or a designated e-mail address.

3. **Follow up immediately with your closest connection at the company.**

   If you were able to get in a few info interviews, follow up with your info sources to let them know that you formally applied. If you have closer relationships, you may even ask them to flag your résumé. *Flagging* your résumé means a person mentions you to the HR department and your résumé goes to the top of the pile.

4. **Ask the hiring manager whether you can answer any additional questions about your application.**

   Often an HR department needs to go through some background checks, maybe even a phone screening with you before it passes on your application to the hiring manager. However, the hiring manager can put pressure on the HR department to speed this process up and even make sure you make it through. So stay in touch with your hiring manager contact as you go through the HR process.

 If the company has a new-employee referral program, your info interview source may have a financial incentive to recommend you for a position. Find out whether the company has such a program and make sure you're seen as the best candidate to stand behind. When I worked at Cisco, I recommended talented people to HR all the time, hoping to collect my $2,500 bonus! However, before I referred people, they had to prove to me that they had a very strong chance of getting the position.

The next sections reveal how to use social media to your advantage, whether you're applying for a position at a larger, more well-known organization or a lesser-known, smaller operation.

Using social media to get an edge when applying to a well-known company

When the barriers to blogging went down along with the economy in 2009, websites like www.bsfshouldhire.me and www.twittershouldhireme.com started to appear, but the strategy of creating such a site isn't very creative or compelling anymore. However, these campaigns do offer the following lessons that are still applicable when applying to a job at a company with a well-known brand:

✔ Growing a social media following is easier when applying to a big company with a brand name.

✔ Building a social media following only works when you come across with authenticity and your story is compelling for others.

✔ Sharing your job search publicly and authentically (like through your blog or website) can demonstrate your credibility.

✔ Having followers rally behind your goal to get a job can feel great and does wonders to your personal brand.

✔ Using the names of big companies on social media channels gets their attention.

✔ Having fun and being creative in your campaign can go a long way.

Not everyone will apply, or is even interested in applying to, a big company. So this advice isn't for everyone. But if you do have aspirations of making it into a large organization, you may consider trying out these techniques to get noticed. You never know what opportunities may arise by putting yourself out there.

Even if you publicly state that you want to work for Company X, that doesn't mean you've limited yourself. Most of these creative job seekers didn't end up getting hired at their target company. But their passion got the attention of other companies who pursued them.

Impressing a smaller company with your social media prowess

Most small businesses compete against their larger counterparts through their market agility. They're able to respond to customer requirements faster, develop features faster, and enter new markets faster. Being cutting edge and responsive in your own online presence is a great way of aligning yourself with the needs of a small business.

By the very fact that you're willing to adopt and use social media to manage your career, you're not only communicating that you're open to change but also demonstrating that you have what small businesses need to remain competitive. Don't be afraid to leave comments on a company's blog, interact with it on Twitter, and write about it to your own blog readers.

You've Applied, So Now What? Helping Out Your Application

After you've applied for a job with an organization, you still have some work to do. Remember that at least 16 other people are likely to apply for the same position (according to the U.S. Bureau of Labor Statistics); in some cases, up to 300 people may apply for one position (according to some job boards). Although, you may be qualified, your application may not even be looked at. I encourage you to do the following after submitting your application in order to lend it a helping hand:

- **Go radio silent on your Twitter account and other networks in regards to that company.** Companies aren't happy when candidates talk about the fact that they've applied to a job or about private conversations they've had with their staff. Now that you've applied, let things fall where they may.

- **E-mail any contacts you've made during your info interviewing and your discussions with hiring managers.** Let them know that you applied, that you're available to answer any questions, and that you're more passionate than ever before about the possibility of working with them based primarily on their generosity of time and information.

If you really want to know where your application stands, follow the company on LinkedIn and pay attention to whether any new hires have been added recently. If you see someone has taken the position you just applied to, move on.

Turning Rejection into a Chance to Improve

Whether you're applying to a particular position or just reaching out to hiring managers to explore possibilities, the results of your efforts won't always go your way. If you don't get the job or if hiring managers don't want to talk to you, it's probably not your fault. Don't take it to heart. Instead, look at what you did well and what you can improve on. Then, the next time you make a move into a company, you'll have an even better strategy.

If you've had personal contact with the hiring manager, he may personally let you know that you weren't chosen. If not, he may just let HR send an impersonal form letter. In that case, you need to ask for feedback so you can learn from your mistakes. When asking for feedback, query the hiring manager, not HR. The decision maker chose someone else for a reason, and that reason may be valuable information to help you do better next time.

Make sure you follow a rejection letter with some of the questions in the following list (don't ask all of them; just pick three):

- Was there something in particular about my qualifications that lead you to this decision?

- Did you have any specific reservations about hiring me that I can know about?

- Is there a particular skill or certification that, if I had it, would have helped me get the position?

- Could I have improved my communication with you in any way?

- ✔ What could I have done better to influence your decision in my favor?
- ✔ Please describe the person who did get the job. What made that person different/better than me?
- ✔ Would you offer me any advice as I move ahead with my job search?

I suggest using e-mail to ask these questions rather than LinkedIn. In most cases, you're alerted of the rejection via e-mail, and all you have to do is reply. If you don't have an e-mail address or an e-mail to reply to, then a LinkedIn message is the next best option. You may use a subject line like, "Quick follow-up on the XYZ position." Just be sure you don't come across as whining or nagging.

Not all hiring managers are willing to answer these questions, but it's worth a try. Preface your reply with a statement like this, "As a professional, I'm always looking to improve myself. Would you be so kind as to answer the following questions for me? Please be as direct as you can." Never get defensive if a hiring manager gives you hard feedback. Just reply with a simple "Thank you."

Part VI
The Part of Tens

The 5th Wave
By Rich Tennant

"I think you're just jealous that I found a community of people on Twitter that worship the yam as I do, and you haven't."

In this part . . .

1f you're a fan of top ten lists and easily digestible information, then this is the part for you. In it, I shine some light on the modern job search. Prepare to discover how the job-searching process has evolved in the 21st century, simple ways you can stay in tune with social media changes, and the most common mistakes people make when using social media. Well? What are you waiting for? Dive in, and best of luck to you in finding your dream job!

Chapter 19

Ten Ways the Job Search Has Evolved in the 21st Century

. . . .

In This Chapter

▶ Discovering the shift from paper-based résumés to online content and relationships

▶ Realizing the importance of an online reputation and what you can do for your target company

. . . .

*I*n this chapter, I guide you through some of the major differences between today's job search (yes, today as in right now) and job searches of the past, as in when your grandparents were looking for a job.

The First Page of Google Has Become Your New Résumé

Recruiters are now using Google searches to find talent, instead of paying for job-board or talent databases like they used to. In fact, many companies even mandate that every new applicant go through a Google screening process. So that means that the first page of your Google search results matter much more than they ever did before.

The problem is that, unlike a standard background check, what Google delivers on a name search isn't regulated and is very difficult for the user to control. Furthermore, Google's search algorithm changes several times a year, making it difficult to know exactly what's going to show up.

So what can you do about this situation? First, become a publisher of your own content and flood Google with lots of great keyword-rich content (I explain how to write such content in Chapter 6). Second, control the results on a Google search with Vizibility (www.vizibility.com). Vizibility is a website that lets you reverse engineer a Google search by making it easy to control what the results will be when people click your Google Me link. (See Chapter 7 for more information about managing Vizibility.)

A Summary Is Enough

Nowadays, you no longer need a multipage résumé that includes lengthy, bulleted lists of all your past working experiences. A paragraph-long summary at the top of a one- to two-page résumé or in an online profile is more than enough to get by in the modern job-search market. Because so many candidates are competing for each job, HR people (or hiring managers if they're tasked with recruitment) often scan résumés or profiles quickly. In fact, the average time these folks spend reviewing a résumé is about 30 seconds. So make your summary paragraph count, whether it's at the top of a résumé or in an online profile. You can go into the details about your career during the interview.

Social Proof Is a Must

Social proof, or the notion that if others think you're cool then you must be cool, is essential because it seriously reduces the perceived risk of you as a candidate. Social proof for a job seeker can be LinkedIn recommendations or even testimonials from ex-bosses. The most costly mistake a hiring manager can make is to hire the wrong person. Some say that if a new hire leaves within three months, it costs the organization 1½ times that person's annual salary. And with the economy as tight as it is, you can understand why hiring managers are so risk averse.

You can set hiring managers' minds at ease that you're a low-risk prospect by offering social proof on your résumé and LinkedIn profile. A good standard is to have the number of recommendations equal to 10 percent of the number of contacts in your network.

Résumés and Cover Letters Aren't Read on Paper Anymore

Most organizations aren't receiving paper résumés in the mail anymore. Instead, they're getting them via e-mail or their application system. Instead of printing and reviewing résumés on paper, most organizations review them on-screen. So expect your résumé and cover letter to be read on a computer screen and format accordingly.

Always format your documents in a way that makes screen-scanning easy. Here's how:

✔ Use headlines to break up content.

✔ Keep paragraphs short.

✔ Use **bold** and *italics* to emphasize key points.

✔ Keep plenty of white space on the page.

✔ Use color tastefully.

✔ Consider adding logos, icons, or charts.

Relationships Come First, Résumés Come Second

Thanks to the popularity of social media, your résumé may not be the first thing a potential employer sees about you. As more and more people connect with each other online through LinkedIn, Twitter, Facebook, and other social media sites, a potential employer is far more likely to see your online profile before ever setting eyes on your résumé. (This trend is a good thing because your online profile offers much more information about you than your résumé does. Specifically, it contains more details about your work history, links to other resources about you, and testimonials from ex-bosses and co-workers, and it offers a peek into your personality.) So shift your priorities from "I have to update my résumé!" to "How can I expand my network?"

If you're running your modern job search right, you'll get unsolicited e-mails from recruiters. Because they may ask you for your résumé at some point, be sure to have a copy ready to share.

Employers Only Care about What They Want

In years past, a résumé or job application focused on what the job seeker wanted. Now an application, résumé, or cover letter must speak to what value the job seeker can bring to the organization. As you write your online profiles, be sure to communicate how you can bring value to a company and how soon that company can realize that value.

Gaps in Employment Are Okay

Large gaps in your résumé aren't as important as they used to be. Not only do employers realize that great and wonderful people get laid off, but they also appreciate when candidates show initiative and volunteer, take a temp job, or try to start their own business or blog. (Some analysts even predict that by 2020, most professionals will use the Internet to generate multiple streams of income in addition to their day job.)

As long as you have a good explanation for the time you weren't working and can show that you've tried to be productive during it, a good potential employer will understand. (And if you encounter an employer who doesn't, then you may not want to work there anyway.)

Nouns Are the New Currency

Screening software and LinkedIn talent searches have introduced an unexpected element to the way a résumé should be written. Because these tools rely on nouns or keywords (rather than verbs) to deliver search results to recruiters, the résumés with the right combination of nouns often win.

If you want to succeed in today's job search, make a commitment to figuring out how to research keywords and how to use them appropriately online. (I show you how to conduct this research in Chapter 5.) Of course, those powerful verbs your college career adviser gave you are still important, too.

Everyone Has a Personal Brand and an Online Reputation

Ten years ago, not many people knew what a personal brand was or really had much of an online reputation. These days, even if you don't know what a personal brand is or even if you've never touched a computer, you still have a personal brand and an online reputation. Because recruiters and hiring managers are looking for red flags to help them narrow down their candidate pools, inconsistencies in your image or messaging and a sullied reputation may prevent you from passing screening. So you have to decide whether you'll control your image or someone else will. Turn to Part II for advice on taking charge of your personal brand and managing your online reputation.

Employers Expect You to Be Prepared

Back in the day, it didn't matter whether your résumé was geared toward a particular company or whether you knew much about that company during an interview other than its stock price. Fast forward to now, where, thanks to the Internet, you have access to more information about a company at your fingertips than generations past. As a result, companies' expectations for preparedness are much higher. To really shine, focus on customizing each résumé and cover letter for the company you're targeting. Sending off a few very targeted applications is a much better strategy than sending out many general applications and hoping they reach the right people.

Chapter 20

(Almost) Ten Ways to Stay Up-to-Date with Social Media Changes

In This Chapter

▶ Getting your hands on social media news

▶ Finding local technology clubs and events to network at

▶ Following social media movers and shakers on Twitter

Staying up-to-speed with social media can be frustrating, even for people who work in the industry. Not only are new technologies emerging every week but also existing companies are merging, splitting, and adapting quickly. As a job seeker, you certainly don't need to be on top of the very latest, but knowing what's out there can help you find new and creative ways to manage your career. Following are (almost) ten ways to make sure you aren't the last to know about a new tool or development in the world of social media.

Read Social Media News Sites

Following and reading all the various sources of information about social media companies (think company-owned blogs, press releases, case studies, and technical releases) can be a real waste of time, especially if you don't work in the social media field. Lucky for you, writers and analysts summarize and comment on these updates on relatively few news sites. Scanning the following sites on a weekly or monthly basis keeps you in the loop regarding all things social media:

- ✔ **Mashable:** Mashable (www.mashable.com) offers the most comprehensive news and commentary on the social media landscape.

- ✔ **Read Write Web:** This site (www.readwriteweb.com) is one of the most widely read technology news sites on the Internet. Many top businesses rely on Read Write Web to inform their decision making.

- ✔ **The Next Web:** This site (www.thenextweb.com) publishes technology news with an international focus. You can drill down into the Social Media channel to reach topic-specific articles. (See the different Channels on the left-side column of the home page.)

- ✔ **Nonprofit Technology News:** This site (www.nptechnews.com) publishes nonprofit-related content with a focus on technology, fundraising, and industry topics.

Set Up Weekly Summary Newsletters

If you don't like to spend your spare time surfing news sites, consider setting up a subscription for a technology summary newsletter so the news comes to you. These newsletters typically contain articles from leading news sites around the web. I recommend SmartBrief on Social Media (www.smartbrief.com/socialmedia), which is the most well-respected social media news summary you can get delivered right in your inbox. (SmartBrief also offers other industry-specific newsletters, including one with job-search tips and career advice.)

View Real-Time Web Updates with RSS Feeds

When you find blogs or news sites related to social media, such as the ones I mention earlier in this chapter, simply subscribe to their RSS feed. *RSS, or Really Simple Syndication,* is a technology that allows you to subscribe to and read various websites all in one place. I scan my RSS reader weekly, looking for news and blog posts that catch my attention. Setting up an easy-to-read listening station with your RSS reader is easy. I suggest using Feedly (www.feedly.com), which generates a magazine-like user interface and runs Google's Reader technology underneath.

Feedly works with Firefox, Safari, and Chrome browsers. After you sign up, it immediately suggests news sites to add. You can create categories and even e-mail or tweet articles without ever leaving the application.

Join a Local Club

Getting involved with a local social media club gives you access to other people passionate about social media who are doing the work of staying up-to-date for you. Most major metropolitan cities have a group of social media enthusiasts. You can search for a club in your area at www.socialmedia club.org or www.meetup.com. Social Media Club has more than 166 chapters in the United States and clubs in more than 40 countries around the world. I'm willing to guess that a chapter of Social Media Club exists in your neck of the woods.

I did a search for "social media" on Meetup and found nearly 3,000 groups around the world, meeting on a regular basis to talk social media, live and in person. Perhaps not all these groups are relevant to you as a job seeker, but they're likely putting on events and inviting guests who have something interesting to say — at least every once in a while.

Make New Technology-Savvy Friends

Take a look at your circle of friends. Are they open to new technologies? Do they talk passionately about the latest and greatest Facebook feature? Or do they cringe whenever you mention the words *text message?* If you don't normally run around in technology-friendly circles, where the words *UX* and *agile* are thrown around like *chocolate* and *shopping* on *Sex in the City,* then you may need to make some new tech-savvy friends.

One great way to get to know the technologically inclined is to attend technology conferences and events. Doing so allows you to meet new people, ask questions, and get motivated about new technology. Here are some ways to find technology events in your area:

- **Use Mashable (**www.mashable.com**) to find annual technology conferences.** If a conference is in your area, consider attending, even if you don't know what's going on.

- **Go to** www.eventbrite.com, www.plancast.com, **or** www.upcoming.yahoo.com **and search for local events with a technology focus.** These event websites have strong technology subscribers and will help you stay current with events.

- **See your local chamber of commerce or business journal.** These organizations spend a lot of time and energy educating their local businesses and quite frequently offer active calendars with training, networking, and educational opportunities.

Listen to Podcasts

Podcasts are digital audio or video episodes that you can download to your computer or MP3 player. New episodes come out regularly and often represent current trends in innovation. iTunes offers a wide array of free social media–focused podcasts and classes. From *Today in Social Media* to *6 Pixels of Separation,* you have your pick of episodes to download and listen to, whether you're running, in the car, or on the treadmill.

Watch Social Media TV

YouTube is the second largest search engine in the world. Companies and analysts can easily produce and upload new video. So cruising YouTube is a fun and informative way to stay up-to-speed on social media. For reliable and constant content, subscribe to a YouTube channel that's focused solely on social media by following these steps:

1. **Type "social media" into the search bar on** www.youtube.com **and click on the Search button.**

2. **Click on Filter & Explore just below the search bar and choose Channel to sort out the social media–related channels.**

3. **Subscribe to Mashable and any other channels you find compelling.**

Read the Tweets from Pundits

Social media thought leaders, not surprisingly, share their thoughts on Twitter (www.twitter.com). Why not follow them and read what they have to say? Of the many self-proclaimed social media gurus, here's a list of *tweeps* (Twitter users) who truly deserve your attention:

@briansolis

@chrisbrogan

@mashable

@mashable/social-media

@jowyang

@charleneli

@TechCrunch

@Pogue

@DaveATNorth

Find Trending Topics through Social Bookmarking

Social bookmarking is a way for Internet users to share what websites they're reading. These sites often track trends and news more accurately than news sites themselves. You can see what articles are being read and shared in real time. Social bookmarking can help you stay up-to-date with social media because people bookmark new and interesting news sources as they come out in real time. Check out www.stumbleupon.com, www.reddit.com, and www.digg.com.

Chapter 21

Ten Common Mistakes People Make When Using Social Media Sites

Social media is probably one of the most hyped-up technologies today. And often, those things that get a lot of hype also come with a lot of misunderstanding. Companies, as well as individuals, have made some *very* damaging mistakes because they didn't take the time to really understand social media.

In this chapter, I share with you the ten most common social media mistakes so that you can learn from them and avoid them. I want you to be comfortable with social media and have the confidence to be authentic, be yourself, and grow a powerful network that propels your career to new heights.

Forgetting That Social Media Is Just a Tool

Social media has a lot of excitement around it today, making it easy to believe all the hype and success stories and expect those same successes to happen to you instantly. Just like Favel thought America was paved with gold in the movie *Coming to America,* new users of social media can sometimes think these tools are magical — but they're not.

Treat social networking as you do in-person networking. Build your relationships over time and with care. Social media is just the tool; you still have to use that tool wisely and effectively.

Failing to Think of What Hiring Managers Need to See

Successful people on social networking sites don't overly obsess about how spiffy their profiles look or what they've done in the past. Masters of social networking have good-looking and well-worded profiles, but they focus their time on interacting with potential employers and talking about how they can help them.

Learn from these masters. Focus your messaging on solving other people's problems and explaining how you can help their business, their career, or their life.

Taking Before Giving

You may have people in your social media network who you met once, months or years ago, and then rarely hear from. Then, out of nowhere, they send you (along with hundreds of other people on their list) an e-mail with their résumé attached, asking for job opportunities. It's not very compelling, is it?

To avoid being seen as someone who takes without giving back, keep in contact with your network and try to be of service to others. Here are some helpful ideas:

- ✔ Write someone an unsolicited recommendation; try doing this once a week.

- ✔ Share interesting and helpful articles with your network via status updates on a daily basis.

- ✔ Connect two people with similar interests without being asked.

- ✔ Make exceptions to your rules; for example, if you connect with only people you've met in person, break that rule every once in a while when someone seems to really need help.

- ✔ Keep an eye out for job opportunities and send them to people in your network who may qualify.

- ✔ Take someone under your wing and mentor him. Yes, even if you're early in your career, you have something to offer.

Being Inconsistent

Many recruiters and hiring managers have told me that any inconsistency in a candidate's application raises a red flag and winds up in the *maybe* pile at best. Inconsistencies to watch out for are saying you do one thing on your résumé and something else on your LinkedIn profile. Or perhaps you say you've worked at one place on your LinkedIn profile, but then you fail to include that company's name on your résumé.

More subtle inconsistencies can happen in your personal image. Perhaps you look nice and professional on your LinkedIn profile picture, but a simple Google search reveals your Halloween party bender where you're taking beer bongs with Viking horns or wearing a toga.

Here are some ways to improve your online consistency:

- **Plan out your personal brand before filling out profiles and résumés.** Decide up front who you are and how you want to look to others. (Turn to Chapter 4 for advice on crafting your personal brand.)

- **Post to your networks on a regular basis.** Having a consistent and regular voice online can help bolster your personality as perceived by others.

- **Ask for feedback from friends and colleagues/professional contacts.** Sometimes what may be perceived as an inconsistency may just be a mistake or even a personality quirk that can be hard to spot. Getting outside feedback can be valuable. Perhaps you only wear jeans and T-shirts but are an executive at a company. Although you may not be willing to change your style, you can play it up as a personality trait.

Having an Incomplete or Outdated Online Presence

If you're going to explore other social networks in addition to LinkedIn, such as XING or Brazen Careerist, don't do it halfway. (I go into detail on other social networks in Chapter 14.) Decide to join a network and then do whatever it takes to complete a profile. Putting your best foot forward is a must. If you aren't prepared to give it 100 percent, then don't open the new profile in the first place.

Having an outdated profile out there means you risk looking inconsistent. As your personal brand changes and evolves, your newer profiles begin to differ more and more dramatically from the old ones that aren't being maintained. And it just looks like you don't care. Nothing is worse for your personal brand than a Twitter account with only three posts from two years ago!

Revealing Too Little Personal Information

Revealing a vast amount of personal information isn't always going to help you in your job search, but leaving out *all* personal information can really hurt your chances of standing out in the job market. After all, the name of the game these days isn't just what you can do but who you are and what makes you different.

Including a few, well-chosen items about your personal life can do wonders for rounding out your image. By opening up about yourself, you make it easy for others with similar interests to relate to you. For example, my friend's son included on his LinkedIn profile that he'd hand-crafted a guitar over the summer. The hiring manager for an internship he applied to turned out to be a guitar enthusiast. Guess who was chosen for the most competitive internship that year!

Not Understanding the Etiquette of the Networks They Use

Not having a good understanding of the rules of one social network versus another is a major mistake because what's acceptable on Twitter may be considered a faux pas on LinkedIn. So reading and understanding what the network is and what the rules are is important. Sometimes, of course, you may have a message that's appropriate on several networks, but for the most part, interacting and engaging with your audience in the way each individual network expects is the best option.

Avoid services that blast out the same message to multiple networks at the same time. You wouldn't show up at a friend's house for beer and pizza and start passing out your résumé, would you?

Not Knowing Their Audience

Make sure your messages are appealing to the people who read them. For example, some people still think blogging is writing personal information about your life for the whole world to see. When, in fact, the best blogs are written for a very specific reason and a well-defined audience.

As a job seeker, your audience will likely be hiring managers and HR professionals. As a general rule, these people don't want to see your political views, religious views, or anything else that may cause controversy. Instead, focus on what makes you different, the value you can bring to the table, and your level of understanding about a field.

Failing to Keep Up with Their Networks When They're Employed

The average time for keeping a job in the United States is two years, which means you may be packing up and looking for a new boss every couple of years. In the traditional job-search paradigm, you'd simply restart your networking, résumé writing, and other job-hunting efforts at each interval. However, these days, such a start-stop approach is inefficient and impractical.

Just because you have a job doesn't mean you can slack on networking and maintaining your outgoing professional image. You may need your network before you know it. I cringe when I see incomplete LinkedIn profiles because one day those people will need a strong network to catch them. Neglecting their profile also means they haven't extended themselves to help others in need. One day they will seriously regret the oversight.

Following are some tips to help you keep up with or expand your network, whether you're employed or not:

- **Update your network regularly, either with LinkedIn status updates or occasional e-mails.** These updates can be as simple as sharing links to articles you've read or news about your professional life.

- **Keep your online profiles current so your network knows what you're up to.** Doing so is just a common courtesy that you probably also expect from others.

- **Continue to invite new people to connect with you.** As your network grows, so does your influence and value. If you're employed, use your status to help others find work or make connections.

Ignoring Face-to-Face Networking

The technology world is not only unpredictable but also volatile. Every connection you have online and every e-mail communication you send via a social network is owned by a company. If you aren't taking ownership of your connections and communications, then you risk losing them later on if that company goes out of business.

The highest impact you can have communicating with someone else is face-to-face, not e-mail. Strive to conclude every online communication with a call to meet in person. Also seek out in-person networking opportunities in addition to the virtual ones. (Besides, you can always follow up from a day of traditional in-person networking by inviting your new friends to connect with you online.)

Index

● Z ●

Apple & Macs

iPad For Dummies
978-0-470-58027-1

iPhone For Dummies,
4th Edition
978-0-470-87870-5

MacBook For Dummies, 3rd Edition
978-0-470-76918-8

Mac OS X Snow Leopard For Dummies
978-0-470-43543-4

Business

Bookkeeping For Dummies
978-0-7645-9848-7

Job Interviews
For Dummies,
3rd Edition
978-0-470-17748-8

Resumes For Dummies,
5th Edition
978-0-470-08037-5

Starting an
Online Business
For Dummies,
6th Edition
978-0-470-60210-2

Stock Investing
For Dummies,
3rd Edition
978-0-470-40114-9

Successful
Time Management
For Dummies
978-0-470-29034-7

Computer Hardware

BlackBerry
For Dummies,
4th Edition
978-0-470-60700-8

Computers For Seniors
For Dummies,
2nd Edition
978-0-470-53483-0

PCs For Dummies,
Windows
7 Edition
978-0-470-46542-4

Laptops For Dummies,
4th Edition
978-0-470-57829-2

Cooking & Entertaining

Cooking Basics
For Dummies,
3rd Edition
978-0-7645-7206-7

Wine For Dummies,
4th Edition
978-0-470-04579-4

Diet & Nutrition

Dieting For Dummies,
2nd Edition
978-0-7645-4149-0

Nutrition For Dummies,
4th Edition
978-0-471-79868-2

Weight Training
For Dummies,
3rd Edition
978-0-471-76845-6

Digital Photography

Digital SLR Cameras &
Photography For Dummies,
3rd Edition
978-0-470-46606-3

Photoshop Elements 8
For Dummies
978-0-470-52967-6

Gardening

Gardening Basics
For Dummies
978-0-470-03749-2

Organic Gardening
For Dummies,
2nd Edition
978-0-470-43067-5

Green/Sustainable

Raising Chickens
For Dummies
978-0-470-46544-8

Green Cleaning
For Dummies
978-0-470-39106-8

Health

Diabetes For Dummies,
3rd Edition
978-0-470-27086-8

Food Allergies
For Dummies
978-0-470-09584-3

Living Gluten-Free
For Dummies,
2nd Edition
978-0-470-58589-4

Hobbies/General

Chess For Dummies,
2nd Edition
978-0-7645-8404-6

Drawing
Cartoons & Comics
For Dummies
978-0-470-42683-8

Knitting For Dummies,
2nd Edition
978-0-470-28747-7

Organizing
For Dummies
978-0-7645-5300-4

Su Doku For Dummies
978-0-470-01892-7

Home Improvement

Home Maintenance
For Dummies,
2nd Edition
978-0-470-43063-7

Home Theater
For Dummies,
3rd Edition
978-0-470-41189-6

Living the
Country Lifestyle
All-in-One
For Dummies
978-0-470-43061-3

Solar Power Your Home
For Dummies,
2nd Edition
978-0-470-59678-4

Available wherever books are sold. For more information or to order direct: U.S. customers visit www.dummies.com or call 1-877-762-2974.
U.K. customers visit www.wileyeurope.com or call (0) 1243 843291. Canadian customers visit www.wiley.ca or call 1-800-567-4797.

Internet

Blogging For Dummies,
3rd Edition
978-0-470-61996-4

eBay For Dummies,
6th Edition
978-0-470-49741-8

Facebook For Dummies,
3rd Edition
978-0-470-87804-0

Web Marketing
For Dummies,
2nd Edition
978-0-470-37181-7

WordPress
For Dummies,
3rd Edition
978-0-470-59274-8

Language & Foreign Language

French For Dummies
978-0-7645-5193-2

Italian Phrases
For Dummies
978-0-7645-7203-6

Spanish For Dummies,
2nd Edition
978-0-470-87855-2

Spanish
For Dummies,
Audio Set
978-0-470-09585-0

Math & Science

Algebra I
For Dummies,
2nd Edition
978-0-470-55964-2

Biology For Dummies,
2nd Edition
978-0-470-59875-7

Calculus For Dummies
978-0-7645-2498-1

Chemistry For Dummies
978-0-7645-5430-8

Microsoft Office

Excel 2010 For Dummies
978-0-470-48953-6

Office 2010 All-in-One
For Dummies
978-0-470-49748-7

Office 2010 For Dummies,
Book + DVD Bundle
978-0-470-62698-6

Word 2010 For Dummies
978-0-470-48772-3

Music

Guitar For Dummies,
2nd Edition
978-0-7645-9904-0

iPod & iTunes For
Dummies, 8th Edition
978-0-470-87871-2

Piano Exercises
For Dummies
978-0-470-38765-8

Parenting & Education

Parenting For Dummies,
2nd Edition
978 0 7645-5418-6

Type 1 Diabetes
For Dummies
978-0-470-17811-9

Pets

Cats For Dummies,
2nd Edition
978-0-7645-5275-5

Dog Training For Dummies,
3rd Edition
978-0-470-60029-0

Puppies For Dummies,
2nd Edition
978-0-470-03717-1

Religion & Inspiration

The Bible For Dummies
978-0-7645-5296-0

Catholicism For Dummies
978-0-7645-5391-2

Women in the Bible
For Dummies
978-0-7645-8475-6

Self-Help & Relationship

Anger Management
For Dummies
978-0-470-03715-7

Overcoming Anxiety
For Dummies,
2nd Edition
978-0-470-57441-6

Sports

Baseball
For Dummies,
3rd Edition
978-0-7645-7537-2

Basketball
For Dummies,
2nd Edition
978-0-7645-5248-9

Golf For Dummies,
3rd Edition
978-0-471-76871-5

Web Development

Web Design
All-in-One
For Dummies
978-0-470-41796-6

Web Sites
Do-It-Yourself
For Dummies,
2nd Edition
978-0-470-56520-9

Windows 7

Windows 7
For Dummies
978-0-470-49743-2

Windows 7
For Dummies,
Book + DVD Bundle
978-0-470-52398-8

Windows 7 All-in-One
For Dummies
978-0-470-48763-1

 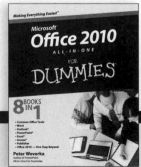  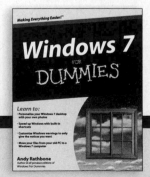

Available wherever books are sold. For more information or to order direct: U.S. customers visit www.dummies.com or call 1-877-762-2974.
U.K. customers visit www.wileyeurope.com or call (0) 1243 843291. Canadian customers visit www.wiley.ca or call 1-800-567-4797.